D0460635

THAT'S ENTERTAINMENT

**RELIVING THE MAGIC OF ICONIC
MOVIES, TELEVISION, RADIO AND MORE**

EDITORIAL

EDITOR-IN-CHIEF Catherine Cassidy
CREATIVE DIRECTOR Howard Greenberg
EDITORIAL SERVICES MANAGER Kerri Balliet

MANAGING EDITOR / PRINT & DIGITAL BOOKS Mark Hagen
ASSOCIATE CREATIVE DIRECTOR Edwin Robles Jr.

ASSOCIATE EDITOR Ellie Martin Cliffe
ART DIRECTOR Raeann Sundholm
LAYOUT DESIGNER Catherine Fletcher
CONTRIBUTING LAYOUT DESIGNERS Matt Fukuda, Holly Patch
EDITORIAL PRODUCTION MANAGER Dena Ahlers
COPY CHIEF Deb Warlaumont Mulvey
COPY EDITOR Mary C. Hanson

EXECUTIVE EDITOR Heather Lamb
ASSOCIATE CREATIVE DIRECTOR Sharon K. Nelson
EDITOR, REMINISCE Matt Phenix
ART DIRECTOR, REMINISCE Gretchen Trautman

BUSINESS

VICE PRESIDENT, PUBLISHER Russell S. Ellis
ASSOCIATE PUBLISHER Chris Dolan

CORPORATE DIGITAL & INTEGRATED SALES DIRECTOR, N.A. Steve Sottile
ASSOCIATE MARKETING DIRECTOR, INTEGRATED SOLUTIONS Katie Gaon

VICE PRESIDENT, BRAND MARKETING Jennifer Smith
VICE PRESIDENT, CIRCULATION AND CONTINUITY MARKETING Dave Fiegel

READER'S DIGEST NORTH AMERICA

VICE PRESIDENT, BUSINESS DEVELOPMENT Jonathan Bigham
PRESIDENT, BOOKS AND HOME ENTERTAINING Harold Clarke
CHIEF FINANCIAL OFFICER Howard Halligan
VICE PRESIDENT, GENERAL MANAGER, READER'S DIGEST MEDIA Marilynn Jacobs
CHIEF MARKETING OFFICER Renee Jordan
VICE PRESIDENT, CHIEF SALES OFFICER Mark Josephson
GENERAL MANAGER, MILWAUKEE Frank Quigley
VICE PRESIDENT, CHIEF CONTENT OFFICER Liz Vaccariello

THE READER'S DIGEST ASSOCIATION, INC.

PRESIDENT AND CHIEF EXECUTIVE OFFICER Robert E. Guth

STEP RIGHT UP!

The glamour of Hollywood and Broadway...the childlike delight in cartoons and comedy...the anticipation of a trip to the beach or the ballpark. In the good old days, we sure worked and studied hard, but we knew how to play hard, too, and reward ourselves with plenty of things to smile about!

Here at *Reminisce*, we've gathered our contributors' favorite stories and photographs about classic American pop culture, and we're thrilled to present *Reminisce: That's Entertainment*! From broadcasts and baseball to radio and recreation, this keepsake collection revisits the quintessential entertainment highlights of yesteryear.

Recall the storied singers and beloved bands that defined a century in "Crooners & Chart-Toppers" on page 6. Revel in tributes to the advent of television from both actors and their fans (see "Same Time, Same Channel" on page 80). Remember excursions to amusement parks, the zoo, New York City and other spots to be seen in "Out & About," page 148. And reconnect with childhood friends including Nancy Drew and Dick and Jane (flip to "Hot off the Press" on page 126). In *Reminisce: That's Entertainment*, you'll find all this and much, much more.

And now, ladies and gentlemen, we invite you to settle in and turn the page...the show is about to begin!

Best to you all,
The editors of *Reminisce* magazine

TABLE OF CONTENTS

CHAPTER 1

CROONERS & ♫ CHART-TOPPERS

Truly the universal language, music frequently provides a soundtrack to our memories of the good ol' days.

"It wasn't surprising that Bob and Ray Eberle made music their careers. There was usually plenty of music in the Eberle house in Hoosick Falls, New York," writes their sister Pat Knapp of Bradenton, Florida.

"It sure was a thrill having brothers who sang with famous bands. Add to that occasional chances to meet Jimmy Dorsey, Glenn Miller, Helen O'Connell, Marion Hutton, Tex Beneke and the Modernaires. They were usually performing in New York, Chicago or California, but we were lucky to be able to hear them on the radio and on records.

"Decades later, my brothers have both passed away, but all four of us sisters now live in Florida, where the radio stations play a lot of good old music. We often hear Bob's and Ray's records and reminisce about those wonderful bygone days."

Whether you love Big Band music, rock 'n' roll, country and western or something entirely different, these tales are sure to bring to life the sounds of the past.

I SAW FDR & FRANKIE
ON THE SAME DAY!

THREE FRIENDS BASKED IN THE PRESENCE OF FAME AND FORTUNE ONE DAY IN 1944.

By Rose Guarino Cianchetti, Wading River, New York

The world was at war in October of 1944, and many of the boys from Lafayette High School in Brooklyn had been drafted into the military or joined up on their own.

Reminders of the war were everywhere—blue star and gold star banners hung in many folks' front windows, and our school activities included collecting scrap metal around the neighborhood and selling savings bond stamps.

Even the Saturday matinee didn't offer an escape, as the Movietone News showed us details of war battles. My best friend, Ellie, and I would grasp each other's hands and shudder with fear over the safety of our brothers and friends stationed overseas.

So when Frank Sinatra came to the Paramount Theater in Times Square, we were ready to let loose and, if only for a few hours, forget the war.

WORTH THE WAIT

Classmates had been cutting school all week to see their idol, but our parents ruled that Ellie and I, plus another friend, Connie, had to wait until Saturday to see his show. It proved to be a real stroke of luck.

The three of us dressed in bobby socks, saddle shoes, skirts and sweaters. We also fashioned large bow ties out of cardboard and fastened them around our necks to imitate Frank's trademark.

There was a steady drizzle all day, but it didn't dampen our spirits. None of us had seen Frank Sinatra before, and we were caught up in the excitement of the crowd that stormed the theater when it opened.

Once inside, no one sat still for a moment. When our idol appeared onstage, all the girls screamed with excitement, "I love you, Frankie!"

ALL DRESSED UP. Author Rose Cianchetti re-created the bow tie she and her friends wore to see Sinatra in 1944 (above). On the right, Ellie, Connie and Rose (left to right) shared the same taste in clothing as in crooners during the 1940s, when they attended high school together.

As he embraced the microphone and crooned *Night and Day*, there was even more screeching, swooning and general hysteria. After the show, we left the theater in a state of exhilaration.

As we crossed the street on our way to the subway station, we noticed the streets seemed unusually crowded. There were people everywhere, standing in the rain. Some had umbrellas or held newspapers over their heads. Flags hung from every building.

Glancing back at the Paramount, where a huge picture of Frank was displayed on the facade, we spotted the real thing. Just to the right of his picture, sitting on the sill of an open window, was Frank himself!

As if that weren't great enough, he looked right at us, mimicked approval of our ties and laughed, then waved!

No one else seemed to notice him. We ignored the cold rain that splashed on our faces as we excitedly acknowledged his warm greeting.

I think we imagined, for a few seconds, that Frank was sitting on that window ledge in the rain just to wave at us. We found out how wrong we were.

Frank's attention was soon drawn away, and he looked down the street. Suddenly we were surrounded by the deafening sounds of sirens as police motorcycles roared past, followed by an open limousine with men in rain slickers riding on the running boards.

A PRESIDENTIAL GREETING

Inside was President Franklin Roosevelt! He had a cape draped over his shoulders and was waving his rain-soaked fedora.

For a fleeting moment, Ellie, Connie and I came into his view. He smiled broadly and appeared strong and gallant. People were shouting, waving flags and blowing kisses.

In a flash, the car was gone, and Frank disappeared from his window, too. But the excitement of seeing both our pop idol and our president (who was visiting New York during his re-election campaign) had us squealing and jumping up and down.

Wet and cold, we huddled close together on the long train ride home. That night, we wrote to our brothers in the armed forces to tell them about that brief moment in our lives we knew we'd never forget.

Frankie! Frankie!

Two weeks after my family moved to Louisville, Kentucky, in July 1943, I began dating Patti Ellen Taylor, my idea of a true Southern belle. Pet, as she was nicknamed, was perfect except for one thing—she was a Frank Sinatra fan.

I had Sinatra's records *I'll Never Smile Again* and *This Love of Mine*, but at the time, I saw him as little more than another good band vocalist. The bonus about his records was that they were great for dancing cheek to cheek.

Ever since I'd heard Glenn Miller's records *Moonlight Serenade* and *Tuxedo Junction*, I was a Big Band fan. My other idols were Count Basie, Harry James, Benny Goodman and Tommy Dorsey.

In August, Pet made me stand in line for 45 minutes to see Sinatra's movie *Higher and Higher*. We were lucky to get first-row balcony seats.

When Sinatra sang *The Music Stopped*, every female in the theater, including Pet, stood up and screamed "Frankie!" As she did, Pet's popcorn descended like hot buttered snow upon many of the main-floor patrons.

I got even after the movie when we had cherry Cokes and fries at our favorite malt shop. I put a quarter in the jukebox and played six Glenn Miller records. When *Moonlight Serenade* came on, we got up and danced cheek to cheek for the next three minutes and seven seconds. It was pure heaven.

—***Bob Langbein,*** *Lakeview, Arkansas*

BIG FANS. Among Dean Martin's admirers were the author (right, in 1954) and her parents (above), owners of the Pronto Pup, a popular teen hangout in San Jose, California.

Dino Charmed Them...in His Driveway

AN ITALIAN-AMERICAN FAMILY MET THIS HANDSOME SUPERSTAR IN A MOST UNCONVENTIONAL WAY.

By Cookie Curci, San Jose, California

Back in the less-complicated 1950s, a promise from Mom and Dad to take us to a Dean Martin-Jerry Lewis film on Friday night was enough to keep us kids on our best behavior all week long.

A singer and television and movie star, Martin's warm charisma appealed to people of all types and ages. The ladies were attracted to his dark and dashing good looks and romantic singing voice; the youngsters adored his shenanigans with Jerry Lewis; and the men envied his bon vivant lifestyle.

My family loved his song *That's Amore*, which we always called the "pizza song." I still play it on a scratchy 45-rpm record on my turntable.

To children of Italian immigrants, including our own parents, Martin's success was especially meaningful. Martin was born Dino Paul Crocetti in a multicultural part of Steubenville, Ohio.

On our annual family vacations to Los Angeles, the first thing we did was drive past Martin's rambling, two-story estate in Beverly Hills, always hoping to catch a glimpse of its owner.

I'll never forget passing Martin's house in 1958, when Dad decided to enter the driveway to get a closer look. Peering through the gates, we were surprised to see a small, well-tended vegetable garden amid the star's lush landscape. Tomatoes, fava beans and long green Italian peppers filled a small portion of the backyard.

We were so enthralled by our discovery that we nearly failed to notice the dazzling red Thunderbird that had pulled up in the driveway behind us.

Imagine our surprise at realizing that the driver was none other than Dean Martin himself!

He had paused to collect his mail and was waiting patiently for us to move our car so he could get into his driveway.

Martin walked over to our car and signed autographs for Mom and me, shook hands with Dad and exchanged a few words in Italian. He was just as easygoing and charming in real life as he was in his onstage persona.

That day, our family drove away on cloud nine, reliving the excitement over and over.

When I Was a Hit On Tin Pan Alley

A CHILDHOOD ILLNESS LED TO A HEALTHY AND PROLIFIC SONGWRITING CAREER.

By Kay Twomey, Wellesley, Massachusetts

MISS WITH HITS. The author (top) felt lucky to meet famous composer Richard Rodgers (below, on left, with Oscar Hammerstein) on her first trip to New York.

The old song that says, "There's a broken heart for every light in Broadway" never applied to me—I made it on my first day in town!

Maybe it was the luck of the Irish—though I hadn't been so lucky with my health. As a child, I'd had rheumatic fever and was bedridden.

Then my family moved to the better climate of Florida. I passed the time reading poetry and taking piano lessons. That got me interested in song lyrics, and as a teen, I began writing.

Years later, when I was 29, my father was looking at my lyrics. "These are really good," he said. "Why don't you go to New York for a couple of weeks and see what you can do with them?"

So in 1942, with Father staking me, I headed for Broadway and the Brill Building, capital of Tin Pan Alley. Songwriting was mostly a man's domain then, with few women in the business.

Luck of the Irish

But talk about luck! I was carrying a big envelope with about 50 lyrics I'd typed and just happened to wander into the right office. There was well-known composer Richard Rodgers!

He was in the middle of casting *Oklahoma!* and asked me, "Can you sing?"

"No," I replied, "I'm a writer."

Richard looked over my lyrics. "Not bad," he said. "I know who you should write with. Your lyrics fit his type of music."

That put me in touch with Al Goodhart, who picked out a lyric I wrote called *Johnny Doughboy Found a Rose in England.*

Dennis Day recorded it and the song became one of the big hits of World War II. Cordell Hull, then Secretary of State, gave me an award for the song at a ceremony in Atlantic City, New Jersey.

My Irish luck continued when, after having been there only a short time, I met Irving Berlin.

He asked me if I had a place to write. I said no—I went from one publisher's office to another. So Irving gave me a room in his suite to use. "You make me think of my wife a lot," he said. "She's Irish." I used that office for three years.

Al and I were a songwriting team for a long time. I also worked with Sammy Cahn. He and I penned *Hey, Jealous Lover.* It was a big hit sung by Nat Cole and Frank Sinatra.

One night, Frank introduced me at a nightclub where he sang *Hey, Jealous Lover,* saying I was the only good songwriter among the women in the Brill Building.

Took Care of Family

In all, I published 116 songs, including *Jeepers Creepers; Put the Blame on Me* for Elvis Presley; *Serenade of the Bells,* recorded by the Sammy Kaye Orchestra; and *One Magic Wish* for Alfred Hitchcock's movie *Under Capricorn.*

I spent what money I made writing lyrics on my family. I sent my sisters to college and bought a house for my mother and aunt. They couldn't believe I could support them all—but they had taken care of me when I was sick, and I wanted to repay their kindness.

I still visit New York about twice a year, and when I go to the Brill Building, they always say, "Come on in, Kay. You want to write something?"

A Trip to the Record Store

The day this photo was taken in 1946, a photographer from Charles Mayer Studios in Akron, Ohio, happened to be in Teddy's Rendezvous record store and caught me checking out a few albums.

My favorite pastime was shopping for records like Tommy Dorsey's *Boogie Woogie* or Eddy Howard's *To Each His Own*. Plus, record stores had booths where you could listen to music and meet friends.

Of course, once you selected your albums and took them home, friends usually came over to "cut a rug"...literally. I wore out my mother's living room rug jitterbugging every night.

Teenagers also spent their money on their wardrobes, but not like they do nowadays. The dress I'm wearing in the photo cost just $4. Zoot suits were "in" for the boys. I loved them.

—**Francie Stopera,** *Akron, Ohio*

Bing Crosby Was 'Regular Army' To These GIs

SONGSTER FIT RIGHT IN WITH HIS OUTFIT.

By Walker W. Smith, Vienna, Virginia

During World War II, I was personnel sergeant major in Headquarters Company, XII Corps, which was the spearhead for Gen. George Patton and his 3rd Army's dash across south France, Luxembourg and Germany.

In September 1944, our unit was bivouacked in a deserted French army camp in the eastern town of Commercy.

One evening, I was walking with my GI towel when I saw a man bent over, washing his hands by the enlisted men's mess tent. As I neared him, he said, "Hey, soldier, can I borrow that?"

I knew all the men in our company but did not recognize him. After a second look, I saw that he was none other than Bing Crosby!

After I got over my amazement, we shook hands and chatted a bit. He dried his hands and thanked me, and I went on my way.

The next morning, Bing, wearing a floppy hat and Army ODs with no insignia or other ID, lined up as the last man in the chow line. When Bing got near the food, the GI serving it asked him, "Hey, soldier, where's your mess kit?"

Bing replied, "Ain't got any. Where's yours?"

The soldier barked back, "What are you, a smart—? What's your name?"

"The name is Crosby," he said, "but everyone calls me Bing."

Bing said later that the man almost passed out, then stammered, "Sorry, Mr. Crosby," and ran out to get a mess kit.

A couple of days later, Bing again showed up at the enlisted men's mess for breakfast and was given a royal welcome this time.

As Bing ate, an officer rushed in and said, "Bing, we've been waiting for you at the officers' mess. The general is eating with us today."

Looking up, Bing replied, "I've been spending a lot of time with you stuffed shirts. Now I want some time with the working men. Give the general and other officers my regrets."

Of course, that made Bing a big hit with our outfit. We all thought he was a real regular guy.

IN THE ARMY NOW. When author Walker Smith (right) was stationed in a unit with entertainer Bing Crosby (together, above) during World War II, celebrity status didn't matter.

*When I was growing up...the
extent of my dream was to sing on
the radio station in Memphis.*

—*Johnny Cash*

WE MET THE MEGASTARS!

Blowing Horns With Louie

In 1940, my boyfriend and future husband, Vernon Boushell, played bugle and trumpet for the Marine Corps Band and was stationed at the Philadelphia Navy Yard.

One evening, the commandant got a call from famed jazz musician Louis Armstrong, who was appearing at the Lyric Theatre in Philadelphia and needed six Marines for his show's bugling contest. Vernon was one of the men chosen. There they are, on the right.

Each of the fellows played a bugle call, and the theater audience decided the winner by applause. Vernon, the tallest Marine in the photograph, was the winner of $50, with the other contestants getting $10 each.

After the show, Mr. Armstrong invited all the fellows back to his dressing room, praising their performances and asking about their duties at the Navy yard. Vernon said the Marines were awestruck to have such a well-known trumpeter and showman chatting with them in such a friendly way.

—*Grace Boushell,* *Merritt Island, Florida*

Driving Miss Horne

I was an executive chauffeur for a large advertising agency in New York City from 1959 to 1979. One day, I was sent to drive the agency's CEO and Miss Lena Horne to lunch at the Lutece restaurant.

After lunch, I helped them into the car and got behind the wheel. When I started the engine, water came shooting up all around the hood—like "stormy weather!"

As I helped them into a taxi, the CEO was a little upset but Miss Horne just gave me a big smile. I drove her many times after that and always thought she was a real fine lady.

—*John Postava,* *Oviedo, Florida*

Nat Hushed Him Up

Back in the '60s, I had the pleasure of "appearing" with Nat "King" Cole at the Chez Paree in Chicago.

He was singing *Unforgettable,* and I, seated at a ringside table, had been singing along. Nat stopped the band and invited me up on stage. He asked if I knew *Everybody Loves Somebody;* it was one of my favorites, so we sang it together.

Upon finishing, Nat said, "Ed, you don't quite know the words, but you have good sound and volume. Thank you. Now sit down and be quiet."

—*Edward Mraz,* *Lombard, Illinois*

A Snapshot With Benny

Not all devout fans of Benny Goodman got to meet their idol like I did in July of 1948.

While vacationing in New York, my pals and I drove up to White Plains, where Benny was playing a concert at a community center.

I'd written earlier to the center's manager saying I'd like to meet Benny. But when we got there, I was content to just bask in the sublime sounds of his clarinet, the piano of Mary Lou Williams and

the clarinet played by a whiz from Sweden, Stan Hasselgard (Benny's protege that summer).

At intermission I found the center's manager and reminded him of my letter. He promptly led me backstage to meet Benny!

Even though I'd fought in the Battle of the Bulge, I was a little scared. But Benny calmed my nerves at once, flashing a genuine smile and telling me how much he appreciated support from his fans. He even recalled a photo I'd sent him way back in 1942!

During our 15-minute chat, his personal photographer, Popsie Randolph, took our picture. I gave him money for postage, hoping he'd send a print to me. He did; it's on the right.

Of course, I was on cloud nine the rest of the evening. I remember what a thrill it was later when we heard Benny and Stan swap choruses on their "licorice sticks."

—**Dan Bied,** *West Burlington, Iowa*

Lawrence Welk Wowed

LED WITH HIS LEFT. In the summer of 1967, a friend got our family tickets for the Lawrence Welk show in Hollywood. Mr. Welk picked our 10-year-old son, Kevin, to come up and lead the orchestra. Kevin is left-handed, and Mr. Welk kept trying to put the baton in Kevin's right hand. But, as you can see, Kevin put it back in his left one.
—Bea Henisey, Acton, California

Spawning a Fish Story

I was recently remembering the time when band director Lawrence Welk came over to our house, in 1953.

My father, Barney Liddell, was Mr. Welk's new solo trombonist. One day, Dad phoned to say he was bringing the boss home for dinner. I was a fussy eater, so in order to head off any problems in front of Mr. Welk, Mom fried up a batch of fish, which I loved.

All was going well at the dinner table, but I couldn't help but notice that Mr. Welk kept reaching enthusiastically, with fork in hand, toward the large plate of fish. In a short time, the plate was empty.

I blurted out, "He took all the fish!" Well, my father looked like he was going to have a heart attack, but Mr. Welk just laughed good-naturedly.

For several days after Mr. Welk's visit, fellow band members ribbed Dad with questions such as "Hey, Barn, how's the fish holding out at home?" and "Have you taken the kids fishing lately?"

Over the next 30 years, occasional jokes continued to pop up about the fish incident spawned by a spontaneous outburst from a 10-year-old denied his favorite food.

—**Terrence Liddell,** *Atascadero, California*

The Day I Saw Rachmaninoff

THE TOP RUSSIAN COMPOSER LEFT A LASTING IMPRESSION ON A 10-YEAR-OLD GIRL WITH HIS MUSIC AND A WARM GREETING IN 1937.

By Elizabeth Ross, Thomasville, Georgia

PIANO LESSONS. A music teacher herself, the author (here in 1973) passes on her love of the art to her own students.

I was a student at A. Harry Moore Elementary School in Jersey City, New Jersey, in 1937. Miss Boltwood, the school's music director, also gave piano lessons to those of us who had pianos at home. One day she told me she had two tickets for a concert at a local high school.

"Maybe you'd like to come with me," she said. "The performing artist is the Russian composer Sergei Rachmaninoff."

I was 10 at the time. My music appreciation included listening to symphonies on the radio during dinner, the Salvation Army band in the park, and pumping the pedal of the player piano when my aunts and uncles came over on Sunday. I also played piano at home for the joy of it, mistakes and all. But I didn't know Rachmaninoff.

"He loved his home in Oneg and hearing the village church bells echo through the frosty air," Miss Boltwood explained. "When he began to write his own music, people say he put into some of it the sounds of his old Russian bells."

In the Spotlight

At the theater, the lights dimmed and the curtains parted to reveal the longest, flattest piano I'd ever seen. Its cover was raised at a slant.

The audience broke into applause as a tall, thin man walked to the piano. He wore a black suit, with a jacket that split halfway down the back.

The two halves of the jacket seemed astonishingly long, and I noticed he was careful not to sit on them as he played his songs.

And what songs! I liked the sounds and rhythms of his music. Some pulsed like a parade. Some whirled like ocean waves. Some made me feel sad.

The last song repeated, "BONG, BONG, BONG, chime, chime, chime, BONG, BONG, BONG." *My goodness,* I thought, *his old Russian bells!*

At the end of the concert, everyone stood and shouted funny words like "brah-vo!" and "my-stro!" Then an usher came and told Miss Boltwood to follow him backstage.

But there wasn't any stage, just a room crowded with grown-ups in fancy clothes. Miss Boltwood kept nudging me into the middle of them.

If I looked around a lady standing near him, I could see the back of the pianist's jacket. There were four satin buttons at the waist. I reached out to touch one.

Suddenly, the jacket turned, and my hand was swallowed up inside both of Mr. Rachmaninoff's. He bent over so his face was right in front of mine. I saw he had a pointy chin, silvery hair and a smile that made me smile back. His dark blue eyes never looked away from mine.

Whispered in His Ear

I couldn't think of any words to say aloud to this important man, so I whispered in his ear, "You played wonderful songs."

He squeezed my sandwiched hand harder and said in funny English, "Makushla, that is the best compliment I haff receive tonight," then gently released my hand.

That night, I wore a glove on the hand Mr. Rachmaninoff had held. As the school year went on, Miss Boltwood remarked on the emotion I laced into my pieces. I felt it, but was not aware my music reflected it.

I'm still not sure why Miss Boltwood asked me along to the concert. I wasn't gifted, just in love with the sounds a piano could produce.

Meeting Rachmaninoff opened the doors to a new world, given to me for a lifetime. I'd spoken with my first hero, and since then, I've savored the sounds he created all the days of my life.

We Danced With Glenn Miller!

AFTER WINNING A DANCE CONTEST, TWO HIGH SCHOOLERS WERE INVITED TO SHARE THE STAGE WITH SOME BIG BAND LEGENDS!

By Walter Newton, Bullard, Texas

Back when the Big Bands were popular, my future wife, Ginny, and I were high schoolers in western New York. Our hometown of Wayland had a population only in the hundreds, but it was a wonderful place to hear the swinging Big Band sound firsthand. Located in the scenic Finger Lakes region, Wayland was a popular stopover for bands as they traveled by bus from New York City to Buffalo.

At one time or another, all the big-name bands played at Wayland's dance hall...and Ginny and I were always there. Everyone said we danced really well together. Whenever we got out on the floor to jitterbug, we'd draw a crowd!

Finally, friends convinced us to enter an Arthur Murray dance contest held in nearby Bath, New York. We called our act "The Newtons." Ginny and I won first place! That allowed us to go on to the New York State "Shag" Championships, held at the State Fair in Syracuse on Aug. 26, 1939.

COMPETITION WAS TOUGH

We needed flying feet and a lot of aerial tricks to stay in competition with 56 other couples. Still, Ginny and I managed to tie for first place.

The prize—awarded by Arthur Murray himself—was $150.00 plus a one-week engagement as opening act with Eddy Duchin (shown left, center) and his orchestra at a theater in Buffalo!

What a thrill it was for us to meet the members of that famous band, including singers Carolyn Horton and Lew Sherwood. But we soon experienced an even bigger thrill.

On Sept. 8, we got a telegram from the manager of the Paramount Theater on the Great White Way offering us a three-week engagement with Glenn Miller (shown top left) and his Moonlight Serenaders! Of course, we accepted.

The Paramount billed us as "New York State Shag Champions," and we appeared along with an up-and-coming musical group called The Four Ink Spots (bottom left).

DANCED WITH A STAR

Glenn Miller's singers at that time were Ray Eberle and Marion Hutton (pictured below). Marion's sister, Betty, visited us backstage at the Paramount before leaving for Hollywood to try her luck as an actress. I didn't know then what a big star Betty Hutton would later become. But I'll never forget jitterbugging with her to the great sounds of Glenn Miller—she was an excellent dancer!

Almost before we knew it, our three weeks dancing at the Paramount were over. Ginny and I returned to Wayland with enough memories to last a lifetime. We performed locally a few more times until World War II put an end to our short "career" on stage.

Now it's been more than half a century since we actually got paid to do what we did for fun. But Ginny and I still fondly recall those magical few weeks in 1939 when a couple of small-town kids got to "kick up their heels" in the big city.

Engaged, At Last

When I became engaged to Amelia Borquez in April 1941, we celebrated by going dancing at the famed Hollywood Palladium, where Glenn Miller was starting a three-week engagement.

Miller was only a day away from completing the movie *Sun Valley Serenade*, so, as a result, many movie celebrities attended what became one of the biggest Big Band openings of all time. When I first heard his band play *Chattanooga Choo Choo*, which was introduced in the movie, I knew they had a hit.

My fiancee and I introduced ourselves to Mr. Miller during one of his brief intermissions and informed him of our engagement. Along with offering his congratulations, he called for a special picture to be taken, and the result is this photo.

Mr. Miller then added, "Amelia and Art, the first number in our next set is for the both of you." The selection was *At Last*, and it has been our song ever since.

—*Art Loya*
South Gate, California

Love at First Listen

PATTI PAGE'S VOICE WARMED A YOUNG BOY'S SOUL ONE FROSTY NIGHT.

By Michael McGarr, South Glens Falls, New York

My Patti Page story began on a bitterly cold winter night in 1950. Mom had passed away five years earlier, so I was living with my father and his parents in Glens Falls, New York.

I was an altar boy, serving midnight Mass on Christmas Eve. After the service, my dad took me to a local diner to warm up with a hot chocolate before heading home. A gentleman there walked over to the jukebox and dropped in a coin. The record he chose changed my life forever.

I listened to the bittersweet lyrics of *Tennessee Waltz* sung by the most beautiful sound I had ever heard—the melodic voice of Patti Page. I'd never experienced anything so wonderful. As tears ran down my cheeks, Dad asked me if I was OK, and I said I was and walked over to the jukebox.

Music to My Ears

I'd just turned 12, but I'd never seen records. My grandparents were wonderful to me, but they felt that music was for the idle and that idleness was the devil's workshop.

Dad gave me a quarter, good for six plays. I played *Tennessee Waltz* over and over.

As time passed, I'd stop in the diner almost daily. The proprietor listened to my tale of woe. He'd drop some money in and let me play anything I wanted to hear.

I listened to other singers—Johnnie Ray, Kay Starr, Eddie Fisher, Teresa Brewer, Perry Como, Rosemary Clooney, Joni James and Guy Mitchell, to name a few—but none could compare to Patti.

I socked away enough pennies from my paper route to buy my first record: Patti Page's *Tennessee Waltz*. I wrapped it in newspaper and hid it in the back of my closet.

As the years went by and her hits began tumbling out, I amassed quite a collection of Miss Page's recordings, including *I Went to Your Wedding, Changing Partners, Old Cape Cod* and *Let Me Go Lover*!

I vowed that when I grew up and left home, I'd do two things: buy a record player and someday meet Miss Patti Page.

When I graduated from the New York State College for Teachers—now the University at Albany—in 1961 and got a teaching job, I bought my first record player and dug out all of the records I had hidden away.

Time to Fulfill the Dream

As time marched on, marriage and three kids made it more difficult to obtain my other goal— seeing Miss Page.

In 1982, I wrote a letter to her through her record label, expressing how much I enjoyed her singing. Within a short time, she replied, saying she was to appear at the Orrie de Nooyer Auditorium in Hackensack, New Jersey. Finally, I was going to see her.

What a joy it was! Her finale, of course, was the hauntingly beautiful *Tennessee Waltz*, transporting me back in time.

The highlight of the evening came as I walked to the parking lot. I saw Miss Page exiting a side door with her entourage. I walked over and asked if she'd sign an LP I had brought along. She signed it, and we started talking.

I told her about my first encounter with her music, and we even talked about our families. Here was this music icon, one of the top-selling female vocalists of all time, taking the time to chat with me.

I've had the honor of seeing Miss Page perform in concert more than a dozen times since then, each time as much a thrill as the first. In 1987, I was named the Patti Page Fan of the Year by a fan club organized in her honor.

In 1997, my wife and I accepted an invitation to attend her 50th Anniversary Concert at New York City's Carnegie Hall—a performance that earned her a Grammy—and had the honor of attending a private reception for her afterward.

Patti Page remains my all-time favorite vocalist because she sang with such warmth in her voice, as though she was personally singing to each individual listener. It's the same feeling I had in a diner so long ago.

the
big
records
of
PATTI
PAGE

Pillsbury
BEST
COLLECTOR'S
SERIES

Tennessee Waltz
By REDD STEWART and PEE WEE KING
RECORDED BY PATTI PAGE FOR MERCURY RECORDS

PUBLISHED BY

WITH MY EYES WIDE OPEN
I'M DREAMING

lyrics and music by
MACK GORDON & HARRY REVE

as Recorded by
PATTI PAGE
on Mercury Record
No. 5345

CRAWFORD MUSIC CORPORATION

One Night Only!
Patti Page

Enjoy such classics as:
"Old Cape Cod,"
"Allegheny Moon,"
"Doggie in the
Window" and her
multi-platinum
"Tennessee Waltz."

Her voice is . . .
"warm and
compelling as ever"
- Liz Smith, Daily News

with special guest
"Peter Nero and the Philly Pops"

Tickets: $60, $40, $30, $20 & $15 available at the box office
or call CarnegieCharge (212) 247-7800 - For Golden Circle
seating and post concert reception call: (212) 581-8566

Carnegie Hall
Saturday, May 31, 1997 • 8 pm

JOIN NOW!
National Radio
FAN CLUB

FEBRUARY
25¢

HIT PARADER
A CHARLTON PUBLICATION

champs

"these are the tops"

Competition for that number one
spot is probably more intense in the
music world than in any other. That's
one reason recording artists prize a
victory in "American Bandstand's"
Annual Poll. This year again almost a
half-million votes from all sections of
the nation were tallied—and The Winners—for 1957:

Patti Page—*Favorite Female Vocalist*
Elvis Presley—*Favorite Male Vocalist*
Rick Nelson—*Most Promising New Male
Vocalist*
Janice Harper—*Most Promising New
Female Vocalist*
Jerry Lee Lewis—*Best Instrumental
Combo*
Danny & The Juniors—*Best Vocal Group*
"All-Shook-Up"—*Best Record*,
by Elvis Presley

PATTI
PAGE

SIXTEEN TONS
IT'S ALMOST TOMORROW
ALL AT ONCE YOU LOVE HER
LOVE AND MARRIAGE
CRY ME A RIVER
ROCK A BEATIN' BOOGIE
C'EST LA VIE
A WOMAN IN LOVE
ONLY YOU
DADDY - O
I HEAR YOU KNOCKING
PEPPER HOT BABY
BURN THAT CANDLE
AT MY FRONT DOOR
BAND OF GOLD

The winners all received these handsome
plaques — permanent reminders of great
days in 1957.

PERENNIAL FAVORITE. In 1957, Patti Page made a strong
showing in *American Bandstand's* Annual Poll. The author
(shown in a 1959 photo, top left) couldn't agree more.

I MADE SWING AN ALL-DAY THING

THIS DEVOTED BIG BAND FAN SAT FRONT AND CENTER FOR SHOW AFTER SHOW AFTER SHOW.

By Shirley Belleranti, Mesa, Arizona

Whenever I hear Big Band music or read about a famous performer of that era, I think back to the '40s when I lived in suburban Milwaukee, Wisconsin.

Back then, the Riverside Theater featured the biggest names in popular music...and when one of my favorites was scheduled on a Saturday night, I'd make the outing an all-day affair.

In the morning, I'd wrap a sandwich, then take the streetcar downtown and wait for the box office to open. When it did, I'd buy my ticket, stake out a seat in the center of the front row and camp there for the next few hours.

Soon they'd show some boring movies, which were rerun between stage shows. Those dull movies got even worse with the second showing!

Gradually the theater filled with fans. My wait was well worth it when master showman Cab Calloway strode across the stage in his blue velvet tuxedo singing *Minnie the Moocher*.

Other times, Lionel Hampton enchanted with vibraphone solos of exquisite delicacy. Then, in a change of tempo, he'd dash to the drums to show why his were "the fastest wrists in the business." From the drums, Hamp would head for the bass fiddle, where he'd strum wildly.

ENJOYED ELLA'S VOICE

Then there was Ella Fitzgerald, who could caress a ballad with a voice of such liquid purity that no one dared unwrap a candy bar or stick of gum, lest the spell be broken.

When Gene Krupa went into a frenzied drum solo, he was sure to break a stick. Sometimes he'd just move to the bongos or the conga drum and beat out the rhythm with his bare hands.

When the Krupa band's male vocalist, Johnny Desmond, stepped to the microphone to croon a medley of ballads, the mood changed to one of romance. But then the tempo accelerated once more as a bouncy Anita O'Day belted out a couple of tunes, sometimes joined by trumpet player Roy Eldridge for a scatting duet.

Of course, everyone in the room enjoyed Count Basie, tickling the piano keys to drive that wonderful Basie band. The Count would sit quietly, almost motionless, while his fingers roamed the keyboard.

I also remember a new trio that was receiving rave reviews in both *Downbeat* and *Metronome* magazines. It was booked at the Riverside as a fill-in act for the stage show of Blackstone the magician. The King Cole Trio was so new that its records were not yet available in Milwaukee. Its biggest hit, *Straighten up and Fly Right*, hit number nine on the charts in 1942.

SAW ACT 20 TIMES!

I liked what I heard so much that I stayed through five grueling performances of Blackstone's magic show just to listen to pianist Nat "King" Cole sing *Sweet Lorraine*.

But as much as I loved the King Cole Trio, my favorite act of all was the wonderful Duke Ellington and his orchestra. They played just one weeklong engagement in my hometown during that period, but while they were there, I made daily pilgrimages to the theater. I must have seen that show at least 20 times!

I'll never forget Duke Ellington's quizzical look one Saturday night when he saw me still seated in my usual front-and-center seat for the fifth straight performance of his show.

When you're a youngster, it's a real treat to think that one of your idols actually noticed you. Now I realize that he must have thought I was a little crazy!

Styles in popular music have changed. But in the echo chamber of my memory, I continue to hear Cab, Hamp, Ella, Gene, the Count, the King and the Duke.

It's still a glorious sound!

She Did the One O'Clock Jump

Friends of mine went to New York City in 1962; he to attend a seminar and she to see what life in the Big Apple was all about. Being a country girl, she was told to be very careful of big-city crime.

Their hotel was across from Central Park, and she went out to do some shopping. Making sure her room was locked, she entered the hotel elevator, noticing three men were standing in the back.

Then one of them shouted, "Hit the floor, lady. Hit the floor." She instantly threw herself down with a thud, frightened stiff, resigned to giving up her purse but not her wedding ring.

The three men started laughing and dashed over to help her. They were astonished at the way in which she had misinterpreted their request to push the elevator button for the floor she wanted.

My friend and her husband enjoyed dinner in the hotel that evening and were pleasantly surprised when the maitre d' arrived at their table carrying an ice bucket and a bottle of Champagne.

"Our apologies for embarrassing you with our New York 'lingo,'" it read. It was signed, "Count Basie."

—**Helen Sojka,** *Danvers, Massachusetts*

COUNTRY HAD ITS
CROONERS

STEEL GUITAR PLAYER WENT ON TO PRODUCE ALBUMS FOR COUNTRY MUSIC SINGERS.

By Don Davis, Gulf Shores, Alabama

When I got my first steel guitar in a swap for a bicycle, I never dreamed that I'd end up playing with some of America's musical heroes.

I grew up poor in the 1930s in Satsuma, Alabama, but I didn't know it. My stepdaddy made $9 a week at International Paper, and we had everything we needed—a car and plenty to eat. We spent $3 on groceries and had to take the backseat out of the car to get them all in.

A year after I got the guitar, my parents bought me a $39.95 electric steel guitar from Sears Roebuck. During World War II, I played for Saturday night dances at community centers, where defense workers in Mobile lived.

Finding the Music

At 16, I moved to Nashville and joined the Pee Wee King Band and played the Grand Ole Opry. Within three years, I'd traveled the 48 continental states and was earning $45 a week.

Much of the money I made was from selling those souvenir music books at the performances. I got a dime for every one I sold. I worked steady and lived well. I never was a millionaire, but I was never out of work. While being on the road was fun, it started wearing thin.

I returned to the studio and earned a solid reputation as a session player, working with Hank Williams, Minnie Pearl, Ernest Tubb and Red Foley. As a musician, I performed on more than 3,000 recordings during the 1940s and '50s. I played on Hank Williams' first records on MGM, including *Mind Your Own Business*, *Wedding Bells* and others.

I gradually moved into the production end of country music and produced several albums, including three for Johnny Cash. In fact, I brought him what may be his best-known hit song of all time: *A Boy Named Sue*—he even mentioned it in his autobiography!

Celebrated poet Shel Silverstein, who wrote the song, had dropped by my office and asked me to record it. I made a demo copy and called Johnny, telling him I had his next hit song.

When I gave it to him, he knew I was right. To show his appreciation, Johnny bought me a black-on-black Cadillac. It was the biggest, longest, ugliest car you've ever seen. I felt like a fool driving it and kept it only about six months.

Back in Alabama, I did the *Alabama Jubilee* early-morning television show for five years. I returned to Nashville and record production, retiring in 1985.

In 1997, I was inducted into the Alabama Music Hall of Fame and was honored to receive a lifetime award for non-performing achievement. I was nominated three times for the Hall of Fame's Pioneer Award, but I lost each time, the last to Jimmie Rodgers.

Looking back, that's the first time I ever lost anything and was happy about it. After all, Mr. Rodgers was a star before I was born.

RADING POST

GENE AUTRY, OKLA.

Coca-Cola

DOUG AUTRY ↓

MINNIE PEARL ↓

DON DAVIS ↓

PEE WEE KING ↑

Hank Williams Impressed

I was 19 years old when I saw Hank Williams Sr. perform in person. It was 1951, about a year before he died on his way to a New Year's concert.

The place was a little barn-like structure called The Riverside Rancho near Griffith Park in Los Angeles. The Rancho's house band was led by Tex Williams, but other performers dropped by from time to time, including Little Jimmy Dickens and Lefty Frizzell.

Before Hank sang that night, it was so quiet you could hear a pin drop—I think we all sensed that we were in the presence of greatness.

Under the hot glare of the lights, in his typical crouching position, Hank sang his heart out.

Lovesick Blues, Move It on Over and *Mansion on the Hill* were only a few of the hits he did for us.

I remember thinking how thin he was and how tall and gaunt he looked with his bony knees protruding from his pant legs.

There was a police officer on duty that night who had mentioned beforehand that he didn't go for this "country stuff" and had never even heard of Hank Williams.

After the performance, I bumped into the officer and asked what he thought. "Well," he replied, "he's different—he's got something."

I had to agree. Seeing Hank Williams perform that night is a memory I'll always cherish.

—*Judy Paris*, *Clearwater, Florida*

ONE UP ON THE KING

ONE LOWLY MEDICAL CORPSMAN POSSESSED SOMETHING MORE PRECIOUS THAN ALL OF ELVIS' MILLIONS.

By Don Haines, Woodbine, Maryland

I was just going on duty as a medical corpsman on the psychiatric ward at the 97th General Hospital in Frankfurt, Germany.

It was February of 1959, and I'd been stationed in Frankfurt for a little over a year. I had said goodbye to my wife and son a few weeks before, watching with an empty feeling as their plane took off from the Rhine Main Air Base headed for the United States. The six weeks I had to wait before joining them would be the longest weeks of my life.

I was coming up the walkway toward the main building when a Jeep pulled up and an officer got out. I snapped him a salute and nodded to his driver. "How're you doin'?" I said.

"Fine," replied the young GI. "How're you?"

That guy sure looked familiar, I thought to myself while taking the elevator up to my ward. As I got off the elevator, a WAC nearly ran into me trying to board it. "Is he still there?" she inquired breathlessly.

A Brush With Fame

"Is who still there?" I asked the young woman, completely befuddled.

"Elvis! You walked right past him—I was looking out the window!"

She began pounding on the elevator button, as if this could close the doors any quicker. When they finally shut, I heard her exclaim, "I can't believe you were that close to him! I hope he's still there...but I'll probably die if he is!"

Walking back to my ward, I was still feeling depressed. Of course, I'd heard that Elvis was coming to Frankfurt—who hadn't? But at that moment, I was more concerned about my own departure than his arrival.

It didn't matter to me that Elvis had rented an entire floor in the best hotel in Frankfurt, or that his father and a host of family and friends had accompanied him to Germany.

The important thing was that I was a short-timer and he was not. As my shift wore on that evening, I remember telling a fellow corpsman that thinking about Elvis made me feel better.

His puzzled expression made me laugh. "Think of it this way," I said. "This guy has all the money in the world. He's living in a luxury hotel, but he's still here! And he'll still be here when I'm home!"

I figured I was one up on the King. Now don't get me wrong—I had nothing against Elvis, even though I was never a big fan. Actually, word got around that Elvis was an OK guy. And as for his life of luxury, any of us would have arranged the same deal if we'd had the money. (Besides, as an Army enlisted man, his life while on duty could not have been all that luxurious.)

We Had the Army in Common

Elvis did his time in Germany just like I did. But that's where the similarities end. I went home to my family and led an ordinary life. Elvis went back to his mansion, his Cadillacs and his ladies, and led a life that was fast, furious and too short.

Today, I'm sorry I didn't recognize Elvis that day in 1959. I'd have shaken his hand and maybe even fibbed that I liked his music.

But as I was leaving, I also would have said, "I'm going home next month."

sock hop with a twist

Chubby Checker's *The Twist* became a No. 1 hit in the fall of 1960, when I was a freshman at Appalachian State Teachers College in North Carolina. College kids everywhere were doing this crazy new dance.

In October, my girlfriend, Nancy Everidge, and I had returned to a sock hop after a football game at our high school in Jonesville.

Someone put *The Twist* on the record player, and Nancy and I (left) and our good friends Bud Reece and Diane Cheek (right) got up and did the twist. As you can see, everyone gathered around to watch these strange moves.

When the music stopped, we felt kind of proud—until the high school coach announced that there would not be another sock hop at Jonesville High if people were going to do that vulgar dance!

Nancy and I were married in November 1963 and still smile when we hear *The Twist*, remembering that night more than 50 years ago.

—**Reg Banner,** *Winston-Salem, North Carolina*

CHAPTER 2

RIDIN' THE RADIO WAVES

Back when radio reigned, popular programs often became the talk of the town. Folks would gather to hear broadcasts, using their imagination to "see" the scene.

"We listened to my favorite radio program, *Grand Ole Opry*, on a radio my mother bought at a Western Auto Supply store," recalls Lem Slayter from Oklahoma City. "It got its power from a 6-volt battery.

"We'd play the radio until the battery got weak, then exchange it for the one in the car. Then we'd jack up one rear wheel of the car, start the engine and recharge the battery.

"On Saturday nights, our house and yard would be full of kinfolk and neighbors listening to *Grand Ole Opry*. I can still see us waiting for 'the solemn ole judge' George Dewey Hay to proclaim, 'This is WSM radio, 650 on the dial in Nashville, Tennessee, bringing you *Grand Ole Opry*!'"

From music and news to mysteries and game shows, turn the page to take a trip back in time and remember those cherished voices of yesterday.

THE SMALLEST
BROADCAST STUDIO

IN 1940, KATE SMITH BROADCAST HER POPULAR RADIO PROGRAM FROM HER SUMMER HOME AT LAKE PLACID. *By Richard Hayes, Newfield, Maine*

Robert "Believe It or Not" Ripley described it as the world's smallest broadcast studio. Strange as it may seem, it belonged to one of the largest radio personalities—Kate Smith.

In 1940, Kate was the top female pop singer in the U.S. Both her weekly program, *Kate Smith Hour*, and her 15-minute weekday series, *Kate Smith Speaks*, were tops in popularity surveys.

Kate lived in New York City and broadcast most of the shows from her Park Avenue apartment. She'd review, rehearse and edit the script; then, before airtime, her cocker spaniel, Freckles, would be whisked away and an engineer would set up a microphone on a table.

Kate also had an island home at Lake Placid, New York, and said she needed her summer vacation to "recharge my batteries."

In the weekday series, Kate spoke about events of the day, food, fashion, home decorating and new books and movies that she deemed worthy. Because of the show's popularity in 1940, CBS insisted it continue during the summer months.

"Only if I can do it from Lake Placid," Kate said.

So a cable was laid to the small village in the Adirondacks and across the big lake to Buck Island. Situated on nearly an acre, Kate's compound was named Camp Sunshine. It consisted of a two-story main house, a guest cottage, a house for the maid and cook, and two boathouses. Kate loved to cruise around the lake in her 1938 mahogany Chris-Craft speedboat.

FAN BECAME FRIEND

I had been a Kate Smith fan since boyhood. How well I remember coming home from grade school every lunchtime. Seated at the table with my mom and sister, we always listened to Kate's midday chats with Ted Collins, her radio partner. We

delighted in their lighthearted banter and Kate's hearty, contagious laugh.

I joined her fan club in 1967 and soon became editor of its publications. A phone call from her in 1968 marked the start of a valued friendship. When I visited her at Lake Placid in 1971, she gave me a tour of the compound and pointed out where the tiny studio had first been, in the guest cottage.

"We had one small room in which Ted and I could sit across from each other," she said. "Then we made the closet the engineer's booth. When it was noon and he got the signal from New York, he threw the finger signal at the soundproof window, and Ted said, 'It's high noon in New York and time for Kate Smith...' and we went on the air."

Perhaps her most fateful show was in November 1938, the twentieth anniversary of the signing of the World War I armistice. That's when she introduced a new song.

"I wanted a new hymn of praise and love and allegiance to America," she told her audience.

She had sent Ted to visit Irving Berlin, who remembered a song he wrote for an Army camp show in 1917 that had been rejected. He made a few changes and sent it to Kate.

"This song is called *God Bless America*," she announced. "When I tried it...I felt, *Here is a song that will be timeless. It will never die. Others will thrill to its beauty long after we are gone.*"

KATE SOLD BONDS

When America went to war in 1941, Kate took on the role of morale booster on the home front.

Besides encouraging everyone to work for victory, she conducted legendary radio war bond marathons and was credited with selling some $600 million worth. She ended every daytime broadcast with, "Remember, if you don't write, you're wrong," urging listeners to send letters to friends and relatives in the service.

In 1946, Kate began to speak her mind about news events that troubled her, and CBS started to censor her editorial comments. The next year, she moved to the Mutual network with a program that ran until 1951, when television was taking over.

Her show expanded, too, and included recorded music. That resulted in a move to another small room, off her trophy room, which was upstairs in the large boathouse. It was here that Kate allowed me to record any and all of the records stored there when I made a return visit three years later.

Aside from many albums, she had a large number of "air checks," individual songs recorded from live broadcasts. I taped six hours of her precious singing voice.

If you visit Lake Placid in the summer and take the narrated boat cruise around the lake, you will hear about Kate Smith, who died in 1986, and the world's smallest broadcast studio as you pass Camp Sunshine.

I'm glad I had the chance to visit.

TRANSCRIPT CAPTURES FLAVOR OF 'KATE SMITH SPEAKS'

Here are excerpts from the *Kate Smith Speaks* program of Aug. 11, 1947, with casual conversation between Kate and her partner and manager, Ted Collins. This program was broadcast from Camp Sunshine.

Kate begins by chatting with Ted about an upcoming fishing competition, the Alabama Deep Sea Fishing Rodeo off the state's southern coast.

KATE: What on earth is a fishing rodeo? Do the men go 'round with a rope, bulldogging the poor fish, or do they do their casting from the saddle?

Ted explains the gathering is a traditional fishing contest with points awarded according to how hard the fish are to catch—500 points for tarpon, sailfish or ling, and 100 points for sharks weighing at least 50 pounds.

KATE: Don't they count any nice little fish?

TED: Well, yes—but not much. The lowest number of points is 10, for Spanish mackerel and speckled trout.

KATE: They make very tasty eating. I think maybe you ought to get more points for them. After all, nobody wants to eat a shark!

TED: Now isn't that just like a woman! Just because you like the taste! It's the fish that are hardest to catch that rate the count. And the prizes, incidentally, are magnificent. The grand prize is a speedboat, and there are outboard motors and many other awards.

KATE: Will they have a fish fry?

TED: Yes, tomorrow night they're having what's advertised as the world's largest fish fry.

KATE: Now there's something I'd like to be in on. However, though we may not have the world's largest up here in the mountains, we can have our own little fish fry. Fresh fish right out of the lake! Cooked right beside the lake!

After a commercial, Kate and Ted return to speak about tea wagons and one she bought at a country auction the previous summer. She uses it for tea and little cakes, and also as a plant stand in the winter months.

Next there is a brief look at news headlines and another commercial before Kate wraps up the show.

KATE: For those of you who love the old songs— the lovely songs that never die—here's a story, a story of how one of those songs came into being. In a hotel room in Riverside, California, many years ago, a woman paused as she was dressing for dinner, just as many of us pause, to watch from the window the fading of day into night.

She'd had a pleasant day with friends she loved, and now, as she stood watching the twilight shadows gripping the earth in a soft gray shawl, she said with a sigh of pure happiness, "It has truly been a perfect day."

Suddenly, acting on impulse, she stepped to a table and began to write. The words began to take shape under her sure fingers. And those words have become familiar to all of us.

In the intervals of dressing, hurrying from dresser to table and back again, she set down two stanzas. Then she tucked the slip of paper away and forgot it.

But the words remained in her subconscious memory and months later, on another summer night, she was driving with friends when she began to sing softly the words she had written that evening in Riverside. The melody came naturally, without thought or effort.

Kate continues to tell how Carrie Jacobs Bond went on to publish A Perfect Day *and was surprised that she had touched the world's heart.*

KATE: Today, Aug. 11, is the anniversary of the birth of the beloved songwriter who not long ago slipped away from this mortal world after she had lived more than fourscore years of usefulness and left as a monument of that useful life music that stirs every heart and lingers like the benediction to remind us of her.

Truly there could be no finer monument to Carrie Jacobs Bond than the songs she left behind, timeless songs that carry the message of love and beauty down through the years.

Thanks for listenin'—and goodbye, folks!

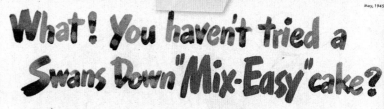

May, 1945

What! You haven't tried a Swans Down "Mix-Easy" cake?

You've been missing the biggest news that's hit cakemaking in years . . . if you haven't yet tried a Swans Down "Mix-Easy" cake!

Making a cake has suddenly become so unbelievably easy . . . so fast . . . so *rewarding!*

Just look how baby-simple this new method is! No creaming—beating time cut in half—fewer dishes to wash.

Then see how rich your Swans Down "Mix-Easy" cake tastes—how long it keeps fresh!

Get a box of Swans Down and try this luscious "Mix-Easy" Lemon Orange cake! Swans Down guarantees it—double-guarantees it!

But remember that guarantee applies only when you use Swans Down—not any other flour!

"MIX-EASY" LEMON ORANGE CAKE

Preparations: Have shortening at room temperature. Grease pan, line bottom with waxed paper, and grease again. Use 9x9x2-inch pan or 9x5x3-inch loaf pan. Start oven for moderate heat (375°F.). Sift flour once before measuring. (All measurements are level.)

Measure into sifter:
1½ cups sifted Swans Down Cake Flour
1¼ teaspoons Calumet Baking Powder
¾ teaspoon salt
1 cup sugar
¼ teaspoon grated lemon rind
1 teaspoon grated orange rind

Measure into cup:
½ cup milk

Measure into bowl:
½ cup vegetable shortening

Have ready:
2 eggs, unbeaten

Now—Swans Down's "Mix-Easy" Part!

(Mix by hand or with electric mixer on low speed.) Mix or stir shortening just to soften. Sift in dry ingredients. Add ⅓ of milk and the eggs. Mix until all flour is dampened; then beat 1 minute. Add remaining milk, blend, and beat 2 minutes longer. (Count only actual beating time. Or count beating strokes. Allow at least 100 full strokes per minute. Scrape bowl and spoon or beater often.) Turn batter into pan.

Baking: Bake in moderate oven (375°F.) 30 to 35 minutes for square cake, or about 50 minutes for loaf cake. Spread with orange frosting.

Or bake in greased cupcake pans in moderate oven (375°F.) about 25 minutes. Cover tops with seven-minute frosting tinted a delicate shell pink. Makes about 15 large or 24 small cupcakes.

Other Ways to Bake this Cake: Double recipe and use three 9-inch layer pans or two 9x9x2-inch pans. Bake in moderate oven (375°F.) 30 to 35 minutes. Or bake in 13x9x2-inch pan in moderate oven (375°F.) 45 minutes, or until done.

Kate Smith says—

"Beating cut in half!"

"No creaming!"

"Fewer dishes to wash!"

"Richer taste!"

"Keeps fresh longer!"

TUNE IN: Kate Smith Speaks —CBS Network

Watch for New "Mix-Easy" Recipes in your Swans Down box!

New "Mix-Easy" recipes . . . developed and tested in Swans Down kitchens at General Foods . . . are constantly appearing in Swans Down packages.

Guarantee—Double the cost of all ingredients back, if you don't think your Swans Down "Mix-Easy" Cake is better than any similar cake you've baked with any other flour! Swans Down itself has not changed—you can still use all your old favorite recipes. Swans Down has made supremely fine cakes for 50 years. And today more women choose Swans Down than all other packaged cake flours put together.

Bake a better cake with Swans Down

SWANS DOWN CAKE FLOUR

KATE SMITH SPEAKS

CBS
11:00 A.M.
C.S.T.

"Give Christmas Menus a Holiday Touch with Post's Bran Muffins!"

"And what could be more delicious Christmas morning than a luscious batch of hot, oven-fresh Post's Bran Muffins? The folks'll love them!"

directions. You can always count on fresh, real-bran flavor because the golden flakes are "FreshProtected." A new, exclusive inner-liner gives their crispy, crackling goodness all the way from the toasting ovens to you.

Crisp and crunchy on the outside, these wonderful muffins are light and tender inside. Each tempting mouthful makes you want to eat more—and more! Play safe and double the recipe.

In muffins—as cereal, Post's Bran Flakes are delicious. And they supply just enough bran to help prevent irregularity due to lack of bulk in the diet. Make them your daily "ounce of prevention."

When "It's High Noon in New York," Kate Smith Speaks—Monday through Friday, CBS Network. 12 noon EST, 11 A.M. CST, 10 A.M. MST, 9 A.M. PST.

It's really easy to make melt-in-your-mouth muffins with Post's 40% Bran Flakes. Just follow the package

Post's 40% BRAN FLAKES

LIFE IS SWELL WHEN YOU KEEP WELL

POST'S CEREALS—FreshProtected FOR CRISPNESS

There'll be bluebirds over the white cliffs of Dover tomorrow, just you wait and see.

—From The White Cliffs of Dover, recorded by Kate Smith in 1942

I Survived the War of the Worlds!

WAY BACK BEFORE ASTRONAUTS, THIS READER MANAGED TO MAKE IT THROUGH A "MARTIAN INVASION."

By Robert Tefertillar, Springfield, Illinois

FLYING SAUCER

Halloween eve fell on a Sunday in 1938, so the usual community festivities in my hometown of Centralia, Illinois, had been rescheduled for the following night.

I was one disappointed 11-year-old, resigned to a boring evening at home, listening to radio programs with the rest of my family. None of my favorite adventures or serials was on. Even Edgar Bergen and Charlie McCarthy didn't seem particularly funny that night.

No one objected when Gramps began twisting the dial in search of more interesting fare. He paused at a music program and was about to move on when we heard a news flash.

The announcer had quickly commanded our complete attention. He said that a Chicago scientist had just observed several big explosions on the planet Mars!

"Mars, huh?" my grandfather grunted loud enough for us all to hear. "That's a million miles away—what's that got to do with us?"

A SPACESHIP LANDED!

The music started once again, but it was almost immediately interrupted by a frantic announcement about "a fiery, unknown object from space" that had crashed in a farm field near Gravers Mill, New Jersey.

Now my ears were really riveted to our old Philco! When the announcer promised to keep us posted on any developments, an awful premonition began to turn my stomach inside out. My fears were not quieted when the music stopped for good a moment later.

"There are fragmented, unsubstantiated reports of many people dead or injured in New Jersey," the announcer said in a trembling voice.

"What in billy blue blazes is going on?" my uncle stammered.

Grandma gasped. "Mercy, that man said people were dead and injured!"

"There's got to be some mistake," Gramps snapped. "I don't care how scared that announcer sounds. There'll be a commercial soon, and we'll find out this is all made up."

COULD IT BE REAL?

This isn't made up! my mind was screaming. *It has to be real!*

After all, I'd read all about Superman coming from another planet, and I kept up with all the adventures of Buck Rogers.

I knew exactly what that thing in New Jersey was: a spaceship from Mars filled with terrible monsters that were killing people. They'd probably get all of us—including me!

On the radio, another voice cut in. It was a reporter actually on the scene at Gravers Mill!

"This is unbelievable!" he gasped. "I am standing on a small hill observing what is just not possible. What has landed here is a silver spacecraft of some sort...

"These creatures," he continued, "are huge, slug-like beings. Their weapons are some sort of ray guns, shooting a deadly green flame. Another

A CONVINCING ACT. Actor Orson Welles terrified a large number of radio listeners across North America—including the author!

cylinder has just crash-landed... the police are moving in... *Arrrgghhh!*"

Just then a tremendous pounding at the front door sent me cowering behind Gramps' chair. Our neighbor Jessie Collins barged into the room, ashen-faced and shaking.

"What's...what's going on?" Jessie managed to stammer. "Is this for real?"

"It can't be real!" my grandfather insisted.

Outside our house, there was commotion in the street. Grandma threw open the front door, and I peered cautiously around her skirts.

Our neighbors were streaming from their houses. Some had guns, others carried pitchforks and baseball bats. All eyes were scanning the clear, star-filled sky, searching for signs of those dreaded silver cylinders from Mars.

Some folks, who'd tuned in the program from the beginning, said it was only make-believe. They tried to convince their hysterical neighbors it was all a put-on. But nobody believed them.

We stayed awake for hours watching for Martians. When we finally went to bed, Gramps was grumbling about how easily people had been taken in. I, on the other hand, was not completely convinced. Just to be safe, I slept on the floor of my grandparents' room. Meanwhile, a few neighborhood diehards kept a lonely all-night watch from their porch swings, with loaded shotguns in their laps!

Next morning, the newspaper revealed the embarrassing truth: *The War of the Worlds* broadcast by Orson Welles had frightened not only our neighborhood, but a good portion of North America!

Welles himself professed amazement that his make-believe performance had been taken literally. (I think he was secretly pleased!)

I know I will never forget the genuine terror I felt that night. Nowadays, modern "space-creature" movies just don't seem as scary. After all, I survived the Martian attack of 1938!

Know Ye the Bearer MRS NORMAN H REYNOLDS has been duly proclaimed "Cinderella," winner of radio program "Cinderella Weekend," Station WBZ Therefore be it known Cinderella REYNOLDS is entitled to all privileges and honors bestowed upon her and her Prince Charming while in New York, Nov 7, 8, 9 '52

Given this date under hand and seal
Nov 7 '52   Barbara Walace

We Won Prizes Galore!

My Cinderella Weekend

Back when radio quiz shows like *Quiz Kids* and *Queen for a Day* were popular, I decided to try to get on a local program broadcast from station WBZ in Boston.

Cinderella Weekend awarded good prizes, and the big winner was flown to New York City for an all-expenses-paid weekend for two. As a young mother living in Everett, Massachusetts, I figured I could use a vacation!

To qualify for the New York trip, a contestant had to win one day during the week, then compete with all the other weekday winners on Sunday.

Despite being a little nervous, I wrote the station and gave them my name. Several weeks later, I was informed that I'd been chosen to compete on the Tuesday show.

I was lucky enough to be the show's daily winner, which entitled me to compete in Sunday's big contest against the other weekday winners.

Here's the question they asked on Sunday: "This is a common slang expression conveying disappointment. Fill in the blank: Oh, _____."

I answered "fudge" and couldn't believe it when they told me I'd won.

Immediately the talkmasters converged, loading me down with all kinds of prizes, as can be seen above—sterling silver filigree jewelry, a watch, salad dressings, cases of soda, and every kind of household item anyone could imagine.

My husband and I were just starting out, so we were thrilled with everything. My mother was equally happy to baby-sit our 1-year-old son,

Normie, while the two of us spent a carefree weekend in New York.

We visited the Empire State Building, saw a play, shopped in the big department stores and ate in some very nice restaurants—all paid for by WBZ.

Looking at our old photos of the contest brings back a rush of memories—the way you feel when you hear an old familiar song. How I wish we could do it all over again!

—**Doris Reynolds,** *Foxboro, Massachusetts*

Mom Had Last Laugh

I was a secretary at an adverising agency at 30 Rockefeller Plaza in New York City in the late '40s, when radio quiz prizes were not astronomical.

Since the NBC studios were located in my building, we received tickets for audience participation shows as perks.

Being a contestant became my hobby, and I never went away empty-handed.

Although I did not win on *Break the Bank*, I did receive $500 and a package containing several Bristol-Myers personal health care products.

Once, I won a Lane hope chest, and over time, I filled it with GE toasters and Oneida silverware.

My least desirable prize was a year's supply of floor wax. When it arrived, my mother beamed.

"Now you can wax the kitchen floor on weekends," she said.

—**Elise Brennen**
Santa Barbara, California

My Pop Wrote for 'Fibber McGee and Molly'

THE WHOLE COUNTRY WAS LAUGHING ON TUESDAYS, THANKS TO THIS AUTHOR'S FUNNY FATHER.

By Susan Leslie Peters, Eugene, Oregon

Every Tuesday night when I was a kid, I'd tune in for another visit to "79 Wistful Vista," home of Fibber McGee and Molly.

Along with countless other radio listeners across the country, I'd laugh out loud at the antics of the McGees (played by the husband-and-wife team of Jim and Marian Jordan) and a cast of crazy characters.

My enjoyment was never diminished by the fact that I often knew what the characters would be saying. My pop, Phil Leslie, wrote more than 1,000 scripts for this classic show.

Pop helped "put words in the mouths" of the wacky bunch that regularly visited 79 Wistful Vista. There was Dr. Gamble, Fibber's obese buddy and insult-trader, and The Old-Timer, who always said, "Hiya, kids! Hiya, Johnnie!"

Remember These Characters?

Mr. Wimple often stopped by with his ever-present bird book, plus Sweetie-Face, his big old wife. And who could forget the stuffy Mayor LaTrivia? Dignified, formal and persistently pompous, he was the character the McGees delighted in deflating!

Audience members young and old were primed to expect and enjoy LaTrivia's "letdowns and blowups," culminating with a long pause and then a drawn-out "McGeeeeee?"

Midway through the program, announcer Harlow Wilcox, in his "perfect sales voice," would tout the virtues of Johnson Wax—with Fibber cracking jokes in the background. The commercial was really an ingenious part of the show. The laughing audience actually enjoyed being sold on Johnson products!

Each year at Christmastime, we listeners knew Teeny, the kid character, would con Fibber into telling her a story like *The Patient Little Star* or *Laura, the Lopsided Pine.*

Sweet Music

As he told the story, Fibber was joined by The King's Men, the musical quartet that appeared on the show each week. Headed up by Ken Darby, they cheerily sang during the Christmas season, and I clearly recall their songs, though it's been half a century since they graced the airwaves.

As good as that popular cast of characters was, the success of *Fibber McGee and Molly* depended on two important ingredients—the incredible sound effects produced by Monty Frazier, and the vivid imagination of every listener.

Both would jump into action whenever Fibber would say, "It's right here in the hall closet!"

"McGee!" Molly'd beg. "Don't open that door!"

Of course, what followed was the most astounding cacophony of crashes, thumps, bumps and booms, followed by a sweet tinkling bell that signaled the end of the chaos.

Then came Pop's favorite "sound effects"—the laughter and applause of the studio audience.

Today, TV comedies don't leave much to the imagination. But in the golden age of radio, listeners really got into the action, visualizing in their mind's eye what they heard through the crackly speaker.

It makes me pleased and proud to think that my pop (pictured below between Marian and Jim Jordan) helped millions of folks make that imaginary visit to Fibber McGee and Molly's place every Tuesday night.

Thanks, Pop—from all of us!

To Know Red Skelton Was to Love Him

THIS KING OF COMEDY HAD A HEART OF GOLD.

By Jean Allen Brown, Tacoma, Washington

In my teen years, I listened faithfully to Red Skelton's radio programs and loved his little boy segments, with the tagline "I dood it."

Well, when World War II was ending, in the summer of 1945, Leo Sweeney, my GI fiancé, and Red Skelton were together at a hospital camp near Blackstone, Virginia.

Leo and I were married on July 13, 1945. After our honeymoon Leo had to report back to camp. I went with him and we took a room at the Blackstone Hotel.

The hotel owner was eager for me to meet Red, so he took me to camp, where we picked up Leo. As we drove around, Red ran up to the car, hopped on the running board, greeted us and then won me over by saying, "Hey, Sweeney, how'd you manage to win such a sweetheart?"

Once I was out at camp when Red was in the hospital. I was sitting on his bed visiting, and across from me on the wall was a pencil sketch he had done of a hospital urinal with a bouquet of flowers in it. I laughed about it—and now wish I'd asked for it.

At an event for officers, one of the soldiers came to the table and asked me to dance. I was no sooner back to the table when another GI asked for a dance. It finally dawned on me that these boys thought Red and I were married and wanted to go home and talk about dancing with Red Skelton's wife. Red said, "Hey, don't tell them any different. Go ahead, dance and give them a thrill."

That night, Red handed me a chain with a St. Christopher medal. I could not accept it, but Leo said he would give me Red's dog tag, as they had switched tags earlier. The tag now hangs beside an autographed photo of Red on which he wrote the following message:

"To Jean, my dear friend who married my best friend. Well, all is fair in love and Blackstone. Love, Red Skelton."

One day, Red and I were talking in the hotel lobby, and he said he was going into the bar. Halfway across, he did one of his famous pratfalls, picked himself up and walked away, his shoulders shaking with laughter. I was in shock—Red Skelton had done a pratfall just for me!

I once asked him how he found time for all that he did. I'm sure his answer will stay with me forever: "Jean, everyone has time to do what he wants to do."

I'm so sorry there was only one Red Skelton. The world could use many more like him.

This Show Can't Be Topped!

My favorite jokes (which I repeat often, to the chagrin of my children) come from the old radio program *Can You Top This?*

When I was a child, my family rocked with laughter at the antics of the three featured comedians, "Senator" Ed Ford, Harry Hershfield and Joe Laurie Jr.

During each show a listener's joke and a joke told by one of the humorists were read to a live audience. Then, a "laugh meter" measured audience reaction to the two jokes, and the funnier was declared the winner for that round.

I always looked forward to new jokes and an evening of fun with the three hilarious stars of *Can You Top This?*

—**Lorraine Walterscheid,** *Manhattan, Kansas*

'Banjo Eyes' Was My Grandfather

Eddie Cantor might've been famous, but to me, he was a terrific grandfather who could make a banana go in one ear and come out the other—or turn into a quarter.

I was a captive audience—I can still see his big "banjo eyes" sparkle when he made me laugh. Here we are in a publicity shot taken in 1954.

When Eddie went on radio, his show was top-rated for many years. And when television came along, the only host of the *Colgate Comedy Hour* to beat Ed Sullivan in the ratings every time was Grandfather. (The two "Eds" were good friends.)

Grandfather died in 1964, but thanks to fans and family, Eddie Cantor will never be forgotten.

—**Brian Gari,** *New York, New York*

'Cinnamon Bear'
Was a Sweet Serial

WOULD THE FEISTY LITTLE IRISH
BEAR FIND THE SILVER STAR IN MAYBELAND?
YOU HAD TO STAY TUNED.

By Carolyn Kolibaba, Portland, Oregon

HI, PADDY! The beloved Christmas tradition of Paddy O'Cinnamon's search for the silver star lives on in this radio fan's home and heart.

Do you remember Christmastime in 1937, when Paddy O'Cinnamon and his friends, Jimmy and Judy Barton, began their search for the silver star?

I certainly do! I sat there with my ear pressed against the speaker of a Sears Roebuck super heterodyne console radio, imagining a golden glass airplane flying over the Root Bear Ocean and Looking Glass Valley.

This charming children's story was created by Glanville Heisch, a talented young writer at radio station KFI in Los Angeles. That autumn, he'd been asked if he could create a serialized children's Christmas tale to begin airing just after Thanksgiving.

"No, I can't," said Glanville. "I don't do children's stories."

"Yes, we can," said Glanville's wife when he told her about the idea. With Glanville writing each night and his wife editing and typing each day for six weeks straight, they managed to create 26 episodes and 12 songs of fairy-tale charm and adventure that captured my heart forever.

The Cinnamon Bear involved the adventures of twins Jimmy and Judy Barton and Paddy O'Cinnamon, the feisty but cuddly Irish bear who spoke with a distinct brogue.

The trio searched Maybeland for a silver star. It was intended to top the Christmas tree, but it had been snatched from an attic trunk by the Crazyquilt Dragon and flown to Maybeland.

Search Led to Magic

In their travels, the trio got lost in the Picture Forest, ate snacks in Goody-Goody Cove and heard S.S. Crocodile sing in The Wishing Woods.

They also ran into the terrible Wintergreen Witch, met the sweet Queen Melissa and saw Niki Frudl, Santa's chief of elves.

During World War II, *The Cinnamon Bear* went into hibernation at the radio station here in Portland. Through the years, I often thought of it at Christmastime.

Then, one wonderful day during the '50s, *The Cinnamon Bear* was back! By then, I had three daughters who could listen just as I had. It became one of our family's holiday traditions.

Realizing *The Cinnamon Bear* could disappear from the radio again, I spent three Christmas seasons taking shorthand notes of every episode (this was before cassette tapes), then typing them into book form.

Each chapter has original illustrations done by our youngest daughter and a detailed map of Maybeland. The book went into a cinnamon-brown binder, and each December, we put it out with our own cinnamon teddy bear.

Not Alone in Maybeland

Some years later, I began to wonder who wrote *The Cinnamon Bear*. In 1977, after a lot of searching through old radio archives and writing letters, Frank Nelson, the actor who played Captain Tin Top on the show, put me in touch with Glanville.

He and I corresponded until his death in 1986. During that time, he sent me an autographed copy of *The Cinnamon Bear* theme song and a photo of him and his wife, which I place next to the silver star at the top of my Christmas tree.

A year after Glanville's death, I was pleasantly surprised to read in our local paper that, in honor of Paddy O'Cinnamon's fiftieth birthday, a newspaper editor in Kenosha, Wisconsin, had formed a national fan club, the Cinnamon Bear Brigade. He wanted to hear from all the grown-up children who recalled the radio show.

I sent a note, and we happily collaborated on his newsletter, *The Bear Facts*. Eventually, we heard from nearly 500 people, bound together by the sweet memory of an old-time Christmas story.

And all those years, I thought I was the only one who remembered!

LOVEBIRDS. Art and Joanna Nugent (left) and Kyle and Shirley Waite were brought together by the radio.

Love on the Airwaves

Rebel Song Roused a Romance

It was July 21, 1958, and I was deejaying a request and dedication show at radio station KONG in Visalia, California, from 7 p.m. till midnight.

Many people called in with an abrupt "Play this" or "Play that," but suddenly there was a nice voice on the phone requesting, "Would you please play *Rebel Rouser* by Duane Eddy? Thank you."

I was so taken aback by her "thank you" that I thanked the caller in return. She called back, and we spent the entire evening talking about life.

Joanna and I were married on April 18, 1959, and we have been going strong ever since.

Just before I retired in 2007 after 50 years in the business, the *Fresno Bee* ran a story about my career and mentioned Duane Eddy's song. Well, someone who knew him faxed him the story.

On my last day, Joanna was at the station, and to our surprise, the famous guitarist called with best wishes. He said he'd never thought of *Rebel Rouser* as a love song, but he said he would from now on!

—**Art Nugent,** *Visalia, California*

We Were Married on Network Radio!

Many young women dream of a big wedding, but few can imagine having *thousands* of guests from all across the America. That's just what happened to me, though, when my husband, Kyle, and I were wed in 1949. We exchanged our vows on the air!

I often listened to the popular radio show *Bride and Groom* in my little apartment in Twin Falls, Idaho. Couples were actually married during the program, and then showered with gifts.

The producers were looking for unusual love stories to share with their listners, so I submitted ours. You see, our relationship began when Kyle, who was working as a cook, served me an awful hamburger. When I said I didn't like it, he threw me into a snowbank!

What a thrill it was to receive a telegram that read, "Your application to be on *Bride and Groom* has been accepted. You have been given the date of Friday, Aug. 26, 1949."

On the program, we shared our love story. Then we exchanged vows and Jack McElroy sang our lovely wedding song, *'Tis You*. Next, we were presented with $2,000 worth of gifts and an all-expenses-paid honeymoon!

Each year on our anniversary, we listen to our recording of that memorable day when we were married on the air.

—**Shirley Pope Waite,** *Walla Walla, Washington*

'... And Now A Word From Our Sponsor'

It seems like only yesterday that I was in the smoky twilight of Pittsburgh, Pennsylvania, in the 1940s, watching for the streetlights to come on.

This was the signal for my buddies and me to end our games and run home to get a seat in front of the family radio.

I could just see—with my vivid imagination—the Lone Ranger and Silver, galloping out of the mesh speaker of our trusty Philco radio.

Fred Foy's exciting voice announced that classic polished opening, "A fiery horse with the speed of light, a cloud of dust and a hearty 'Hi-Yo, Silver!'—The Lone Ranger!" and then word of a special premium offer from Cheerios, or some other type of cereal.

No matter what I was doing, I always made sure that I was home in time to thrill to that classic opening of gunshots, hoofbeats and the *William Tell Overture*.

For the next 30 minutes, the voice of Brace Beemer as the Lone Ranger cast a spell that no one could interrupt.

And every kid across America waited to hear the deep-voiced announcer exclaim, just before the show's middle commercial break, "And now a word from our sponsor!"

If you were a Lone Ranger Deputy or a Safety Scout, you knew this message just might mean another Lone Ranger premium would soon be available for one thin Mercury dime and a Cheerios box top.

First there was always the frantic hunt for a sharp pencil and a piece of paper. Once you had the information and that all-important General Mills address in Minnesota, you had only to convince your parents to buy the cereal at the store so that you could tape your dime to the box top and mail them immediately.

The long three- to six-week wait began. Every day after school, you came home and asked, "Did I get any mail?"

Then, one day, sitting on the dining room table, was that special brown package from Cheerios with your name on it.

I still remember those warm, humid summer evenings, sitting on the front stoop of our row house with my buddies, proudly showing them my newest Lone Ranger premium.

And somehow I knew, at that very moment, that everything was right in the world of my youthful dreams.

—*Lee Felbinger, Green Lane, Pennsylvania*

MY YEARS WITH
'TRUTH OR CONSEQUENCES'
PRODUCED FAMOUS MEMORIES

IT'S THE TRUTH—ALL THE CONSEQUENCES WERE GOOD
WHEN HE WORKED FOR RALPH EDWARDS ON THIS POPULAR '40S SHOW.

By William Burch, Sacramento, California

Sometimes good luck and timing alter the course of our lives. Such was the case with me one day in 1945.

My new bride and I were returning to Hollywood from our wedding in her hometown of Rushville, Indiana.

We stopped in Las Vegas for the night, and I called my office. (I'd recently returned from the Air Force and was working for NBC.) It was lucky I called in—my boss, Howard Wiley, wanted me to handle an assignment for *Truth or Consequences*, one of the most popular radio programs in the country.

TRIBUTE TO WOUNDED MARINE

Back in California, I met Ralph Edwards at his home in Beverly Hills. Ralph told me about an idea for a special broadcast to honor a wounded Marine at a hospital in Honolulu.

The Marine's hometown was Salem, Oregon. Ralph's idea was to have the young serviceman, through the magic of radio, "walk" down the main street of Salem. On his walk, the Marine would greet the mayor, druggist, barber who cut his hair, a buddy from high school and, finally, his parents.

My job was to go to Salem and line up all the people for this remote broadcast, then record background sounds to add realism and bring the Marine as "close to home" as possible.

The magic worked—that show won awards. A month later, I went to work for Ralph Edwards Productions as writer/director for *Truth or Consequences*. The next few years were a ball!

There were four of us "idea men" who met every Wednesday morning at Ralph's house to come up with the popular gags and stunts. Each of us thought up six "consequences" each week, and Ralph selected the ones for that week's show.

HILARIOUS SKITS

Of the thousands of stunts we did, two of the funniest and probably best-remembered were those we called "Amateur Comedian" and "Thump Melons."

The Amateur Comedian stunt required a woman to read a very bad joke from a card. It was a joke no one would laugh at—but when the woman read the punch line, the audience howled.

What she didn't know was that every time she read the punch line, we'd dunk her husband in a tank of water just out of her sight! She'd tell the joke over and over without the slightest idea of why the audience was laughing so hard.

The "Thump Melon" stunt started with Ralph asking for a woman volunteer from the audience who thought she was a good shopper.

After being shown a table with five smooth-skinned melons, the female contestant was blindfolded and told to pick out the ripest of the melons by thumping them.

What the woman didn't know was that after she was blindfolded, we substituted her husband's bald head for one of the melons. Believe me, no matter what the woman said, she got a laugh!

As funny as both of those stunts were, the most talked-about and publicized of all was one we called "Mr. Hush."

The March of Dimes had asked Ralph to come up with a fundraising promotion. Rather than "just another stunt," Ralph got the idea of having a celebrity record a jingle that would contain a clue to his identity. Each week the clue would change, getting easier, as more prizes were added.

NAME HAD A FAMILIAR RING

But who would be named as Mr. Hush? We didn't want to disguise his voice, so most familiar radio and movie personalities were eliminated right off the bat. It wasn't until the night before the broadcast that Ralph and I finally decided on boxer Jack Dempsey.

The two of us were the only ones who knew the identity of Mr. Hush. For the next eight weeks, hundreds of thousands of people sent in donations along with their guesses. I don't remember who finally figured it out, but the March of Dimes was the big winner.

After Mr. Hush, we also featured a Miss Hush (silent film actress Clara Bow) and The Walking Man (comedian Jack Benny, so named because of his hometown, Waukegan, Illinois).

In those days, working for Ralph was a family affair. But a few years later when television came along, one show a week became five. Seven employees grew to 50—and the office over Ralph's garage became an entire building.

After that, at least for me, it was never quite the same. Ralph didn't change, though. I visited with him in the 1990s, and he looked much the way he did on that fateful day in 1945 when he sent me off to Salem, Oregon.

NBC HOST. Tour guide Bob Vesel of Belen, New Mexico (far left), awaits a happy group of visitors at at New York's Radio City. This landmark was the headquarters of NBC, the radio network that broadcast *Truth or Consequences*. "Note the newspaper held by the man on the right," writes Bob. "It's heralding an early victory in World War II."

Cracking the Case

'Gangbusters' Fugitive Nabbed by Hero Listeners

"Crime isn't the way...crime doesn't pay." That was the message of the popular radio program *Gangbusters*, which aired nationally from 1935 to 1957. The show was known for thrilling stories and the weekly "call for help from listeners" to locate a wanted criminal.

Pauline Virgin, then 12, of Gearhart, Oregon, and her family were big *Gangbusters* fans. Every Saturday, they'd listen to the announcer "calling all Americans to war on the underworld" as real-life cases were presented and solved.

At the end of each broadcast, the announcer gave a description of a wanted criminal and asked listeners to help find him. Usually by that time, Pauline yawned and got ready for bed. But on one spring night in 1947, she recognized the fugitive being described!

"I've always noticed details about people," Pauline explains. "And the description given that night made me suspect that the man they were looking for, John Harvey Bugg, was my riding instructor at the Gearhart Riding Academy—otherwise known as 'Cowboy Jim Williams.'"

According to *Gangbusters*, Bugg had been working near Seminole, Oklahoma. Needing money, he wrote a check on his employer's account, then fled by car to Missouri. He'd been arrested by a Missouri sheriff but later escaped.

Pauline remembered that Cowboy Jim had a limp, like the fugitive from *Gangbusters*. The tape on his fingers was suspicious, too.

"My girlfriends and I were already curious about that," Pauline recalls. "When we asked why he wore tape on his fingers, he'd never tell us." Pauline suspected the tape covered the tattooed letters L-O-V-E on Cowboy Jim's hands, yet another part of Bugg's description.

Despite all this incriminating evidence, Pauline didn't want to get her friend into trouble.

The day after the broadcast, Pauline confided in her cousin, Navarre Smith, who was 14. As a Boy Scout, Navarre decided he must do his duty, even if it meant blowing the whistle on a man who was popular with folks in Gearhart.

After school, Navarre rode his bike to the police station in nearby Seaside, Oregon, and said he and his cousin knew the whereabouts of the fugitive.

Word spread quickly that the police were looking for Bugg. He fled east to Hillside, Oregon, but was captured a few days later at a friend's house. He surrendered without a struggle.

The crime-stoppers became celebrities in no time. Saluted on *Gangbusters* and interviewed on radio station KEX in Portland, they got fan mail from across the country, and received about $500 from various rewards.

But the story continues. John Harvey Bugg was eventually released from prison, returned to Gearhart and went back to work at the stables.

"One day I was riding my bike home from school and saw him outside the stables," Pauline says. "He waved and called to me, but I was afraid to stop."

That night, Bugg visited Pauline's family, and she discovered her fears were unfounded. "He wanted to thank me," she explains. "He had been tired of hiding and just wanted to forget the past." Bugg had lived in fear of capture for five years. He'd even given up a career on the rodeo circuit to avoid being recognized.

The citizens of Gearhart were ready to welcome the man they knew as Cowboy Jim back into the community. They always believed in his basic goodness. "And," Pauline adds, "he became one of my dad's closest friends!"

—*Jan Holden, Vancouver, Washington*

CRIMEBUSTERS. Navarre Smith and Pauline Virgin became celebrities when they "ratted" on a *Gangbusters* fugitive.

No 'Coming on Like Gangbusters' for Her

The radio program I least liked was *Gangbusters*. I wasn't allowed to listen to it, but I could still hear it from my room after I was sent to bed.

The scariest part of the show came at the end of the program, when they described an escaped convict or wanted person. The announcer would say that if we saw this person, we were to call the police immediately.

I'd bury my head under the pillow so I wouldn't be able to identify a murderer or a robber!

After that, I'd try to fall asleep so as not to hear the squeaking door that kicked off *Inner Sanctum*, which aired afterward.

—**Evelyn McCarthy,** *Lyme, New Hampshire*

Thrillers and Chillers

My brother, Chris, and I liked almost every radio mystery program, but *Inner Sanctum* was high on our list. I was really thrilled when its host, Raymond Edward Johnson, replied to my fan letter. He even sent me Christmas cards for a couple of years.

Later, while at Lone Ranger Camp (Camp Kemosabe) in Michigan, Chris got "hooked" on *The Hermit's Cave.*

Back home in Louisiana, we waited eagerly for cool weather (radio reception improved considerably in those months) so we could get a Detroit station and hear that spooky cackling voice saying, "Ghost stories! Weird stories! And murders, too! The Hermit knows them all. Hee hee hee!"

But our favorite radio serial of all was *Lights Out.* Since it came on quite late, our parents made Chris and me go to bed at the usual time and set the alarm for 11 p.m. so we could get up and listen.

The stories on *Lights Out* were truly fearsome, and Chris took advantage. One evening after the show had ended, he sneaked up behind me and frightened me half to death with an icy hand he'd "primed" in the refrigerator!

After that, I always made sure to climb the stairs to my bedroom backward so I could keep an eye on him.

—**Marguerite Wilson,** *New Brighton, Minnesota*

THEY KNEW WHO KNEW. "Our daughters, Patricia and Jean, were dedicated fans of *The Shadow*," writes Victor Bennett of Horicon, Wisconsin. "They were virtually glued to our Majestic console radio during the program, as seen in this photo from 1950." In the '30s, actor Orson Welles was the voice of Lamont Cranston, who fought crime as the Shadow.

WHAT'S YOUR I.Q.?

My Brother Was Dr. I.Q.!

Back in the '30s, after homework and chores were done, our family gathered 'round the radio to listen to shows like *Fibber McGee and Molly*, *Amos 'n' Andy* and *One Man's Family*.

Those old shows were great, but another network program was our household favorite. It was called *Dr. I.Q.* I happen to remember it well because the star of the show was my big brother, Lew Valentine!

Dr. I.Q., which aired Monday nights on NBC, was one of the first radio quiz shows. Folks all over the country won cash for answering questions from Lew, posing as "Dr. I.Q., The Mental Banker." That was a lofty title for a fellow who never finished high school!

At the time, my family lived in San Benito, a small town in the Lower Rio Grande Valley of Texas. Lew was bitten by the radio bug at age 17 and dropped out of high school just six months before he would have graduated.

The school superintendent consoled Mother by telling her Lew was so intent on a career in radio that he'd probably do OK. And he did.

Lew's first job was at a station in Houston. From there he went to San Antonio, where he worked at WOAI, opening his daily broadcasts with a lusty "Good morning, everyone!"

Mother would turn up the radio so my brother's voice boomed throughout the house. Around 1935, the *Dr. I.Q.* show was born.

It was first aired nationally in 1939, sponsored by Mars Inc., maker of Mars bars, Snickers, Milky Way and Three Musketeers.

The show was broadcast live from different movie theaters in large cities across America. After

A 'Smart' Suitor

In 1949, I dated a girl whose parents always listened to *Dr. I.Q.* At that time, I was working in the mail room at American Broadcasting in Chicago, where the program's scripts were printed.

One week, the girl and I played a trick on her parents. I memorized the answers to every question on their favorite radio show, including the infamous "Thought Twister" and the "Biographical Sketch."

When I arrived for our next date, she was deliberately late getting ready so that I'd have to listen to the program with her parents. I calmly answered each question before any of the studio contestants even had a chance to speak. Her mother and father were amazed, but I acted as if it were no great feat.

Later, as my date and I were leaving the house, I nonchalantly handed her father a copy of the broadcast script.

—**Tom Cantrell,** *San Luis, Colorado*

THE DOCTOR IS IN. Lew Valentine got his start at Texas station WOAI in the early 1930s. He later starred on one of radio's first quiz shows, *Dr. I.Q.*

the movie, Lew would take the stage while several assistants with hand-held microphones spread out in the audience.

An assistant would select a contestant and exclaim, "I have a lady right here in the balcony, Doctor!" Lew would reply, "I have 10 silver dollars for that lady if she can tell me..." and then he'd ask a question.

The amount of prize money would vary with the difficulty of the question.

If the lady in the balcony (or any other contestant) missed the question, she or he would receive a box of Mars candy bars and two tickets to a movie.

In addition to the questions, there was an impossible tongue twister that hardly anyone got right. Called "The Monument to Memory," it was spoken only once by Dr. I.Q. and then had to be repeated by the contestant.

One that I recall was, "'Jim is slim,' said Tim to Kim. 'Jim is slim, Tim,' to him, said Kim."

Another game was "The Biographical Sketch," which was worth 75 silver dollars. The contestant got a clue about a famous person. If the contestant guessed the name after the first clue, he or she won $75. The amount decreased with each clue. Whatever the game, residents of San Benito were very proud of their hometown boy. But none was prouder than Mother.

Lew traveled with the show until the start of World War II, when he enlisted and entertained the troops. Family and friends never grew tired of Lew's stories about all the people he met and the fun he had being Dr. I.Q.

Lew passed away in 1976, but I'm sure many listeners out there still remember him—and all those ladies in the balcony!

—**Madelyn Harris,** *Las Cruces, New Mexico*

MEET A TRUE
COUNTRY-LOVIN' DEEJAY

"MISS DEEJAY USA" STARTED AS A SECRETARY FOR GENERAL MOTORS.

By Pat Boyd, Grand Rapids, Michigan

While most of my high school classmates were dancing to the Big Bands in the late 1940s, I was keeping record shops in business buying the music of Roy Acuff, Eddy Arnold and Hank Williams.

I was born and raised in Grand Rapids, but my mama and daddy had come from Roberts Switch, Tennessee, so I grew up listening to the *Grand Ole Opry*.

After graduating in 1950, I became a secretary at General Motors and also presided over the fan club of Del Wood, "America's Ragtime Sweetheart." Her song *Down Yonder* was an international hit in the '50s.

This experience gave me the courage to write to Joe Hooker, station manager at WMAX, and ask for the job as disc jockey on the morning "drive time" country music spot.

I was amazed when Joe wrote back and said, "Come on down!"

From 1955 to 1965, my day started by running to the station, doing two hours on the air, dashing home to dress for my job at GM, then back to the studio after work for another two hours. I closed each program by saying, "Put the coffeepot on, Mamma—I'm coming right home."

Whenever recording artists came to town to perform at the Civic Auditorium, the station asked me to emcee. Imagine the pleasure this lifelong fan had when finally meeting Roy Acuff and his Smoky Mountain Boys! I also introduced Roger Miller, George Jones, Ernest Tubb, Ray Price, Faron Young, Johnny Cash and June Carter and the Carter Family.

Many of those country stars had appeared on the *Grand Ole Opry*. But in 1957, it was my turn. I was selected "Miss Deejay USA," an honor Opry station WSM gave to female disc jockeys who had contributed to the promotion of classic country music.

It was an absolute thrill! I got to host a live show at the WSM mic, and while I was on the air, my dear friend Del Wood and recording artist

George Morgan (singer Lorrie Morgan's daddy) dropped by for interviews.

The next night, George Morgan introduced me on stage to the audience in the Ryman Auditorium, then home of the *Grand Ole Opry*. It was a weekend I'll never forget!

In 1965, I left the airwaves when classic country was overtaken by "uptown" country.

I was happily surprised a few years ago, however, when "Uncle" John Lubinskas of WBYW-FM, an all-volunteer station in Grand Rapids, called me. He invited me to "come on board" with my classic country sound, so I dusted off my LPs from the '50s and '60s and went back on the air with my *Function at the Junction* show at the ripe age of 65.

Fans from the good ol' days have registered their approval, and we're getting new recruits for our classic country fan base. It just goes to show: You're never too old to give it a shot!

NICE IN NASHVILLE. The stars were out the night author Pat Boyd was on the *Grand Ole Opry*. Gentleman Ernest Tubb (right) was good for a hug and Minnie Pearl (above) for a laugh.

PICKIN' AND GRINNIN'. When she was growing up in Grand Rapids, Michigan, the author could only dream of meeting her heroes. But the dream came true in Nashville, where stars like Faron Young (left), Roy Acuff (below, left) and Stonewall Jackson (below, right) proved country folks never get too big or too popular to meet their fans, and maybe even let them take a few licks on their guitars.

FARON YOUNG

Soap Fans Adored 'Stella Dallas'

The Day Stella Dallas Came to Visit

Her radio voice was known to millions, but Anne Elstner Matthews (second from right, above) could travel anywhere without being recognized. You see, she was better known as Stella Dallas, a dramatic radio role she played from 1937 till 1955.

When the radio soaps were eased off the networks in the mid-'50s, Anne and her husband, Jack, opened a restaurant along the banks of the Delaware River in Lambertville, New Jersey. The restaurant was a success, but Anne never forgot her glory days and often entertained guests with inside stories about her popular program.

During the late '60s, I was manager of an area radio station and thus had something in common with Anne. She often welcomed me to her corner table, where we'd swap stories.

Once she remarked that she still received plenty of mail addressed to "Stella Dallas." Many listeners actually believed that Stella, her daughter, Laurel ("Lolly Baby"), and other characters from the serial were real people solving real-life problems.

To illustrate, she told me about the time she and Jack were vacationing in the South and decided to visit New Orleans.

Upon reaching the Gulf Coast town of Biloxi, Mississippi, Jack reminded Anne that a Biloxi woman named Rose was not only a true believer in Stella Dallas, she was one of the most persistent correspondents Stella had ever had.

Rose's lengthy handwritten letters arrived at NBC studios almost daily. She offered endless advice to the long-suffering Stella and confided her own misfortunes. Rose invariably ended her letters by extending that familiar Southern invitation, "You come see me, you hear?"

Anne, who cherished her fans, made a spur-of-the-moment decision to look up her faithful listener. She also decided she'd stay in character to give the good woman the thrill of a lifetime.

Stepping up to the porch of a modest frame house on a quiet side street, she rang the doorbell.

"Who is it?" called a female voice.

"Stella Dallas," Anne answered.

At that, the door flew open to reveal a stout, middle-aged woman in a housedress and apron, her cherubic face lit up with a huge smile. "Stella, darling," she said, "I knew you'd come!"

Anne stayed for half an hour, took tea and joined Rose in a discussion of their "mutual problems." She didn't have the heart to tell this kindly soul that she was only an actress playing a part.

When she left, she received a tearful hug from the happiest woman in Mississippi!

—*Ed Ramsey,* Trenton, New Jersey

Taking a Break With Stella

During the Depression, my parents were farmers in southeast Oklahoma and had 10 children. All of us were accustomed to hard work, but when we weren't in the fields hoeing cotton or corn, we could listen to *Stella Dallas.*

If we were in the fields, Mother would send one of us to the house for some fresh drinking water, with permission to listen to *Stella Dallas* so we could all keep up with Stella and her "Lolly Baby."

I really enjoyed the program when it was my turn to sit by the radio, then relay the story to the others when I returned to the fields. Somehow, the work didn't seem so hard when we had *Stella Dallas* to look forward to.

—*Myrtle Beavers,* Destin, Florida

he could carry a tune

At the start of World War II, I was a sales promotion manager for General Electric in Los Angeles. GE had just released a unique new portable radio, and I was looking to give it some publicity.

I called a GE dealer in Hollywood who seemed to know everybody in show business. He said he knew somebody who knew Bing Crosby, so I asked if he could get Bing to pose for a picture with the radio.

The dealer called back later to say Bing would be happy to do it, in exchange for one of the radios. I could hardly believe it!

The picture proved to be quite a publicity bonanza for GE. It was my last marketing coup, however. Shortly thereafter, I joined the Army Signal Corps.

Now, whenever I show someone the picture, they ask, "Is that really Bing Crosby?"

When I assure them it is, they look at me (on the left) and ask, "Is that really you?"

I've lost some hair and added some pounds, but I've never forgotten the excitement of having my picture taken with a legendary star!

—**Lee DiAngelo,** St. Petersburg, Florida

THE SILVER SCREEN

Do you remember your first visit to the cinema? Was it a 50-cent Saturday matinee or perhaps an evening under the stars at the local drive-in?

"My favorite theater memory is of my first movie, *The Sound of Music*, when I was 5," says Rhonda Savage, one of our Facebook fans.

"We walked in and sat down in the most wonderful seats of deep-red velvet. When the lights went down, I was reminded to sit still and be quiet. That wasn't a problem! I was in awe as the red velvet curtains parted and the giant screen flickered to life.

"When Julie Andrews began twirling and singing on that green mountaintop, I was enthralled. The music! The dancing! It was magic. From that day I've been a movie buff. Classics and new movies, I love them all."

Read on for many more star-studded memories, from everyday folks who had chance encounters with celebrities to those who worked behind the scenes and on set.

THE GOLDEN
MOMENT

WRITING SONGS FOR WALT DISNEY CHANGED MY LIFE.
By Richard M. Sherman, Beverly Hills, California

I vividly recall the very moment, more than half a century ago, that completely altered the course of my life.

For years, my brother, Robert, and I had been toiling in the pop song market and had had dozens of songs published and recorded, but with modest success. Then a little rock ditty called *Tall Paul*, recorded by young Mouseketeer Annette Funicello in 1959, became a big hit and brought us to the attention of the Disney record people. They encouraged us to write more songs for Annette, and we enjoyed a string of successes with her.

It turned out that Walt Disney himself was noticing our work. Robert and I wrote more songs for Disney film and TV productions.

Then one day in the summer of 1960, after we'd demonstrated our latest song for Walt, he gave us his official seal of approval. "That'll work," he said, and handed us a small book.

"Do you know what a nanny is?" he asked.

We both replied, "A goat."

"No, no," Walt said, "I'm talking about a children's nursemaid. Read this and tell me what you think."

"STICKS, PAPER AND STRINGS"

RECOGNIZE THIS? The sheet music here is an early rendition of *Let's Go Fly a Kite* from the *Mary Poppins* score.

He didn't talk about needing a title song or production number, as he had done on previous occasions...and from his look, we knew this was much more than a song assignment.

HARD AT WORK

For the next two weeks, we worked with enormous enthusiasm on the little red-jacketed book called *Mary Poppins* by Pamela Travers. The stories were wonderful, but as there was no storyline, we created a workable one utilizing six delightful chapters. These stories and characters inspired ideas for songs such as *Jolly Holiday, I Love to Laugh* and *Feed the Birds*.

I recall how nervous we were when we asked Walt's secretary if we could have a half-hour meeting with him. Usually, Walt's meetings were brief and to the point, but we knew we had a lot to talk about. Our half-hour meeting ended up lasting more than two hours, and when we were through, Walt was as enthusiastic as Robert and I were about creating a musical film based on the Poppins stories.

I remember him saying, "You think 'story.' That's good. And I do like your idea of changing the time period to the turn of the century."

Walt leafed through our notes, glanced at the chapter headings we had underlined and

smiled. He then showed us the headings he had underlined in his copy of the book—they were exactly the same!

At that point he noted, "Looks like you fellas really like to work."

"Yes, sir," we both blurted out.

"Well, how would you like to work for me?"

That was the Golden Moment! It was the beginning of our 10 years as exclusive Disney songwriters, and our almost 50-year creative relationship with the Disney organization.

A LIFE OF SONG

Today, decades after the release of the film, the stage musical version of *Mary Poppins* is a smash hit on Broadway. To top it off, the show has premiered at various venues around the world, with stellar reviews.

My latest project is *Pazzazz!*, a musical that I wrote in collaboration with my friend Milt Larsen. It tells the story of Broadway's early years—the 1890s, when performers including George M. Cohan and Lillian Russell were on stage—and how it shaped the fabled place known as the Great White Way.

That Golden Moment launched so many wonderful experiences. Turn the page for more enchanting Disney memories.

WALT'S WORDSMITHS. After Walt Disney (center) hired the Sherman brothers to write the music for *Mary Poppins*, they composed scores for numerous Disney films, including *Bedknobs and Broomsticks*, *The Aristocats*, *The Jungle Book* and *The Tigger Movie*. The brothers also wrote the song *It's a Small World* for the 1964 New York World's Fair. Having created the score for *Chitty Chitty Bang Bang*, the brothers wrote new songs for the current successful stage version of the popular film in the United Kingdom.

A Budding Artist

My father-in-law liked to tell about the time he managed a restaurant in Chicago's Loop in the early '20s.

The owner insisted that busboys be quick and thorough. My father-in-law hired one busboy who was very nice, but unfortunately not very efficient. In fact, he was more likely to be found drawing little pictures on the paper tablecloths than clearing vacated tables.

One day my father-in-law called the young man aside and asked him what he would most like to do in life, since being a busboy obviously was not his chief aspiration.

Young Walter answered that he wished to draw. So my father-in-law said, "Then you should go and do what you most like to do." The boy did just that, and surely everyone knows the rest of Walt Disney's success story.

—*Bob Vanderham,* Holland, Michigan

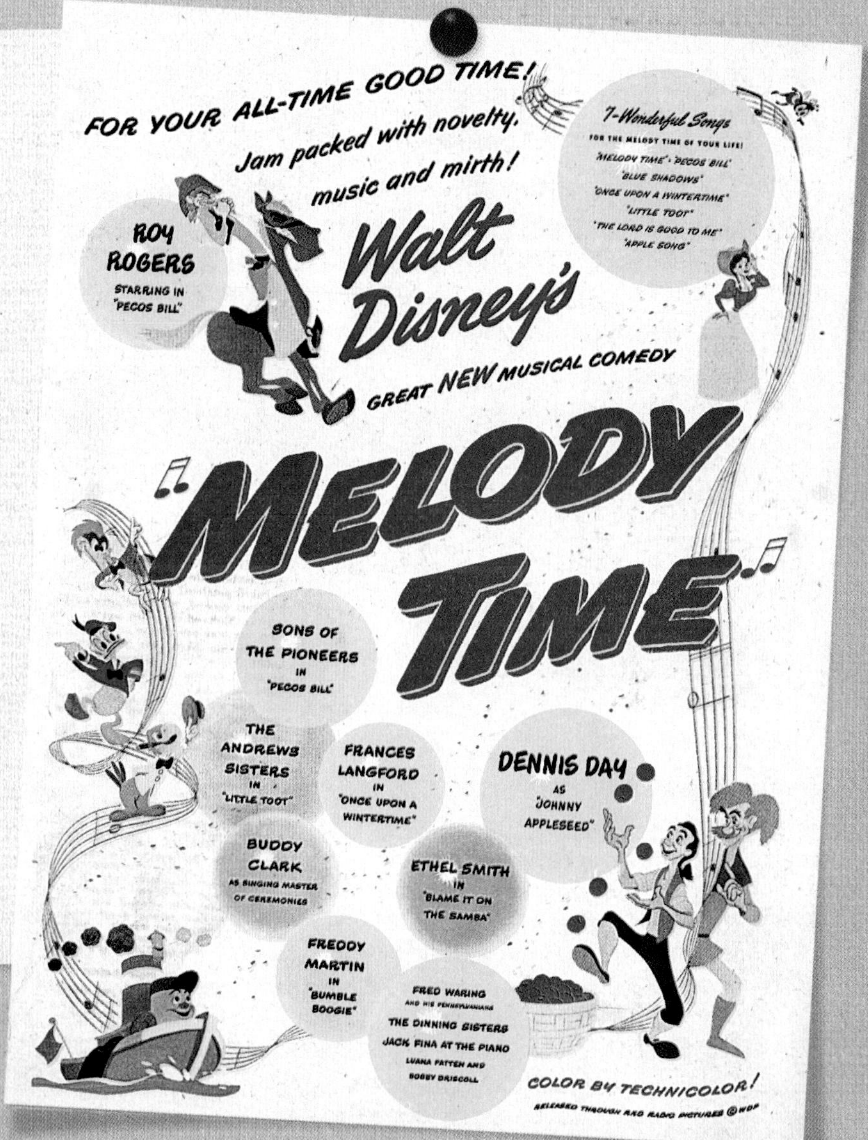

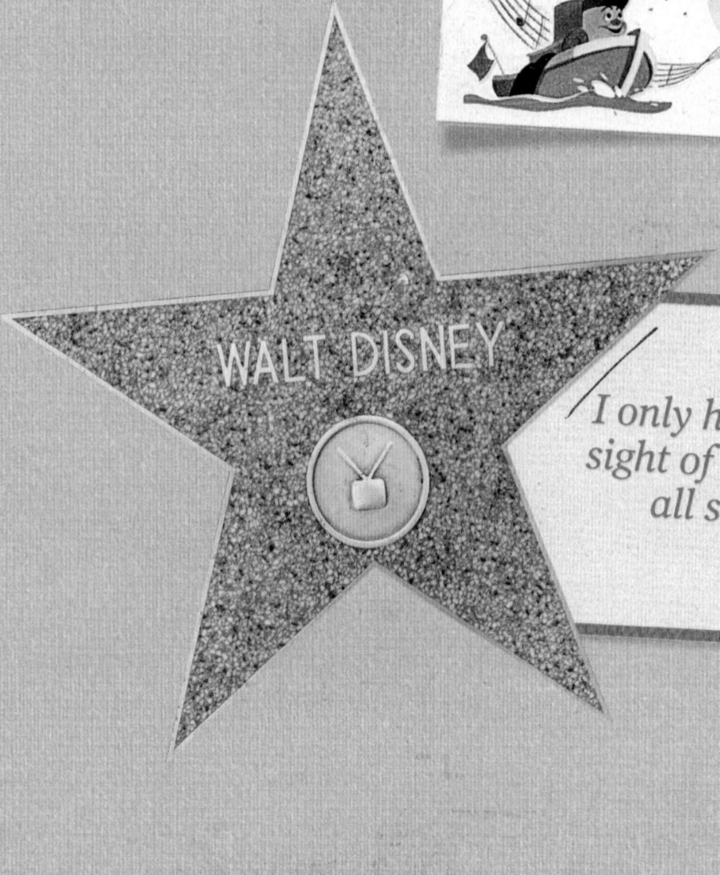

WALT DISNEY

I only hope that we never lose sight of one thing—that it was all started by a mouse.

—*Walt Disney*

BEHIND THE SCENES

I Was a Messenger to the Stars

Can any girl ever be the same after she's been asked by Tyrone Power to run down to the corner drugstore to buy him some cigarettes?

I'm certainly not. I worked at Columbia Pictures for five years in the '50s, and I came away with numerous memories of people I would never have met under any other circumstances.

It started in 1955, when I moved from Long Beach, California, to Hollywood. Like just about every other 19-year-old then, I wanted a job with a movie studio. I made the usual rounds but saved Columbia Pictures for last, because it was only a few blocks from my home.

As I was leaving, the personnel director told me, "Just forget you ever came in. I may call you tomorrow, or then again, I may never call you." Three days later, he called asking if I'd like to be a messenger girl. Would I!

I learned there were strict rules for employees. Studio owner Harry Cohn insisted none of us could be photographed on the lot with anyone. And asking actors for autographs was cause for instant dismissal. Also, no employee could accept a part in any film...they'd have to quit their job before that.

The first sound stage I walked onto was the set for *Queen Bee*, starring Joan Crawford. I had a telegram to deliver, but as I edged my way up to where she was standing, an assistant grabbed it out of my hand, saying, "Is that for Miss Crawford? I'll give it to her for you."

I was crushed. But there were to be many more deliveries. One day on the back lot, Miss Crawford smiled at me and said, "I'm certainly keeping you busy these days." What a treat!

One of the most stunning sets I ever saw was the ballroom set for *The Eddy Duchin Story*, starring Tyrone Power and Kim Novak. It was the hottest day of the summer, and all the extras were sweltering in their fancy evening wear and mink coats. (If you saw the picture, you'd have never known it.)

If I had to pick a favorite personality, it would be Dick Powell: He was a joy to be around.

His office was on the second floor, and every morning I'd hear him get off the elevator singing at the top of his lungs. At the time, he was directing his wife, June Allyson, and Jack Lemmon in *You Can't Run Away From It*.

One day June said to me, "All my life I've wanted red hair like yours."

"You'd have to take these freckles, too," I quipped.

"I wouldn't mind that one bit!" she laughed.

Once I delivered a script to Cornel Wilde, who talked me into holding it while he practiced retrieving it with a bullwhip for a picture he was doing with Jane Russell!

But my biggest thrill was when some stage-hands sneaked me into a booth overlooking a recording stage. For three heavenly hours, I watched Frank Sinatra record *The Lady Is a Tramp*, *I Didn't Know What Time It Was* and *I Could Write a Book* for the soundtrack of *Pal Joey*.

I didn't know it at the time, but those would be the last years of the Old Hollywood studios as we knew them. Before too long, Columbia's sound stages would be filming television commercials, and one by one, studios were being taken over by big corporations.

The Hollywood of today can't compare with the studio system I knew. But it was certainly wonderful while it lasted!

—*Patricia Martin,* La Quinta, California

3-D Disaster

I worked as an usher and part-time doorman at our local theater in the early '50s, when Hollywood began making 3-D movies.

We handed out special paper-framed polarized glasses to each customer and cautioned them not to touch the lenses. But it seemed as if no one could eat a box of buttered popcorn without getting fingerprints on their glasses.

Much of our time was spent cleaning off the fingerprints with alcohol or getting new glasses for customers who'd dropped or bent theirs.

Of course, Hollywood exploited the 3-D effect to the maximum with films featuring a continual stream of objects hurled at the viewer. My favorite 3-D picture was *Bwana Devil*.

Lions, tigers, spears, rocks and numerous other dangers headed directly toward the viewer. The objects seemed so real, audience members ducked or dodged by reflex action.

During one memorable showing, a young couple tried to avoid an incoming object. He dodged left while she dodged right, bringing their heads together with a resounding bonk.

That sound was followed by simultaneous cries of "Yeeeowww!" which caused the entire crowd to laugh. For the rest of the movie, any time an object was launched from the screen, there'd be a chorus of "Yeeeowww!" from the entire audience, followed by roars of laughter.

Those people were certainly entertained—though not exactly the way Hollywood intended!

—John Kosidowski, *Winona, Minnesota*

Wedding Night at the Fox

I worked at the Fox Theatre in Hutchinson, Kansas, and enjoyed some memorable promotions, including my night standing in for Elizabeth Taylor.

When the Fox opened in 1931, it was a big deal. The *Hutchinson News* called it "one of the finest theaters it is possible to build." The theater marquee was said to be Kansas' first display of flashing neon lights. (It still works today and is a colorful feature of the restored theater.) A special bonus was "refrigeration," the term once used for air conditioning.

The theater also had live music shows after the movies, bringing in Xavier Cugat, Les Brown and His Band of Renown, and other big names.

I worked at the Fox 30 hours a week at 40 cents an hour in my last two years of high school. That $12 went a long way toward school needs and spending money.

Employees would wear cowboy and cowgirl outfits when a western was coming to town, and there'd even be horses outside the theater. In those days, movie-going was truly magical.

My best memory of working at the Fox Theatre is from the summer of 1950, when I participated in a promotion for the Elizabeth Taylor movie, *Father of the Bride*.

A replica of her gown was on display for a couple of weeks before the movie arrived in Hutchinson. Finally, on July 29, the movie premiered at the Fox and we had a big event that evening to celebrate. The C.O. Mammel Bakery even contributed a wedding cake. I was the lucky girl who got to wear that beautiful dress and serve up cake to moviegoers!

—Joan Nelson
Wichita, Kansas

Winning Westerns

Well, I'll Tell Ya, Pilgrim

I'd ridden my bicycle across the channel from my home in Ocean Beach, California, to spend the day at the old Muscle Beach Plunge public swimming pool one day in 1950.

Unknown to me, Johnny Weissmuller, Olympic swimming champion and Tarzan in the movies, was putting on a swimming exhibition.

As a 12-year-old, watching Tarzan movies at Ocean Beach's Strand Theater was a weekly ritual for me. But I was even more surprised when it was announced that John Wayne was there to watch Johnny perform that day.

I'd recently seen John Wayne in *Wake of the Red Witch*, a seafaring movie.

Screwing up my courage—I was pretty bashful—I walked up to him as he sat beside the pool and asked a question that had been burning since I saw the movie.

"Mr. Wayne," I said, "you know, in the movie *Wake of the Red Witch*, well, I can't understand how you could hold your breath as long as you did when you were fighting the giant octopus down under the water."

He probably didn't have time to explain all the intricacies of filming, so he just gave me that famous John Wayne smile, chuckled and drawled, "Well, it wasn't easy."

That was one of the most exciting episodes of my young life.

—Pat Cochran, *Waxhaw, North Carolina*

Squadron Shutterbug

When I enlisted in the Air Force (that's me above), I never imagined I would meet with John Wayne.

Besides our field training, we took a battery of tests, and my scores led me to photography. By early 1951, I'd made corporal in Headquarters Squadron, 116th Air Base Group, George Air Force Base, Victorville, California. I became a photographer and lab technician, and my group took and developed all the photographs of the activities on base.

That included photos of all VIPs who visited, which is how I was assigned to take publicity photos of the filming of *Jet Pilot*, part of which was made there. It was Howard Hughes' last film and starred John Wayne and Janet Leigh.

For weeks, we followed Mr. Wayne and Miss Leigh around the base, taking candid photos (such as the snapshot at right) for our base publication as well as civilian newspapers. The two stars could not have been nicer. Mr. Wayne even posed with me for a photo, shown above.

I had always addressed John Wayne as "Mr. Wayne," until the day he put his hand on my shoulder and said, "Look, my friends call me 'Duke,' so no more of this 'Mr. Wayne' stuff."

When the filming was finished, both Duke and Janet came to the base photo lab to thank us for the time we spent showing them around. They were really down-to-earth people.

—William Cozine, *Spring Green, Wisconsin*

Greeting Gene Autry

When my buddy Billy Morris and I were both 12, our favorite cowboy movie star was Gene Autry.

Were we ever excited to learn he was coming to our town, Enid, Oklahoma, to promote a new movie at the Cherokee Theater! Gene would arrive on a private plane at nearby Woodring Airport.

On the big day, Billy and I skipped school and rode our bicycles to the airport to await the plane. When it arrived, local photographers gathered around and took pictures of Gene stepping onto the runway.

They also got a picture of Billy and me standing next to our hero with his hands on our shoulders. Billy and I were delighted beyond words.

The next day, Billy, Gene and I were on the front page of the *Enid Morning News*. Unfortunately, the paper came out after we'd both explained our previous day's absence was due to illness.

That newspaper photo earned us each a trip down the hall to see the principal. Even so, Gene Autry will always be my favorite cowboy.

—*Perry Choate,* Pampa, Texas

I Sang With the King of the Cowboys!

I'd wangled an invitation to the grand opening of a new fast-food restaurant in Philadelphia. As I ascended a red-carpeted ramp, I peered over the heads of the crowd and instantly spotted a familiar white hat. Broad-brimmed and double-dimpled, it was surrounded by a swarm of people.

Under the hat was my boyhood hero—he stood above The Shadow and Daniel Boone, greater even than Abe Lincoln or Jack Armstrong, "The All-American Boy." Standing 10 feet from me, in the flesh, was Roy Rogers, "King of the Cowboys!"

At night, after acting out backyard Wild West melodramas with my buddies in full garb (there I am, below), I lay in my "bunkhouse" bed praying that someday I'd sing with Roy Rogers.

Now here he was, only a few feet away! As I nervously awaited my "ambush," he drifted from his admirers. I neared, and he turned and smiled.

I introduced myself. "You were my boyhood hero, Roy," I said. "Your movies and music have had a great influence on my life."

"Well, thank you, John," Roy said, smiling. His eyes sparkled. "Nice to meet you."

Unbelievable! Here was Roy Rogers, gripping my hand and calling me by name! I took a chance and asked if he'd sign a couple of photographs I'd brought along.

Backs to the crowd, we sat at a small table, where Roy autographed the old photos. We talked for more than 15 minutes. No one interrupted us... maybe everyone assumed we were friends or were discussing business. Whatever the reason, I knew it wouldn't last, so I decided to act.

"Do you remember *Twilight on the Trail*?" I asked. I began humming the melody line.

"Sure do," Roy said, quietly joining in.

I harmonized when I could, and we sang softly for a few exquisite, fleeting moments—until some other people approached for autographs.

Though my treasured time alone with Roy Rogers had come to an end, my childhood dream had come true. I finally did it—I sang with the King of the Cowboys!

—*John Buchholz,* Paoli, Pennsylvania

I WAS 'SHOOTING STARS' IN THE '40S

TINSELTOWN ONCE FELL UNDER THE SPELL OF THIS LOVELY "CAMERA GIRL."

By Rae Roma Gray, Gainesville, Texas

CAUGHT ON CAMERA. The author made a lovely subject herself, posing above with some suave servicemen in 1944.

Working in Hollywood gave me the exciting chance to mingle with some of the era's most famous performers. I even had to shoo millionaire director Howard Hughes away from my camera and hide actor Richard Jaeckel in my dressing room! But that's getting ahead of the story...

I'd recently graduated from Belmont High School in Los Angeles in 1941, when I saw an ad for employment at the Hollywood Palladium, a popular nightclub.

So, I put on my graduation dress, dyed my white shoes blue to match the dress and took the streetcar downtown. There must have been a hundred girls applying for the same job, and they all looked like ex-showgirls—they were beautiful!

After the interview, I just knew I wouldn't get the job. Then as I was waiting for the streetcar home, it started to rain. My crepe dress began to shrink to above my knees, and my blue shoes reverted to white. I'm sure my face was red by the time I boarded.

A few weeks later, I got a call from the Palladium asking me to start working that same night! I began immediately as a camera girl, taking photos of the patrons.

HIATUS LASTED TWO YEARS

I loved my job, but the fun soon ended when a jealous classmate turned me in. I was too young to work in a nightclub and was terminated, but I promised my boss I'd be back when I turned 21.

For the next two years, I worked as a carhop, usherette and waitress. I even bucked a few rivets with "Rosie the Riveter" at the Douglas Aircraft plant in Santa Monica.

On my 21st birthday, I was back at the Palladium as promised. This time I sold gardenias and operated the photo booth, where I met more celebrities. From backstage, I was able to watch Gene Krupa bang the drums and lead his band.

One night, actor Richard Jaeckel told me I saved his life. I had let him hide in my dressing room from a girl who was chasing him. When he came out, Richard said, "Hey, I liked the picture in there." It was one of him that I'd clipped from a movie magazine.

Every night was filled with music, glamour and excitement. But when the war ended, I "retired" from the nightclub scene. My fiance, a combat correspondent, had been killed on Iwo Jima, and I couldn't handle being around all the servicemen who came to the club.

By the late '40s, I needed to return to work. I took a position with a company that had the photo concessions at many of the best-known nightclubs in Hollywood, Beverly Hills and Los Angeles.

The Beverly Hills Hotel provided plenty of star-gazing opportunities. I can still see Mickey Rooney dashing across the lobby, doing a flip off the lobby couch, and yelling, "Ta-da!"

Other frequent visitors included Phil Harris, Peter Lawford, Joan Bennett, Hedy Lamarr, Alice Faye, Betty Grable and Harry James.

SHOOING HOWARD HUGHES

One time at the Town House, I met the beautiful Linda Darnell, who was dining with Howard Hughes. When I approached them and asked if they'd like their picture taken, Mr. Hughes said "No!" and tried to send me away.

I returned later and asked Miss Darnell if I could take a photo of her for my personal collection. Mr. Hughes was about to say no again, but Miss Darnell said it would be fine.

When I got ready to take the picture, Mr. Hughes cuddled next to Miss Darnell and put his arm around her. Now it was my turn to "shoo" Mr. Hughes away!

I later regretted not getting Mr. Hughes into the picture. After his death, everyone seemed to be looking for photos of him.

SLAPSY MAXIE'S MADE MEMORIES

One of the more exciting nightclubs was Slapsy Maxie's on Wilshire Boulevard in Hollywood. Among the great stars who appeared there was Lena Horne, who brought down the house with her rendition of *I've Got the World on a String.*

Lucille Ball was at her reserved table every night for Desi Arnaz's performances. You could certainly tell this famous couple was in love. I also remember seeing the "new" comedy team of Dean Martin and Jerry Lewis.

One night Jimmy Durante asked me to take a picture of him dancing with a young lady who was shy, he said, and wouldn't pose for a photo. He asked me to stand at the edge of the dance floor and be ready, and he would dance toward me.

I waited, and sure enough, Jimmy and his "mystery lady" danced over and I got a shot of both of them smiling into the camera. Jimmy was quite pleased and gave me a generous tip.

It's all gone now, those great bands and the glamour of Hollywood when it was at its peak. But one thing remains—my fond memory of it all.

PHOTOGENIC. When Rae Roma Gray was a "camera girl" in Hollywood nightclubs, she photographed the likes of Jimmy Durante (above) and Linda Darnell (right), who was having dinner with Howard Hughes.

THE STARS WERE OUT! The author loved to watch drummer Gene Krupa (above, right) and his band play at the Palladium, where she worked selling flowers and operating the photo booth. Not Rosie, but Rae the Riveter posed for photos at Douglas Aircraft (left). The beautiful Lena Horne also was among her camera subjects (above, left).

We Sure Liked Shirley!

HER FAMILY COULDN'T BELIEVE WHOM DAD WAS BRINGING HOME FOR LUNCH.

By Sharon Clymer, Renton, Washington

D ad never ceased to amaze Mom, but one day he really surprised her. A man who loved working with horses, Dad heard about a job at the Jack Warner Horse Ranch in Canoga Park, California.

Mr. Warner was making a movie about the great horse Seabiscuit and the famous jockey Georgie Woolf. He needed an experienced jockey to exercise the horses and do some riding for the race scenes.

RIDING HIGH. Author Sharon Clymer's father, Jack Leonard, was riding at 16. His knowledge of horses led to lunch with Shirley Temple (top right with Sharon's sister, Sally).

This was the perfect job for Dad. He was hired, and we moved into a little ranch house on location. I can still smell the fragrant alfalfa fields and see the eucalyptus trees that lined the long driveway. What a neat place to live!

Every day Dad worked closely with the film crew and several movie stars. Each night he'd tell us whom he'd seen and what was happening with the movie. It was fun, but after a while, even that became "old hat" for us. We settled into a routine.

Shocked to See Celebrities

One day, though, the routine changed. My brother and I came home from school to find Mom frazzled. At the time, we were too young to appreciate what Dad had done.

He'd come home at noon as usual, asking, "What's for lunch?" But on this particular day, Mom turned around to find Dad, Shirley Temple and Lon McCallister, two stars of the movie, standing in her kitchen!

To this day, Mom says she has absolutely no idea what she served them. She imagines it was probably soup and sandwiches. What she does remember is how gracious they were—especially

Shirley Temple. They acted just like everyday folks and didn't put on airs.

Mom felt honored that Dad liked her cooking enough to bring home lunch guests (especially stars), but she made him vow to warn her next time. It never happened again, but Mom said just one lunch was enough to provide many memories.

The movie was released in 1949. It's called *The Story of Seabiscuit* and stars Shirley Temple, Lon McCallister, Barry Fitzgerald and Rosemary DeCamp. It hasn't been released on DVD, but we keep hoping. Watching that old movie would certainly bring back fond recollections.

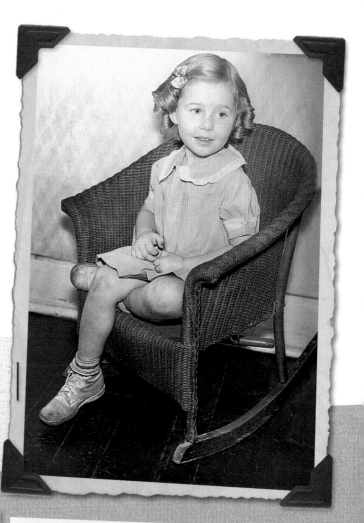

CURLED CUTIE. Due to the Hollywood princess, I endured hours of hair curling. It was all worth it when my young son asked, "Why does Grandma have a picture of Shirley Temple in her living room?"
—Nancy Owen, Rocky Mount, Missouri

SHORT ROMANCE. In April 1945, I was a cadet at Childress Army Air Field in Texas. I worked on charts and records while waiting to start preflight training. Unknown to me, some fellows in my barracks wrote to Shirley Temple, asking what she could do for this guy with a crush on the "All-American Girl." To our surprise, I received several studio photos from Miss Temple, but my fantasy romance was short-lived. A month later, she announced her engagement!
—Robert Schaffhausen, Birmingham, Alabama

SATURDAY NIGHT AT THE **DRIVE-IN**

Preparing for a Saturday night at the drive-in movies called upon the best of Mom's Girl Scout skills. Sleeping bags, pillows, flashlights, mosquito repellent, coloring books and stuffed animals were all loaded into our station wagon to be brought out later as needed.

Just before sunset, Dad would ease the Olds Custom Cruiser into the huge clamshell-shaped lot at the Route 17 Drive-in.

My sister and I, sporting Roy Rogers pajamas, would bounce around in the backseat until the old gas-guzzler was properly centered on the ramp in the family area. (An unwritten house rule reserved the other parts of the lot for teenagers in "souped-up" Chevys.)

Then we'd dash off to the Kiddie Playground. While we played, Mom and Dad stood nearby with the rest of the parents, chatting and watching us run around in our pajamas. It was Mom's job to decide when we'd had enough.

The next stop was the concession stand—a gleaming palace serving up a cornucopia of flash-fried foods in little paper boats. Long, shiny counters were lined with delights we'd never find in Mother's kitchen—corn dogs, crinkle fries, Jujubes, Good & Plenty and extra-salty popcorn. The best part: We got to eat it all in the car.

As dusk fell, something magical happened. The huge white screen took on a warm, unearthly glow, and the ramp lights came on. My

sister and I peered over the top of the front seat, anxiously watching the preview clock tick its way down to zero. Finally, it was showtime!

A brief welcome was followed by previews of coming attractions—strictly "B" movies. A cartoon was next, and my sister and I squealed with delight as our favorite characters raced across the 120-foot screen. After the cartoon, a dancing hot dog and chocolate bar appeared the screen to remind everyone to make one last visit to the concession stand before the movie started.

After we'd slurped down a large "Delicious Soft Drink," this was also a good time to visit the restroom. With those big outdoor speakers blasting dialogue across the parking lot and into the restrooms, you didn't have to worry much about missing an important scene.

Back in the Custom Cruiser, my sister and I made bets on who would stay awake until the very end of the feature. Of course, neither of us won—safe and cozy in our sleeping bags, with our parents sitting inches away, we were usually sound asleep by Elvis' first big number.

Sometimes we wouldn't wake up until we were headed out of the parking lot. But even in that groggy haze, we'd secure a firm promise from Mom and Dad that we'd be able to return and do it all over again next Saturday night.

—*Jennifer Leonard, Saddle River, New Jersey*

NOW SHOWING.
The Redwood was Sonoma County's first drive-in. My parents took me there when I was just a few weeks old because they wanted to experience the new outdoor theater. Years later, when I was in high school in the mid-'60s, I would go to the Redwood or one of the other drive-in theaters around Santa Rosa.
—Edd Vinci, Tucson, Arizona

865 Home of Bud Abbott, Encino, California

Home of Lou Costello, North Hollywood

2B-H471

crazy for
ABBOTT & COSTELLO

Times Square To-Do

During the mid-1940s, many New York City theaters featured stage shows that accompanied their films.

When I was 15, Abbott and Costello were to appear on the opening day of one of their movies. I decided to skip school and try to get their coveted autographs.

Most theaters lined up fans and brought in a few at a time to get stars' photos or autographs, but the Times Square theater hadn't prepared for such a big crowd and had to turn some of us away.

We were disappointed but hung around the stage door anyway. Then someone called out, "Heyyy, Abbbbooot!"

We kids laughed, and the fellow repeated it even louder. He was joined by others until there was a chorus of people yelling, "Heyyy, Abbbbooot!"

Suddenly a window on the third floor opened, and there was Bud Abbott. We started yelling greetings up to him until Lou Costello appeared. Then the cheers got even louder.

The two stars talked with us and said they were sorry management wouldn't let us come in. One of the boys asked if they'd sign his book if he tossed it to them.

"Why sure," said Costello. "Send it up."

For 10 minutes, whoever had an autograph book threw it skyward. Every time Costello dropped it down, he'd make a noise like a dive-bomber, keeping up a steady stream of chatter with us fans below.

I got my book up to the window on the third try and was thrilled when I got it back autographed by both men.

Later, we were talking about how nice they'd been when one of the girls said, "You know, since they signed in pencil, you should cover it with clear nail polish in order to save it better."

That's exactly what I did. Now, many years later, those autographs look just like they did the day I got them...a delightful remembrance of a funny and personable comic duo.

—**Carmen Sarro,** *Santa Clarita, California*

She Gave Dad the Last Laugh

During the '40s, Dad took us to the Avalon Theater on special occasions. We enjoyed those outings, sometimes riding the streetcar to the show. To save money, we'd buy popcorn and candy before the movie at a little store next door.

Abbott and Costello movies were popular then, and some of them had scary monsters (scary to little girls, at least!). I can recall spending half the movie with my face buried in Dad's hat.

Dad passed away at age 89. But whenever movies were mentioned, he'd tell my children and grandchildren, "Margaret watched many a movie through my hat!"

—**Margaret Castellarin,** *Burnham, Illinois*

'GONE WITH THE WIND'
BLEW US AWAY

Frankly, He Gave a Darn

The Aerial Gunnery School commandant at Tyndall Field in Florida moved down our formation that day in 1944, pinning on our silver wings and shaking hands with each of us.

Then the first sergeant whispered to me, "The 'old man' wants to see you." With a knot in my stomach, I headed for the commandant's office.

What had I done wrong? Was I going to lose my promotion? Instead, I and four other new aerial gunners were pleasantly surprised.

"Lt. Clark Gable and his cameraman, Lt. Andy McIntyre, are coming," the commandant advised. "They'll take the same training you just completed, and you've been chosen to be their instructors.

"The class will last four weeks, and they'll be your only students. Upon completion, all five of you will have your choice of any combat bomb group and overseas command."

What a relief! At 18 years of age, I'd enlisted in the Army to fight, and the 8th Air Force was exactly where I wanted to be.

Later in the day, the commandant brought Lieutenants Gable and McIntyre to the main classroom, introduced us and departed. We were in awe at first, but Gable quickly put us at ease when he smiled and said, "Tell us what you're going to tell us."

He was referring to the classic Army training method: 1. Tell them what you're going to tell them. 2. Tell them. 3. Tell them what you told them.

We all laughed and loosened up, then briefed them on the training.

Lt. Gable asked, "Will there be any skeet shooting?"

Weapons was one of my subjects. "In four days of small arms training, we'll do some skeet shooting," I assured him.

That brought out the Clark Gable smile again, as he said, "That's great." We all began to feel comfortable with him and Lt. McIntyre.

On our first day on the skeet range, Lt. Gable missed one or two clay pigeons each round. After that, he didn't miss a single bird and even set a range record for consecutive birds.

A couple of days later, while we were having a soda at the PX, he told me with a lopsided grin, "I guess you know after that first day on the range, I called a friend in California and had him send my special skeet gun by air."

I smiled and said, "Well, your gun sure didn't look like a GI shotgun."

The training went fast, and the night before Gable and McIntyre departed, we instructors threw them a going-away party. Before leaving, Gable said he and McIntyre were going to England to make a movie of bomber crews in combat.

"Who knows," Gable added, "maybe we'll meet again in jolly old England."

His prediction was right. Soon after arriving at Polebrook Air Base, I ran into the newly promoted Capt. Clark Gable.

He invited me to the Church Army Canteen (kind of like our Salvation Army) for tea and crumpets. The first thing he said to me was, "I like your mustache. You trying to copy mine?"

"Yes," I said, "but I have to darken mine with burnt cork."

He laughed, then, smoothing his mustache, he said, "Don't tell anybody—I do, too."

Gable had only two more combat missions to go before returning to the States to put together his movie. With his arm around my shoulder, he said, "Bill, you be sure to come to MGM if you ever get to Hollywood. I'll introduce you to my friends and show you around."

As it turned out, my first combat mission was Gable's last. Back at the base afterward, everyone was talking about Gable being with us that day.

A warrior and a gentleman, Clark Gable (most famous as Rhett Butler in *Gone With the Wind*) really did give a darn, and I'm proud to have known him.

—**William Cramer,** *Hopkinsville, Kentucky*

DAVID O. SELZNICK'S
PRODUCTION OF MARGARET MITCHELL'S

GONE WITH THE WIND

Music From The Original Motion Picture Soundtrack as Monophonically Recorded in 1939
Music Composed and Conducted by
MAX STEINER

A REAL BLOCKBUSTER. Since it premiered in 1939, *Gone With the Wind* has grossed more than $390 million!

The Crowd Roared For Rhett

The burning of Atlanta during the Civil War may have been the most notable event in the city's history...but the world premiere of *Gone With the Wind* had to be a close second. I'll never forget that night in December of 1939, when Atlanta glowed and sparkled with a Milky Way of movie stars.

Daddy took me to the star-dusted parade that ran down Whitehall and Peachtree Streets. The night was bright with klieg lights as bands blared and police sirens wailed. Banners fluttered from every building.

The grand parade ended at Loew's Grand Theater, where the movie premiere was held. The theater had become "Tara," the story's plantation house, dressed in white columns and festooned with vines.

I saw my first movie stars that night. Vivien Leigh was the very soul of Scarlett. I thought she looked like a fairy princess, while her husband-to-be, Laurence Olivier, melted into the background.

Clark Gable's new wife, Carole Lombard, dazzled the crowd almost as much as her husband did. But everyone screamed when Gable flashed that million-dollar smile—he had played the handsome Rhett Butler. Olivia de Havilland was warmly received by onlookers, as well.

Mother kept a scrapbook of the festivities for me. After all those years, the newspaper clippings have yellowed and the photographs have faded, but I still like to look at them and remember my night among the stars.

—*Dorothy Beaudoin, Sarasota, Florida*

'Gone With the Wind' Kept Me Standing in Line

When *Gone With the Wind* came to town in the winter of 1939, I ran downtown with a dime and three pennies clutched in my red-mittened hand. Lots of moviegoers had lined up early. I took my place at the end of a long line.

At last I reached the window...and I was told that all the seats were filled. I and all the people behind me would have to wait for the second showing at 5 o'clock!

I was so disappointed, and also freezing cold. Dejectedly peering through the glass doors, I happened to catch the eye of the theater manager. I was so cross, I stuck out my tongue at him.

Imagine my shock when I couldn't pull my tongue back in! It had stuck fast to the metal door. Despite my rude behavior, the kind manager came and "rescued" me. Inside the theater, as soon as I could speak, I apologized, and he must have believed me, too, because he found me a single seat and let me buy a ticket for the first showing! I was even allowed to sit through a second viewing: The movie was truly that unforgettable, even though, in those days, popcorn was a luxury I couldn't afford.

The theater manager never forgot me, either. When I approached him five years later looking for a job, his answer was simple and direct.

"Of course you can have a job," he said. "You might be the only girl in town who doesn't stick her tongue out at me...and the only kid who can sit through six hours of film without popcorn!"

—*Rita Cashin, Louisdale, Nova Scotia*

Unforgettable Encounters

Secret Was Hard to Keep

A friend and I skipped classes at Nutley (New Jersey) High School one rainy day in 1940 and hitchhiked to West Orange to see the premiere of the movie *Edison, the Man*.

Arriving about noon, we picked a spot about 300 yards from the theater to view the parade. We were drenched, hungry and alone—I don't recall there being any huge crowds.

Suddenly, a limousine pulled over to the curb in front of us. The rear window lowered and there was Spencer Tracy, with that *Boys Town* glow.

"Hi, boys," he said. "Thanks for coming out in this terrible weather to see the parade and *Edison, the Man*. The parade's been called off, but not the premiere. What're your names?"

We stammered our names, and he shook our hands and told us he would give our names to the theater manager and we'd be admitted as his personal guests.

At that, a female voice from inside the limousine said, "That's a very nice thing to do, Spence."

My pal and I argued long afterward over whether the voice belonged to Katharine Hepburn or the movie's costar, Rita Johnson.

Playing hooky in 1940 was not tolerated, so we had to keep secret our joyful news about meeting Spencer Tracy until long after the fact.

But the excitement lasted a long time.

—*Edward Quigley,* Pompton Plains, New Jersey

Sunny Day

My roommate and I were vacationing in the Grand Tetons in the summer of 1954, staying at Jackson Hole Lodge. We noticed Paramount Pictures trucks and equipment on the grounds and learned they were filming a segment of *The Far Horizons*, a movie about the Lewis and Clark Expedition.

We got a pass to go on location and watch filming of rafting scenes down the Snake River. When they broke for lunch, we were invited to eat in the mess tent with the crew and actors Donna Reed, Charlton Heston and Fred MacMurray.

After lunch, I was snapping photos and spotted Mr. Heston sunning himself atop a truck.

As I was about to click the shutter, he rose on one elbow and said, "You won't get a good picture because you're taking it against the sun."

So I ran around to the other side and took this slide. He asked me to send him copies for possible use by his fan club.

I sent them and got a thank-you letter from Mr. Heston. What a thrilling experience!

—*Dorothy Stepan,* Lincoln, Nebraska

PHOTO OP. Actor Charlton Heston was filming *The Far Horizons* when author Dorothy Stepan ran into him while on holiday in the Grand Tetons.

His wish came true.

The pilots in the squadron were treated to lunch with the beautiful young star, as this photo shows. Fenton is pinning on Miss Durbin's aviator wings.

—**Katherine Butler**, *Portland, Oregon*

Package Gave Him Entree

During summer vacation from high school, in 1955, I worked as a messenger in New York City, delivering letters and small packages.

One day, I was given a package addressed to Anthony Quinn, the movie star, who was aboard a ship sailing to Europe in a few hours.

At the ship, since I wanted to meet a movie star, I told them that the package had to be delivered to Mr. Quinn in person. They let me come on board, and I found Mr. Quinn talking with his agent.

When I gave him the package, the agent pulled out a $5 bill and gave it to me. That was a lot of money then—I was making only 75 cents an hour.

Later, I found out from the delivery company that the package contained the script for the movie *Lust for Life*, about the life of Vincent Van Gogh. Mr. Quinn won an Oscar for best supporting actor for his role as Paul Gauguin.

—**William Sullivan**, *Massapequa, New York*

Cemented Relationship With Jane Wyman

My son Larry and his family moved to Reseda, California, in 1952, so soon after they'd settled in, my husband and I decided to take them to see Hollywood. One of our stops was Grauman's Chinese Theatre, where the stars put their footprints and handprints in the concrete.

When we got there, they were having a drawing for a miniature casting of Jane Wyman's prints. When the winning ticket was drawn, I was shocked to learn it was mine!

I was shaking so much when I went up to meet Ms. Wyman that I had Larry come with me. I was presented with this picture (above), which was in all the local papers.

Larry still has the miniature casting in his home.

—**Lena Evaristo**, *Woodstock, Georgia*

Durbin Was Their Sweetheart

In late 1942, the 330th Fighter Squadron was transferred from Olympia, Washington, to the air base at Glendale, California.

At the time, I was dating (and later married) the squadron commander, Capt. Fenton Butler.

Just before leaving, he told me he would be stationed so close to Hollywood that he intended to have his favorite screen star, Deanna Durbin, made "sweetheart" of the squadron.

Getting to Know
JIMMY

My Double Date With Jimmy Stewart

Not often does a girl from Newport News get to spend a day with the likes of Jimmy Stewart and Olivia de Havilland...but that was just one day of a star-filled week I spent around Hollywood in 1940.

I'd had some prior experience with stars—my best friend was Kay Aldridge, who in the 1930s was one of the 10 most photographed girls in the world. After eight years as a model, she was in the movies for eight more years, appearing in 21 features and three serials.

Kay had moved from rural Virginia to live with relatives in Newport News, where she and I were classmates. Later, after she moved to Hollywood, we corresponded occasionally.

In 1940, Kay was pictured on the cover of *Life* magazine. Feeling mischievous, I dug out an unflattering girlhood photo of her and sent it with a letter to the editor.

Well, *Life* ran the letter and photo, and Kay saw it. She immediately wired me an invitation to visit her in Hollywood. I saved enough money to take the three-day train ride across the country and spend a week with my friend.

Besides seeing movies and meeting movie stars, I also got to "double-date" with Jimmy Stewart and Olivia de Havilland.

At the time, Kay was dating John Swope, a photographer who shared a house with Jimmy Stewart and Henry Fonda. John and Jimmy both had remote-control model airplanes and were eager to fly them in the desert, so a picnic was scheduled at Mirage Lake. Kay was to be John's date, and Jimmy would bring his steady, Olivia.

As luck would have it, Kay had a wardrobe fitting that day for her next film, so John invited me to "pinch-hit." I was ecstatic but determined not to act like a star-struck fan. I didn't ask for autographs and took only a few snapshots.

I felt perfectly comfortable, as I'd been with all three of them two days before at Jimmy's house for dinner. Jimmy had played the piano and sung silly ditties before we went to MGM for a private movie showing.

It was a fantastic picnic. Olivia brought a delicious catered lunch with matching paper plates and napkins. What I recall most of all is that Jimmy—whether playing piano or flying model airplanes in the desert—seemed just like he was in the movies.

Now that Jimmy is gone, I often think back to that day in the desert and my double date with that tall, dark and handsome "gee, whiz" guy.

—Elsie West Duval, *Newport News, Virginia*

LIFETIME OF MEMORIES. Author (on the left in the photo at right) and her actress friend, Kay Aldridge, posed for *Life* magazine in Los Angeles in '40, but the photo ended up on the cutting room floor. The other photos (from left) show Olivia de Havilland and her picnic, as well as Jimmy Stewart.

Hardware Store Humbug

Many times during the late 1930s and early 1940s, my grandfather and I would visit a huge hardware store in Indiana, Pennsylvania, which was operated by the father of actor Jimmy Stewart.

While Jimmy was away at war, his Oscar statues were displayed along with scrapbooks and photographs heralding the young actor's successes.

Jimmy's father was very proud of his son's fame, but he had no use for actors as a whole and was annoyed by people coming into his hardware store "just to see Jimmy Stewart's father."

The store's handyman, Andy, was getting on in years and could often be found in the back room sleeping in a big old chair beside a potbellied stove.

When people came into the store and asked to see Jimmy Stewart's father, Mr. Stewart would take them into the back room and point a finger at old Andy slumped in the chair.

They weren't too impressed...but then, Mr. Stewart really didn't care!

—**Homer Shaffer,** *Burkburnett, Texas*

A Man of
MYSTERY

ILLUMINATING APPEARANCE. Famous director Alfred Hitchcock earned the last laugh as he gave author Bill Sadler a light at a televised promotion of a new movie. Actress Anne Baxter (second from left) takes in the gag.

I Met My Match in Alfred Hitchcock

When I switched careers from radio to television production in 1948, everything was new and untried. There were no lists of things you couldn't do, so not knowing any better, we just went ahead and did whatever seemed like a good idea.

I was working at WFAA-TV in Dallas, when Alfred Hitchcock, actress Anne Baxter and actor Roger Dan came to our station to promote Hitchcock's new movie, *I Confess*.

Hostess Jean Oliver was to handle the interviews, but I had an idea I thought might produce a laugh. Hitchcock was already a legend, well-known for his trademark "walk-on" in each of his movies. So, for our TV production, I suggested that I walk onto the set during the interview and ask someone to light my cigarette.

When this happened, Hitchcock would ask who I was, and Jean would explain, "Oh, that's our director—he always makes a cameo appearance on each of his shows."

Hitchcock said he thought it was a great gag. Little did we know he had one of his own in mind. He asked for a candle, so I sent a crew member to the prop room to get one.

Hitchcock lit the candle and set it out of sight. We didn't know what he planned to do with it, and he wasn't about to tell us.

We found out when I came onto the set for my cameo. Hitchcock pulled out the lighted candle and lit my cigarette with a great flourish. Then he turned to the camera and said, "This definitely proves that Alfred Hitchcock can more than hold a candle to Bill Sadler as a producer/director."

His comment broke up everyone, including the camera crew and yours truly. That show turned out to be one of the most fun we ever did. I'll never forget how gracious Mr. Hitchcock was and how thoroughly he seemed to enjoy himself that day.

—**Bill Sadler,** *Brownsville, Texas*

Feather-o-Vision

A college friend of mine, Ken Johnson, tells of the time he and two of his dorm buddies went to see Alfred Hitchcock's 1963 thriller *The Birds*.

They'd heard about the movie from others and decided to each catch a pigeon and take it to the Uintah Theater in Provo, Utah.

They hid the pigeons under their jackets. The birds made noise from time to time, and the usher began to watch the three boys closely.

In spite of the increased surveillance, when a critical moment in the movie arrived, the pranksters released the birds.

The pigeons were drawn to the projector's flickering light, and that, in turn, cast their silhouettes onto the screen. And if that weren't enough, one of the birds flew down and landed on a patron. Pandemonium!

The pigeons were caught and released, as was one of the culprits, who'd run out of the theater and down a blind alley just as the police arrived. His punishment was nothing more than a warning to not do that again.

—**Orson Haynie,** *McMinnville, Oregon*

look both ways, kids

As a professional photographer in 1952, I was snapping pictures on a rainy day in downtown St. Louis, Missouri, and caught this young mother and her kids. They were crossing the street in front of the Ambassador Theatre, where the marquee featured Vivien Leigh, who won an Oscar, and Marlon Brando in *A Streetcar Named Desire*. A second feature was *This Woman Is Dangerous* starring Joan Crawford.

—Jack Zehrt, *Wildwood, Missouri*

CHAPTER 4

SAME TIME, SAME CHANNEL

As televisions skyrocketed in popularity, they became part of most people's daily lives. But some folks, including Linda Fitzhugh of La Mirada, California, were lucky enough to be seen on the screen!

"When I was a sophomore at Neff High School, my 'bestie' Robin Moore and I went to some happening clubs with my brother Tim," she writes.

"Tim invited Robin and me to dance on *New American Bandstand*. We taped three shows and signed up for the mailing list. Just six weeks later, we were back on the ABC lot with six different outfits—and we wound up dancing for the next two seasons.

"Oh, what fun days those were! We got to see so many guest stars, including Freddie Prinze, the Spinners and Tony Orlando and Dawn."

In this chapter, reminisce about the classic American variety shows, sitcoms and dramas on television, plus the famous faces we still love today.

LUNCHES WITH 'GRANDPA BUB' AND A
SECRET ASSIGNMENT

THE YOUNGEST STAR OF "MY THREE SONS" SHARES A
BEHIND-THE-SCENES MEMORY OF FELLOW CAST MEMBER
AND LOVABLE CURMUDGEON WILLIAM FRAWLEY.

By Barry Livingston, Los Angeles, California

TIM
CONSIDINE

FRED MACMURRAY

DON GRADY

WILLIAM FRAWLEY

*that's me—
Ernie!*

STANLEY LIVINGSTON

GET THE SCOOP. To learn more about William Frawley and other stars Barry Livingston came to know, check out his autobiography, *The Importance of Being Ernie*, available in stores and through online outlets.

From 1963 to 1972, I played Ernie, the youngest son on *My Three Sons*. We filmed at Desilu Studios, next door to a great Hollywood restaurant called Nickodell's. At lunchtime, June Lockhart of *Lassie*, Bob Crane of *Hogan's Heroes* and William Shatner of *Star Trek* all vied for the best table in the back. Lucky for our cast, that spot was forever reserved for a member of our show, William Frawley.

Frawley played Grandpa Bub on *My Three Sons*; before that he was known for his role as Fred Mertz on *I Love Lucy*. In real life, he was the embodiment of his TV persona, a sweet grouch. As a 10-year-old, I adored his eloquent profanity. When he forgot his lines, he'd yell, "Who writes this cockeyed crap, anyway?" I'd hit the floor laughing. Frawley was also a lifelong bachelor, and Nickodell's was where he ate almost every meal—and drank booze.

A GRAND ENTRANCE

Frawley would usually lead our gang into the restaurant's kitchen through the back door and bellow out, "This place stinks like an armpit. Too much garlic!"

Laughter and greetings rang out.

"Hello, William!"

"Having the usual, Mr. Frawley?"

"Bring me half a cantaloupe with ice cream in the hole!" he'd reply. I saw him eat so many cantaloupes that he started to resemble one, with his big round face.

Whenever I slid into our booth, my butt would immediately drop into a deep depression in the seat. This was Frawley's spot, day in and day out.

Soon lunch was served, along with Frawley's whiskey. I loved cheeseburgers; Frawley preferred steak. Then the cantaloupe dessert arrived, and another whiskey.

When our lunch hour ended, almost everybody hurried back to work, not wanting to tick off the boss. Only Frawley and I remained. He moved when he was ready. If a studio flunky arrived to retrieve him, he'd roar, "I'll be back after I finish this lousy cantaloupe!" Then he'd eat it right down to the rind, taking his sweet time.

TOP-SECRET BUSINESS

As for me, I stayed because I had a secret assignment. Our production supervisor, John Stephens, knew that Frawley softened like putty around children, so he had me coax my pal back to work.

"Look at the clock—we gotta go!" I'd chirp.

"No!" he'd insist. Then he'd look at the practically deserted restaurant and sigh.

"We're in the scene after lunch, remember?" I'd whine.

"Yeah, I know." He'd pat my head, down his drink and bark, "What's the holdup, kid? Back to the salt mine!"

Off Frawley and I would go, back to work. The ploy must have saved the studio thousands in production overruns.

Nickodell's is gone now, but the memory of Frawley's dessert remains. Cantaloupe and ice cream: I heartily recommend it.

Just Who Was That Masked Man?

AFTER LISTENING TO THE "REAL" LONE RANGER ON THE RADIO, ONE YOUNG BOY
WAS DISAPPOINTED WHEN THE MASKED MAN CAME TO TELEVISION.

By Esmond Fatter Jr., Houston, Texas

I'll never forget the first time I watched television...and walked away disappointed! The year was 1949, and I was an 8-year-old radio fan living in New Orleans.

At 5 o'clock every Monday, Wednesday and Friday, I'd settle in front of my grandparents' radio to listen intently as "the daring and resourceful masked rider of the plains, along with his faithful Indian companion, Tonto, led the fight for law and order in the early western United States."

The Lone Ranger was the hero of my childhood imagination—the strong, kind, selfless embodiment of Old West manhood.

One day a neighbor kid, Jeffrey Hirsh, told me his father had just brought home a television—one of the first on our block! Jeffrey invited me and some other friends over to watch *The Lone Ranger* on the new set. Having never experienced this thrilling medium, I was one excited kid!

When the clock struck 7:30, Mr. Hirsh turned on the television and started to adjust it. I staked out a spot right in front, my backside about two inches off the floor.

The Ranger Appears

Suddenly I heard the familiar theme music...and there he was.

Riding at a full gallop down a dirt trail came my hero! The Lone Ranger and Silver made a 180-degree switchback to the right, then a 90-degree left turn. The Masked Man rode up a hill and reined in, and the great white stallion reared up, his front legs slashing the sky. Wow, just like in the comic books!

Then a voice echoed: "Hi-Yo, Silver, away!"

That was when the bubble burst. It wasn't the same voice! Gone was the deep, resonant, manly tone I had grown to admire so much on the radio. In its place was the high-pitched bleating of some obvious impostor.

"That's not the Lone Ranger!" I blurted out. Mr. Hirsh's eye narrowed and my peers expressed their collective disdain of my observation with gems like "Shut up, Fatter!" "Yeah, be quiet!" and "Clam up, Ezy!"

In mumbled embarrassment, I begged their general pardon. But I felt cheated by the popular new medium.

When Friday came, 5 p.m. found me back in front of the radio. My imagination ran alongside a "fiery horse with the speed of light...." Then I heard that familiar deep, resonant voice calling, "Come on, Silver! Let's go, big fella!"

UNMASK THE MASQUERADER.
Will the real Lone Ranger please stand up? This reader was shocked to discover that a TV impostor had replaced his Western radio hero.

The Night I Went 'Person to Person'

STORMY WEATHER, SECRET VISITORS AND A MAN IN A TRENCH COAT MADE THIS OFFICER'S DUTY SHIFT ANYTHING BUT ROUTINE.

By Herbert Benson, Corvallis, Oregon

As a veteran of World War II and Korea, I have plenty of unforgettable memories. But one peacetime recollection remains as vivid as any—it was the night I risked my military career on the strength of a handshake.

In early November 1957, I was stationed at Stewart Air Force Base, north of New York City. My 24-hour shift began routinely. But by nightfall, an early winter storm had slowed air traffic to a point where my dispatcher and I would have welcomed even the rumor of a flight.

The break came at 1940 hours when the door swung open and, with a blast of cold air, a tall, lean man in a rain-soaked trench coat blew in. His first words were, "I'm Edward R. Murrow."

Shock of Recognition

My reply was automatic. "I'm Capt. Herbert R. Benson, Airdrome Officer this evening. What can I do for you?" Meanwhile, I was thinking, *Who's Edward R. Murrow, and what's he doing here on a night like this?*

"Captain Benson," he said, reaching out for a firm handshake, "I have some people coming. I'd like to wait here for them."

"Well, sir, you'd better make yourself comfortable," I replied. "You may have a long wait."

"I can understand that," he said, sitting down on one of the benches and lighting a cigarette.

Then it hit me! Edward R. Murrow was the world-famous journalist and television personality!

He said he was expecting friends from Canada, who were to be his weekend houseguests—if they made it through the storm.

We began talking about our war experiences, and it wasn't long before he was interviewing me, "Person to Person." What struck me most was that, despite his status, Murrow was more interested in me than in talking about himself.

Before I knew it, an hour had passed. The phone rang, and the dispatcher relayed word that a Canadian flight had touched down. With that announcement, Mr. Murrow took me aside.

Mum's the Word

He revealed that the friends he was waiting for were the prime minister of Canada and his wife. He emphasized that they wanted to slip quietly into the country, without fanfare.

"But, Mr. Murrow," I protested, "regulations require that I notify the base commander when any VIP arrives."

"I admire you for your dedication," Mr. Murrow replied persuasively. "But as a favor to me, I hope you'll agree to ignore protocol. Your convictions are your conscience, but sometimes you have to do what you have to do."

I envisioned kissing my captain's bars goodbye as we escorted the guests to Mr. Murrow's car. "If your CO gives you any problems," Mr. Murrow said as he shook my hand, "refer him to me."

Fortunately, there were no problems. I watched Mr. Murrow and his guests drive off into the storm with the sound of his parting words, "Good night and good luck," ringing in my ears.

THESE STARS SHONE!

Before He Moved to 'Mayberry'

In the early 1950s, I was just out of school and working for Allison-Erwin, a wholesale distributor in Charlotte, North Carolina.

I especially remember my first company Christmas party, which was quite an event. The entertainment was provided by a young man from Mount Airy who did funny monologues; one he called "What It Was, Was Football."

But the highlight of the night for me was when he started up a dance called "The Bunny Hop." Being one of the youngest in attendance and the newest employee, I got to be first in line behind this wonderful entertainer. What a thrill!

He wasn't that well known then, but today, Andy Griffith is a star we all love.

—**Betty Reeves,** *Charleston, South Carolina*

He Loves Lucy, Too!

For years, I worked as a freelance assistant director in Hollywood. In 1951, a production company was shooting a pilot TV show at the General Service Studio, and they seemed to be short of money.

Even the pretty redheaded leading lady was doing some of the janitorial work at the studio. I remarked to her one day that there were other people to handle that work, but she told me she wasn't happy with their methods.

The pilot they made sold after a few months, and it wasn't long before the whole country had heard of *I Love Lucy*. A few years later, Lucille Ball and Desi Arnaz bought their own studio!

—**Richard Evans,** *Carson City, Nevada*

ANDY GRIFFITH, ZUMA PRESS INC. / ALAMY; LUCILLE BALL AND DESI ARNAZ, BETTMANN / CORBIS; JOHNNY CARSON, EVERETT COLLECTION

He-e-e-re's...Johnny!

In February 1946, I was on my way home from World War II along with many other Navy veterans. Hundreds of us were billeted at Treasure Island in San Francisco Bay, and from there we boarded a special train that was headed east.

The train had a dozen Pullman cars and a diner. The passengers were all enlisted men, except for one young lieutenant, of the type known then as a "90-Day Wonder."

This young ensign was extremely personable, though, and he kept us entertained with card tricks, stories and jokes.

Our group dubbed him "Kit Carson" after a famous Carson we knew. This young man soon became famous on his own, however, as Johnny Carson, television star and longtime host of *The Tonight Show*.

—**Herb Klipp,** *Waynesboro, Pennsylvania*

Have TV Series, Will Travel

I was a high school student in 1958 in Gallup, New Mexico, when I met a very funny and huge man—actor Richard Boone.

My father, Capt. Arey E. Adams, was commander of a small military radar site just outside town. The film company for Mr. Boone's TV series *Have Gun Will Travel* was shooting a segment for the show nearby.

It was our good fortune to entertain Mr. Boone and his entourage for a day—one filled with laughter and food.

My mother, Cleo Parker Adams (between Mr. Boone and my dad in photo), was almost giddy as she hugged the big man and grinned with delight.

—**Jim Adams,** *Pink Hill, North Carolina*

There Was No Bogarting Her!

Working as a waitress in The Chestnut Room of Purdue University's Union building in the mid-'50s, I had many opportunities to meet celebrities visiting for lectures, concerts and variety shows.

When Ed Sullivan came to town, his group reserved the private party room for their post-rehearsal dinner. He was a friendly, pleasant man to serve and talk with.

During the meal, an elderly couple who'd been unable to find seating in the crowded main dining room appeared at the door. They waited patiently, then asked if I could accommodate them.

A corner table was unoccupied, and since they were such a nice couple, I didn't explain that the room was reserved for a private party. Instead, I went to Mr. Sullivan's table and discreetly asked if the couple at the door might use the small table.

Glancing over at them, he turned back to me with a smile and a gracious "of course."

As I escorted the couple to their table, the lady pointed to Mr. Sullivan, tugged on her husband's sleeve and gushed for all to hear, "Look, dear—it's Humphrey Bogart!"

—**Cie Chaikin,** *Huntsville, Alabama*

KING OF THE WILD FRONTIER

Campers Watched Davy Crockett in Battle

My family was camping in the Great Smoky Mountains National Park in North Carolina in 1954, when we spotted some Native Americans in warlike regalia one morning. They were following a trail near our campsite.

We knew we were near the Cherokee Indian Reservation, and we had also noticed that the forest trail the Cherokees were following was marked with red arrows.

Our kids demanded that we follow them down the trail, and soon we heard shouts and shots. There, in a natural bowl, was a Native American-frontiersmen battle of fierce proportions.

We had found ourselves in the midst of moviemaking! The Walt Disney Company was filming a Davy Crockett movie in the deep woods with the Cherokees participating.

My wife and children positioned themselves on a hill where some Native American families had gathered to watch the filming. I sneaked up behind a Disney cameraman and snapped pictures with my 35mm camera, then with my movie camera.

The scene being shot was a battle between Chief Red Stick and his warriors against Davy Crockett and his frontiersmen. The battle had to be re-enacted three times because the Cherokees couldn't restrain their laughter.

The director warned them to stop their hilarity or they'd be fired. When I rejoined my wife and children, I found out why the Cherokees were having so much fun. An Indian woman told my wife that each summer, their village of Oconaluftee staged a pageant called "Unto These Hills." It was the story of the Cherokees from the days of the Spanish explorer DeSoto to their eviction from the area to Oklahoma along the Trail of Tears.

The woman said the pageant's leading actor was a Cherokee who portrayed a beloved chief. He died the year before and was replaced by a white actor from the University of North Carolina.

The Native Americans resented this.

The white actor had gotten a part in the movie as one of the frontiersmen. The Cherokee woman pointed him out to my wife and explained that every time there was a fight scene, the Cherokees knocked him down and roughed him up.

"The Cherokees love it," the woman said to my wife. "It's all a big joke. The more takes the better."

We returned home and waited impatiently for the movie to appear on TV. It finally was broadcast as *Davy Crockett, King of the Wild Frontier* in three parts. The first installment was *Davy Crockett, Indian Fighter*.

We delighted in watching the fight between Crockett, played by Fess Parker, and Chief Red Stick

FLICK FILMING. Author Clavin Fisher stealthily snapped these photographs during the filming of Walt Disney's *Davy Crockett, King of the Wild Frontier* in 1954. Behind the scenes, the Native Americans were winning.

that our family had viewed while staying in the Great Smoky Mountains.

Our son Peter soon had a coonskin cap and bragged to his friends that he had actually witnessed the battle.

Shortly thereafter, all of America was awash in Davy Crockett memorabilia and children were joyfully singing the show's ballad theme song. Coonskin caps adorned not only the heads of children, but adults as well. One commentator later noted, "Every raccoon in the country had to run for its life."

—**Clavin Fisher**, *West Simsbury, Connecticut*

Dad Was a Crockett Convert

We were the last family in the neighborhood to get a television set. My husband had proclaimed he wouldn't spend his hard-earned money on such foolishness, adding, "Besides, it's bad for the kids."

One day, I found my 5-year-old daughter watching the neighbors' TV when they were not in the room. I was embarrassed and told my husband we were getting a set.

He knew better than to argue, but after he bought the TV, he rearranged the furniture and faced his chair to the corner!

That first Saturday after we got the set, the kids were watching *Davy Crockett* and rolling around on the floor with laughter. My husband peeked over his shoulder to see what was so funny, then promptly turned his chair around. He was hooked!

—**Doris Bachstein**, *Litchfield, Illinois*

DOIN' THE TWIST. Here, the author's sister Terri is in the middle sporting a barrette in her hair. The author is near the front with blond curls, and Toni, far right in the back, is also wearing a barrette.

Meeting a TV Family

My dad, Ralph, worked in the paint department at General Service Studios in Hollywood, where *I Love Lucy, Our Miss Brooks* and *The Adventures of Ozzie and Harriet* were once filmed.

In 1962, when extras were needed for a TV episode of Ozzie and Harriet's show, my sisters, Terri and Toni, and I got to be on the show with the help of our father. I was 7, and my sisters were 10. They were older and taller than the rest of the kids, and I think my father fibbed about their age to get them on the show.

We were to appear in the episode "The Tigers Go to a Dance." The Tigers were a group of young boys on the show who would take part in a dance planned by Harriet's women's club.

We had to learn to dance The Twist, so we worked for two days. Part of the time was spent rehearsing and filming, and part was spent with a tutor for our schoolwork. But the highlight of those two days, for me, was meeting Ricky Nelson.

We extras were paid $25.47 per day, quite a lot for a child back then. In fact, it wasn't much less than my father's daily pay rate of $32.24 a full five years later.

My father's car, a 1940 Mercury, was used as David Nelson's car in a few episodes as well, for which Dad was paid $25 each time. Dad went on to work at The Walt Disney Studios. We kids loved that because we got free tickets to Disneyland!

—**Trudi Fisher Cabrera,** *Palmdale, California*

1950

Kodak TV stars invite you to the most exciting camera show ever !

See Kodak's "The Adventures of Ozzie and Harriet," ABC-TV. Check local listings.

For movies

Kodak's greatest home movie value Precision 8mm Brownie Movie Camera with fast f/2.3 lens is snap-shot-easy to use. Was $39.75—now reduced! **$29.95, or $3 down.**

Brownie Turret Cameras get normal, telephoto, wide-angle shots. New, lowest priced turret ever—f/2.3, **$59.50**, f/1.9 was $84.75, now **$74.50, or $7.50 down.**

Simplicity itself—Handsome Kodak Medallion 8 Camera magazine-loads in 3 seconds, weighs only 23 ounces. Just one setting: f/1.9 lens. **$106.50, or $10.50 down.**

Big-screen 8mm shows—Brownie 300 Movie Projector has forward, reverse action. Top value! **$64.95, or $6.50 down.** For movies 5 feet wide, Cine-Kodak Showtime 8 Projector, **$123.50, or $12.50 down.**

See the carousel of cameras . . . and the world's most modern line-up of projectors and photo-aids!

With spring here and summer not far off, it's time to get set for picture-taking. And the *place* to get set is at your dealer's Kodak Camera Carnival.

During this exciting event, your Kodak dealer is demonstrating three rings-full of values! You'll see everything new from Kodak that makes it easier for you to take beautiful snap-shots in color or black-and-white . . . sparkling color slides you can show big as life . . . glorious color movies that capture all the action, too! And because everything is made by Kodak, you know it's good!

Come to your dealer's Kodak Camera Carnival—in time for this weekend's fun! (*Prices are list, include Federal Tax where applicable and are subject to change without notice.*)

EASTMAN KODAK   Rochester 4, N.Y.

Kodak
TRADEMARK

A large part of the public said, "An extra $100? For that I can get up from my chair!"

—**Robert Adler,** co-inventor of the TV remote control, on the public's lack of enthusiasm for the new gadget

BLOOPERS
We'll Never Forget!

Early Stations Ruled by the 'Law of the Jungle'

I worked behind the scenes in early television production and advertising...a fun and funny experience. In the '50s, when television was in its infancy, most people on screen either memorized their lines or used cue cards.

On-camera announcers took pride in delivering their lines without being distracted. Unfortunately, the crew took greater pride and satisfaction in being able to break up those "steely nerved" folks.

One time, for an on-air announcement, the young studio crew rigged a surprise. Prior to the show, they put up a trapeze and had one of the propmen hanging from it by his knees. When released, he would swing over the announcer's head, out of camera range.

All waited patiently until "Mr. You-Can't-Break-Me-Up" reached the peak of his presentation. Then, clad in a loincloth and silently beating his chest, "Tarzan" was released. The announcer had clearly seen him, yet he never missed even a word in his commercial. Finally, it was over.

Looking directly into the camera, he said to the crew, "Ladies and gentlemen, I have never broken up on the air, and I'm not going to today." Then he turned and walked out into the hallway, where his laughter could be heard through the closed door.

Meanwhile, the crew was so incapacitated, they couldn't continue—they locked their cameras in place and joined the announcer in the hall. The director in the control booth had no other option but to return to the movie.

—*Jack Brussel,* San Diego, California

Drama Behind the Camera

I was a scriptwriter for early live TV dramas—when anything could happen—and often did.

In a show with several sets, actors often had to quickly maneuver around backstage. They didn't always make it in time, so the other performers on screen would ad-lib to cover the gap.

Clothing changes were made en route. One outfit was worn over another so that layers could be peeled off in a hurry. During one show, an actress had donned four different outfits in the

MAKING A SPLASH. Because early TV was live, every event viewers watched was really happening, such as this indoor rain shower.

wrong order. In a crucial scene, viewers saw her in a denim jacket with an evening gown underneath!

There were many such harrowing moments: An actor who'd just "died," thinking he was no longer on camera, rose like Lazarus and walked away. And during a production of *Hamlet*, Maurice Evans began his famous soliloquy, "Now I am alone..." as a stagehand walked across the set, realized he was on camera, and scrambled frantically off the scene.

—*Eric Arthur,* Williamsburg, Virginia

Last-Minute Change

Early in the '50s, I was appearing on the live soap opera *The Guiding Light*. In an adjacent studio, a new daytime drama was making its debut.

There was a commotion in the hallway, so some of us went out to investigate. One of the actors explained the problem: The powers-that-be had to quickly come up with a new name for the show, which was to air in one hour.

You see, during rehearsal, the announcer had read his copy aloud for the first time: "This is *The Inner Storm*, sponsored by Ex-Lax."

Thus was born *The Secret Storm*.

—*Mark Weston,* Jamaica, New York

RAINING ON SET, RALPH MORSE / TIME & LIFE PICTURES / GETTY IMAGES

We Won BIG on TV!

The Secret That Saved Christmas

It was September of 1955 and here I was, stuck in our trailer in Acushnet, Massachusetts.

It was really my own choice—with no childcare back then, my 3-year-old daughter, Candace, deserved my full attention. Still, there was little to do for entertainment, and we were "dirt poor."

One evening as I was watching *I've Got a Secret*, I thought to myself, *If only I had a secret!*

My one claim to fame was that an ancestor, John Howland, came over on the Mayflower—not exactly earthshaking. But wait a minute! John had had a secret of his own—he was a klutz who'd fallen overboard on his way to the New World!

I decided to send in my "secret." Two weeks later, I answered the phone to hear, "This is Roger Williams of *I've Got a Secret*." I was told to send proof that I was related to John Howland and that he had actually fallen overboard.

After the show received my responses, they paid our expenses for a trip to New York to appear on the program.

The guest star that night was Debbie Reynolds, and her secret was that she had learned how to play the French horn.

Host Garry Moore was very friendly, but when he told us beforehand that 6 million people would be watching, I nearly panicked and left the studio!

I was so nervous that I don't even remember seeing television cameras as I whispered my secret: My great-great-great-great-great-great-great-great-grandfather came over on the Mayflower and fell overboard, but he was rescued—and that's why I'm here.

The panel didn't guess my secret, so I received $80—a fortune!—and a carton of Winstons.

The best part of the experience was attending the Macy's Thanksgiving Day Parade the next morning. Candy remembers it to this day.

But the $80 was absolutely terrific, too. It was our ticket to a real Christmas. I had a wonderful time buying presents, including some special toys for Candy.

My one regret now is that I was never able to see the program I had appeared on. Those were the days before VCRs!

—**Nancy Stoughton Ovitt,** *Chelmsford, Massachusetts*

To Tell a Lie

My uncle Jack worked in New York City and had many friends in the television industry, among them the producer of many Goodson-Todman productions. Naturally, I nagged my uncle to get me on one of the company's quiz programs.

In my eighth-grade year in Arlington, New Jersey, I was given an audition to be on *To Tell the Truth*. A girl named Marian and I were chosen to play the liars opposite Kaye, an Iowa farm girl who had raised a $64,000 Hereford steer.

Now, picture a city girl who summered at the Jersey Shore and had never come closer to a barnyard than watching *The Real McCoys*; and I was expected to lie my way through assorted farm expertise. I had an excellent memory, though, and knew I could do the script and perform.

The only panel member who selected me as the farm girl was Kitty Carlisle. She asked me, "How many roosters do you need for 100 chickens?"

Well, in my day and age and with my naivete, I had no clue what she was talking about. However, being one who always had an answer—true to my Irish heritage—I blurted out, "Well, I guess it depends on the rooster."

The audience roared with laughter, and I couldn't understand why. However, I did receive the one vote from Kitty, who said I looked like a farm girl, and went home a happy person, $187 richer with a neat gift box of Anacin products.

The show aired in early 1961 and allowed me to buy a brand-new washing machine for Mom. That made her day...and many more afterward—no more wringer washer!

—**Corliss Welch,** *Tinton Falls, New Jersey*

LIKE THIS, GARRY. Nancy Ovitt shows Garry Moore how her ancestor fell off the Mayflower when she appeared on television's *I've Got a Secret* in 1955.

SHE LEARNED PLENTY OUTFITTING
'MR. TELEVISION'

MILTON BERLE WAS TALENTED, BUT THIS YOUNG COSTUME DESIGNER FOUND OUT NO ONE WORKED HARDER.
By Grace Case, San Diego, California

In 1955, I signed on as a costume designer for Milton Berle's television program. For production people, this Tuesday night show was known as the roughest to work on, as Mr. Berle was a workaholic and a perfectionist. To top things off, the show was live, so mistakes couldn't be edited out of the tape.

My career in design had begun earlier when a foot ailment ended my dance career, which included a stint with the Rockettes.

I was fortunate to then become a costume designer's assistant and "gofer," running for samples and swatches for shows at the 1940 New York World's Fair and several Broadway shows.

Eventually, I continued on to design costumes for more than 40 shows, seven films and countless television programs.

LONG DAYS, LOUD LAUGHS

The year I joined Milton Berle's NBC show was its last in New York. Aside from his tremendous comedic talent, he worked tirelessly—and expected his staff to do the same. For me, it was the best training possible for the hectic pace of live television.

Show days on Tuesday began at 7 a.m., when my cab pulled up to the NBC-TV studios in Radio City. Our "day" didn't end until 2 or 3 the next morning, when the whole crew went to Lindy's, Milton's Broadway hangout. I'd plead exhaustion, but Milton enjoyed an audience, and his jokes continued at the table!

Other comics envied the way he could make bad jokes funny—even stolen jokes. Around Broadway he was called "The Thief of Bad Gags."

LEARNING THE ROPES

Working with Milton Berle provided a crash course in show business production. One challenge I recall involved Sophie Tucker, a portly singer who rose to fame in the early part of the century and billed herself as "The Last of the Red Hot Mamas."

I was told to make her look like the teenager she'd been when she first started out. I managed to accomplish this with an unusual gown design and some clever backlighting.

Another day, just 90 minutes before airtime, Milton fired one act and replaced it with 12 kids hired to sing *The Ballad of Davy Crockett*. My job was to round up 12 coonskin caps for the kids to wear...but where would I find them with all the stores closed?

"Get them, Grace," Milton ordered. "I'll get Macy's to open for you." And he did!

That's how I found myself in the darkened toy section of the world's largest department store, shopping for coonskin caps accompanied by an armed security guard and three salivating German shepherds.

Almost as funny as seeing Milton's act on the air was watching him being fitted for a woman's dress while three seamstresses crouched on the floor, sewing the hem. Meantime, five writers

HER OWN MODEL. Author, who worked as a costume designer for Milton Berle, modeled one of her outfits in 1955.

stood pressed against the dressing room wall, pencils in hand, rewriting jokes as Milton waved his cigar in rapid rejections of this gag or that.

A SERIOUS STAR

As hectic as it all seemed, little was left to chance. During the last four minutes before airtime, Milton could be found backstage, pacing in circles and silently mouthing his opening monologue like a praying monk.

No one dared approach him during those moments, and it occurred to me week after week—comedians were the most serious people in show business!

I owe much to Milton Berle. Like other great stars—Ray Bolger, Ethel Merman and Bert Lahr—he taught me the value of hard work and of leaving nothing to chance.

I'll never forget those long, long Tuesdays when I learned so much about putting a show together. Thanks, Uncle Miltie.

TRIPLE THREAT. Uncle Miltie could ham it up with the best of them. But to pull off his comedy shows, he and his staff did some serious work.

HOORAY FOR HOPALONG!

He Sat in the Saddle
With Hopalong Cassidy

Hopalong Cassidy captured the hearts and imaginations of millions of kids in the 1950s. Remember? Astride his white stallion, Topper, in movies and on television, Hoppy—played by William Boyd—was our Western hero.

I was a huge fan from the time I was 8 years old. Some liked Hoppy's wavy silver hair or his sparkling blue eyes, but for me, it was his warm and friendly smile—the smile of a confident hero.

As a birthday treat one year, Aunt Mary took me to Madison Square Garden in New York City to see the Cole Brothers Circus—with Hopalong Cassidy among the headliners!

Dressed in my black Hoppy hat, black shirt, black pants and a pair of genuine Wyandotte Hoppy cap guns strapped on my hips, I'd waited for hours for Aunt Mary to arrive.

Then there was the mile-long walk to the station in Plainfield, New Jersey...and a 30-mile train ride to New York City. The trip itself was a blur.

Our seats at the circus were in the third row near the number-one ring. I could smell the elephants as they went past my corner seat. Hoppy just had to notice me there in my outfit!

Normally I loved a circus, but this day found me squirming in my seat waiting for each act to end, hoping Hoppy would appear next. I do remember watching 10 oversized clowns try to stuff themselves into a tiny car. That was when I heard the soft jingle of spurs and distinctive creak of saddle leather. I think I stopped breathing!

I knew Hoppy was there even before I looked.

Slowly turning my head, my heart almost in my throat, I looked straight into the brown eye of Topper his trusty steed! Hoppy was astride his stallion on the other side of the railing right next to me. When our eyes met, he smiled and said, "Howdy, son, hope you like the show."

I nodded, unable to utter a word.

"I see you're a cowboy, too," he chuckled. "Maybe you'd like to sit on Topper for a minute." Reaching over the railing with his black-gloved hands, Hoppy lifted me out of my seat and sat me in the saddle with him. I remember my amazement at how big Topper was.

There was an explosion of flashbulbs and hoots from other kids. I sat there, too dumbfounded to say anything.

"What's your name, son?" Hoppy asked in a fatherly voice.

"J-J-Joe," I stammered.

"Well, Joe, it's time for me to go to work." He lifted my Hoppy hat and kissed my brow. "It was a pleasure meeting you."

Before I realized it, I was back in my seat, with Aunt Mary squeezing me and shouting something I couldn't hear over the roar of the crowd.

Hoppy and Topper were in the spotlight as they rode out and circled all three rings. Aunt Mary says I was in a trance for the rest of the performance and the ride back home. (We still laugh about it when I visit her.)

Bill Boyd died in 1972. Occasionally I'd see his widow, Grace, when she wasn't busy working with children's hospitals here in Southern California. We'd talk about Hoppy the character and Bill Boyd the actor...and how they both loved kids.

—**Joseph Caro,** Long Beach, California

BIRTHDAY BUCKAROO. Author Joseph Caro wore his Hoppy outfit (left) on the very day he met his hero.

Howdy, Hoppy

Hopalong Cassidy was one of my favorite cowboys. He was also the grand marshal of the Tournament of Roses Parade on Jan. 1, 1952.

Several of us couples celebrated the holiday with a day of bowling in Los Angeles on New Year's Eve. Then around midnight, we headed for Pasadena so we could get good seats for the parade. As you can see from the photo on the top right, we succeeded. Some of the folks are bundled up with blankets and coats—it was quite chilly out there!

We really welcomed the sunrise that morning after sitting for so long in the cold.

—*Joan Stewart, Chula Vista, California*

Fashion by Hopalong

A TV set was not something my parents were eager to buy, since they didn't think that television would outlast radio.

We did, however, visit often with Aunt Florence, who owned the first TV set in the family—a Muntz with a six-inch screen encased in four feet of bulky cabinet. Uncle Steve could hardly wait for the evening news and wrestling matches, and Aunt Florence always accommodated my love of Westerns.

TV serial Westerns were all the rage back then, and my all-time favorite was *Hopalong Cassidy*. I was the happiest little girl in the world when, for my birthday in 1950, I received my beloved cowgirl outfit with accompanying six-shooter, as you can see on the right.

—*Jan McCanless, China Grove, North Carolina*

Honk If You Loved Clarabell

My father, Sanford Betker, was the manager of a small department store in Columbus, Ohio. He and the manager of another store down the street were always trying to outdo each other for business.

I don't know how he did it, but in August 1951, Dad managed to get Clarabell the Clown from the television program *The Howdy Doody Show* to appear at the store.

We were so excited! On the day Clarabell came, the people who worked in the store, and their children, got to be there before the store opened. We really felt like big shots.

Then a man came into the store. Everyone was whispering that he was Clarabell. He said a quick "Hello," and went into my dad's office. A little while later, Clarabell came out!

The older kids tried not to show how excited they were. But the younger ones, like my 6-year-old sister, Arlene, couldn't take their eyes off him.

In the photo (right), you can see my sister on the left. The woman is trying to get her to look at the camera instead of at Clarabell.

Clarabell was so nice—and funny! Every once in a while, he would pretend to squirt someone with his seltzer bottle.

Even after more than 60 years, we still talk about what an exciting day that was.

—*Jan Rosansky, Columbus, Ohio*

Out of This World

I was a kid who loved anything that had to do with outer space and things of the future so I watched *The Jetsons* every time it was on.

—*Ellen Marie Leach, via Facebook*

SURF'S UP In the early 1960s, there was a TV show called *SurfSide 6*. Remember? It was about three private investigators who worked out of a houseboat tied up next to a Miami Beach hotel. This is the actual houseboat, with my wife, Lou, standing in front. We were in the area when the show was still on and stopped by. —Bob Crawford, Apple Valley, Minnesota

CLOWNING AROUND.
A Columbus, Ohio, department store was abuzz when Clarabell the Clown of *The Howdy Doody Show* paid a visit. Read all about it on the opposite page.

Saturday Night With Snooky Was a Hit With Mom

Like most kids growing up in the '50s, I was glued to the television set on Saturday morning. Saturday night, on the other hand, was reserved for taking a bath, laying out church clothes and a quiet game or bedtime story.

Then Mom developed a crush on Snooky Lanson, the handsome singer from *Your Hit Parade*. That's when I got my first taste of popular music, as well as my first chance to watch an adult program on TV.

Your Hit Parade had been a popular, long-running radio show featuring such singing greats as Frank Sinatra, Buddy Clark and Doris Day. The television version debuted in July 1950.

Of course, the most exciting part of the show was at the end, when the No. 1 song of that particular week was finally revealed.

Mom's favorite, Snooky Lanson, was one of the regulars, along with Russell Arms and "songbirds" Gisele MacKenzie and Dorothy Collins. And because this was television, they couldn't just sing a song—they also had to act it out.

I think *Your Hit Parade* was such a smashing success because the cast members were so clean-cut and enthusiastic, and the music was always singable, with catchy tunes and lyrics.

Not long ago, while looking through some family keepsakes, I came across a letter Mom received from Snooky Lanson. She must have written him a fan letter and he'd graciously replied.

The letter was warm and personal, just like the show had been. In it, Snooky explained how the cast rehearsed from Tuesday through Saturday. He said everyone had to be very prepared because the show was broadcast live and they had to perform flawlessly—or be clever enough to cover up their mistakes.

I still recall the lyrics of the show's closing song:
So long for a while,
That's all the songs for a while.
So long from Your Hit Parade,
And the beautiful music we played.

What a wonderful memory. And what a wonderful show!

—Jan Holden, *Vancouver, Washington*

Say Cheese!

Candid Camera was one of my favorite shows as a child—we watched it as a family. The show I will never forget is the one where the car rolls into a gas station and the driver tells the attendant at the pumps to check the oil...the attendant raises the hood, and there's no motor! As a child, I was amazed by that and wondered how in the world they did it. When I saw the same show as an adult, I realized the gas station was located at the bottom of a small hill. Ohhhhh!

—Diana Cervantes, *via Facebook*

My, How TV Has Changed!

An Old Family Member

If you were interested in the Gemini and Apollo space flights of the '60s, you just had to have a big color TV—unless you could be there for a launch.

My old black-and-white set had about had it, so I looked at a number of color sets and bought a build-it-yourself Heathkit 25-inch set. It arrived in two huge boxes—one with the picture tube and the other full of hundreds of little parts.

After a few weeks of soldering parts to circuit boards, with the final assembly on the picnic table in the garage, the kids got in their favorite seats in the station wagon and imagined they were at a drive-in movie. All 22 tubes in the back of the set lit up, and the first thing we heard was the theme song to *Green Acres*. Appropriately, the picture was all green because nothing was adjusted yet. But then, we breathed a sigh of relief and watched our first color program.

I soon turned my attention to designing and building a legless console that was supported on two walls (below). The set would slide out for repairs, and a small fan moved the heat to a kitchen cupboard on the other side of the wall.

Next, a stereo was built and that added to the TV's sound output. Now, when there was a space launch and the volume was turned up full, the whole neighborhood thought our house was going to blast off!

After one picture-tube replacement, many small repairs and more than a quarter-century of use, I heard a "psszt," and the picture shrunk to a small dot in the center of the tube.

I found it impractical to fix that old set and even harder to get rid of than it was to build. So now it just sits there and serves as a shelf for vases and wedding pictures.

—**Elmer Schmitt,** Pittsburgh, Pennsylvania

WEDDING GIFT. Newlyweds Wilbert and Lula Mae Gibson (above) of Hammond, Louisiana, were overjoyed to receive a TV from their family in 1954. It was the couple's first piece of furniture. Nephew Oscar Williams Jr. of Kirkland, Washington, shared the photo.

IN LIVING COLOR. The Cartwright men appear in this 1965 ad for RCA televisions.

The Power of Television

Memories of our first TV came flooding back when I came across an agreement that was penned by my father and signed by us three boys in 1954.

The first part of it read:

"State of Illinois, County of Cook, City of Chicago.

"We, John R. O'Connor Jr. (age 15), James Lee O'Connor (12) and Jerome O'Connor (5) do hereby swear and affirm that we, as a group and individually, will adhere to the following rules in regards to the television set when it is installed.

"1. We will eat all our meals at the table and at the time we are called, and further, we will not gulp our food down in order to hurry back to the aforementioned television set....

"2. We will be cooperative in the selection of programs."

Tacked onto the end were rules about curfews, bedtimes, homework and music practice.

I don't know how long the rules lasted, but I clearly recall that several years later, homework didn't get done first. I'd settle down to watch *The Mickey Mouse Club* at 3 in the afternoon until my brothers came home and switched the TV to *American Bandstand*.

—**Jerry O'Connor,** *Lansing, Illinois*

Cartwrights in Color!

One day in 1959, my dad was in an appliance store that had black-and-white televisions next to the new color models.

"What a difference!" Dad yelled when he got home, telling us about the woman on the show he'd watched in the store. "You could see her blue dress, her red lips, her blond hair!" Then he exclaimed, "I bought a set!"

My frugal mom, Mamie, went nuts, asking Dad if he was crazy and reminding him of the bills to be paid and the old roof that would need to be replaced. But the set, a gigantic console with a 24-inch screen, arrived a few days later.

Bonanza was to have its color debut later in the week, so Dad invited neighbors over to watch.

We all watched the whole show, but my young friends and I especially adored Little Joe, played by Michael Landon, with his blue eyes and green suede jacket. What a doll!

That night was like a Hollywood premiere in our little town of Phillipsburg, New Jersey.

—**Weda Mosellie,** *Phillipsburg, New Jersey*

Captain Video's One-Man Cleanup Crew

FOR THIS '50S HERO, MOPPING UP OUTER SPACE CRIME WAS A SNAP COMPARED TO DEALING WITH SYRUPY YOUNG FANS.

By Albert Sohl, Port St. Lucie, Florida

In the early '50s, our 6-year-old son, Albert, would sit much too close to our 10-inch TV watching his hero, Captain Video, every weekday evening before supper. Much like Flash Gordon in the '30s, Captain Video captivated '50s kids with his outer space crime-fighting.

Attired in his silvery Nehru-style space hat, a safari bush jacket, white breeches and boots, Captain Video was Earth's crusader against alien wrongdoers. No star was too far and no unearthly perpetrator went unpunished.

One memorable autumn day in 1953, Captain Video stepped out of his spaceship and invited young fans to come see him in person!

"Space Rangers," Captain Video announced, "it's easier than zapping a Martian worm-rat! Simply have your parents remove the label from a jar of my Mallowmarsh Syrup and carefully print your name, age and address on the back.

"Send it to me in a self-addressed envelope, and tickets to my Empire State Building headquarters will be mailed to you posthaste. First come, first served!"

Blast-off Set

We did as the space master bid, but it wasn't until the following July that a familiar self-addressed envelope reappeared in the mail at our Levittown, New York, home. The promised tickets had arrived, and Albert's joy knew no bounds!

The day of our visit to the show was sweltering hot. Arriving at Studio C on the 66th floor of the Empire State Building, we and the other bewildered parents were herded into a large room where a harried-looking guide waited.

"At precisely 4:45," she explained, "the children will be escorted to the set for a quick warm-up. At 5:02, Captain Video will appear and interview his young Space Rangers. Parents will sit in the adjacent viewing room with a TV monitor.

"Last, but far from least, the rest rooms are at the far end of the corridor. Please make sure that all, uh, precautions are taken before we go on the air," the guide concluded.

At that point the door opened, and in walked Captain Video himself. He was greeted with

STUNNED SPACE RANGER. Young Albert Sohl was surprised when his hero, Captain Video (above right), landed back on the planet Earth.

shouts of joyous recognition from the children and polite applause from the adults.

Doffing his silver cap, he bowed modestly, saying, "Thank you. Thank you, one and all."

The Captain had even more instructions. At the end of the show, his Space Rangers were to line up and accept a jar of Mallowmarsh Syrup.

"It is most important that you take the gift with both hands," the Captain emphasized. "Both hands," he repeated, looking at his young charges. "How many hands, Space Rangers?"

"BOTH HANDS!" the kids yelled.

"Excellent. Now, let's blast off!"

In the parents' viewing room, out-of-focus images of our children faded in and out. We struggled with the controls, but it was 20 maddening minutes before we got a tiny but clear picture of Albert accepting his jar of Mallowmarsh...with both hands.

A Sticky Situation

The show over, we hurried down the hall to join our junior celebrities. Happy and excited, Albert ran toward us. Then the unthinkable happened—our son dropped his jar on the marble floor, where it shattered into what must have been a thousand pieces!

Like a giant amoeba, the syrupy puddle extended sticky tentacles in every direction. For a moment the room was frozen in a stunned silence, which was then broken by Albert's loud, anguished shriek.

We were attempting to console our son when, from the corner of my eye, I saw someone rushing toward us with a mop and a pail. It was Captain Video himself!

"Just an accident...couldn't be helped," the actor muttered to no one in particular, dropping to his knees and swinging the mop in sweeping arcs. When Albert saw his space hero kneeling on the floor still dressed in full uniform, his crying stopped.

Later, as our family took the elevator back down to Earth, my son, gingerly holding his new jar of Mallowmarsh, looked up at me with a wisdom beyond his years.

Yes, I'm afraid that the humbling sight of the Champion of the Universe mopping up that sticky, gloppy mess had probably shattered Albert's youthful dreams forever.

Got a Super Handshake

I grew up in Pomona, California, in the 1950s. Since my parents were busy running their store, I often visited my oldest sister and her husband, both of whom lived a few blocks away.

In 1955, I was 10, a few years older than my two cousins. My sister invited me to join them for the Hollywood Christmas parade; I declined.

"But this parade will have a lot of TV personalities," she said. "I know you like Danny Thomas and Art Linkletter, and I think even Lassie will be there." That clinched it!

We arrived at Hollywood Boulevard, and the place was filling up. We had gotten there early enough, so we found a good spot in the front.

My sister was right—a lot of my favorite TV stars passed, riding in convertibles and waving.

Then I saw him, my favorite person in the whole world: George Reeves, who played Clark Kent and Superman in the 1950s TV series.

As if by instinct, I scooted under the yellow tape that separated the crowd from the celebrities. My brother-in-law reached to stop me, but I was too quick—almost as quick as Superman himself!

A policeman ran toward me, but George Reeves waved him away.

He smiled at me and I smiled back and offered my hand so he could shake it; he crushed it!

The crowd laughed, but I didn't care. My hand had been crushed by Superman.

"Now you be a good citizen," he said. "Nice to meet you." I was speechless.

I went back to my place in line and was severely scolded. I didn't hear a thing, and I told myself, "I am not ever washing my hand again."

The next day at school, I told my classmates about my adventure. Many wanted to shake the same hand that had touched Superman. A few days later, I absentmindedly washed my hands.

—**John Montes,** *Hauula, Hawaii*

They Loved Them...
YEAH, YEAH, YEAH!

GIRLS' FIRST GLIMPSE OF THE BEATLES ON TV LED TO MUSICAL INFATUATION.

By Sharon Eastman, Redford, Michigan

Feb. 9, 1964, was a calm winter's night as my family and I visited my uncle Glenn and his family in Livonia, Michigan.

Actually, my cousin Barbara and I wanted to be together to watch the most famous export from modern Great Britain—The Beatles— on TV. We had heard of the band and had heard their music, and our curiosity made us feel like two cats staking out a mouse hole.

Gathered around the 17-inch, black-and-white television set, we sat on the Danish-modern furniture eating pizza— a cheese-and-bread concoction that was new to us. Real Cokes, not the diet variety, fizzed down our throats, and we smiled with delight as we enjoyed such a rare and delicious treat.

Anticipation rose as we waited for *The Ed Sullivan Show* to begin. The adults whispered about Frank Sinatra and Elvis Presley and the similar reactions of hysteria.

Barbara and I, in our Sunday-best chartreuse dresses, talked about our favorite subject—boys. We were in junior high school and happy that we could wear lipstick and nylons. We smoothed our satiny, bubble-cut hairdos and adjusted the clip-on bows that crowned our heads.

After we endured a songstress and a comedy act, Ed Sullivan finally shuffled to center stage. He shouted to a studio filled with screaming girls,

"Ladies and gentlemen— The Beatles!"

Barbara and I rushed to the front of the small TV screen to see every detail of these impish men. The band's quirks mesmerized us. Their hair looked silly, and they shook their heads as they sang.

We were used to the diluted rock of the early '60s. We enjoyed artists like Bobby Rydell and Connie Francis at the time, but The Beatles' music was a return to the origins of rock and roll. These four men amazed us.

They sang five songs that night. Barbara's favorite was their finale, *I Want to Hold Your Hand*, because she liked the lyrics. My favorite was *She Loves You*, with its bouncing beat. They also sang *All My Loving*, *Till There Was You* and *I Saw Her Standing There*.

We had missed *Bonanza* that night, but it was worth it. The adults were happy that Barbara and I enjoyed the performance, never realizing the cultural impact The Beatles had made.

As we departed, we asked each other, "Who's your favorite Beatle?" Barbara's was Paul. Mine was George. And our hearts were filled with joy—"yeah, yeah, yeah."

Today, when I see kids going crazy over musical groups that I just "don't get," I try to be patient and recall the days when I, too, was crazy over a new, unique group—a fabulous foursome from Liverpool, England.

ghost in the machine

On a 1965 visit to my sister's family in Richardson, Texas, I took this slide of my niece, Lisa, soon to be 4 years old. It was Saturday-morning cartoon time. Fortunately, I had my camera handy when Lisa took her Casper doll with her to get a closer look at her favorite program, *Casper the Friendly Ghost*.

—**Don Rose Jr.,** *Cypress, Texas*

CHAPTER 5

GREAT PERFORMANCES

Seeing people's talents come to life on stage—whether on Broadway or in your own hometown—is truly enchanting. For the performers, the experience is just as magical.

"I've spent many years in the entertainment field, but none compare to my roots in the Toby Tent Shows," writes Mike Lacey of Rogersville, Missouri, who, with his parents, made performing a family affair in the '40s and '50s. "For almost a century, hundreds of these shows served as rural America's entertainment lifeline.

"Our performances commonly featured a three-act comedy or drama play with variety and vaudeville acts in between. The undisputed star of every production was Toby Ticklebush, a red-wigged, freckled country bumpkin who always 'out-slickered' the city slickers. Country folks loved him.

"I'm proud to have been a part of those Toby Tent Shows, rural America's 'Broadway Under Canvas.' I'll forever treasure the memories."

All of us have been awed by drama, inspired by dance or uplifted by comedy, and we know that great performances, such as those on the following pages, are impossible to forget.

SHOWGIRL
STILL KICKING

HIGH-STEPPING DANCER—AND GRANDMOTHER—HAS BEEN WOWING AUDIENCES FOR OVER SIX DECADES.

By Dorothy Dale Kloss, Palm Springs, California

I was 13 and about to go into high school when Miss Comerford, a great tap-dance teacher, told me, "I'd like to train you to teach for me."

That's how, in 1936, I first embarked on my dance career and I've never stopped.

Bobby Fosse was in my first class at the Academy of Fine Arts in Chicago. He and I were from the same neighborhood, just a couple of blocks apart, on Chicago's north side. He was three years younger than I was, and I began giving him tap lessons; he had a style that was different from that of most dancers.

He became one of the greatest dancers and choreographers in American musical theater, winning an Academy Award for directing *Cabaret* and earning eight Tony awards for choreography.

After I taught for a couple of years, I needed a change of scenery. I wanted to perform in the Loop, where all the dance action was.

The Merriel Abbott Dance School taught high-kick, character, ballet and tap, but not jazz back then. I checked out the school to find out how much classes cost. They were $15 a month.

My mother, a widow raising three kids, told me she had enough for three months of lessons, so I went down and registered.

As the three months were ending, Miss Abbott was in Hollywood with her dance troupe. Eddie Shavers, the tap teacher, said Miss Abbott would return next week and have a tap contest.

"You can win," he told me, assuring me the contest wasn't fixed.

I won, and that's when I got into show business.

Miss Abbott booked The Palmer House and put me in the 10 p.m. "little show."

On opening night, I came out to Irving Berlin's *A Pretty Girl Is Like a Melody* as the emcee said, "And now, Dorothy Dale." (My real name was Dorothy Hunn, but Miss Abbott changed it.)

The audience was very generous and applauded me, calling out, "Come back, Dorothy. Come back, Dorothy."

QUITE A SIGHT. Winning over sailors at the Great Lakes naval base, in 1941, was the author, Dorothy Dale Kloss.

What did I know? I was just 15 years old. Miss Abbott put me in the two big shows at the Empire Room and gave me a new costume.

The pay for my first week of dancing was $35; I've still got the canceled check. I used it to buy my mother a dress.

STARTING SHOWBIZ

At 17, I decided to get an agent and go out on my own. I told Miss Abbott I wanted to be an act—a solo ballet tap dancer.

"What makes you think you're sprinkled with stardust?" she asked.

"You did," I said. She loved that.

I went on tour with the Eddy Duchin orchestra for a year, worked with famed comic Cantinflas in Mexico City and performed through World War II with Big Band leaders such as Ray Noble and Skinnay Ennis.

As television became popular, I was getting older and started doing more dates at clubs, such as Chicago's Chez Paree. I was the first tap dancer on TV at WBKB in Chicago, then began teaching, got married, opened my own dance school on the city's north side and had a son, Craig.

About 20 years ago, I was in California and not feeling well. A doctor told me the diagnosis: I had cancer. I underwent surgery, then began chemotherapy treatments.

One day, he started talking about the few years I had left.

I stopped him right there: "I don't want to hear about that, about how long I've got," I said. "Don't tell me. When the time comes, that's it." That's my philosophy of life. And after that, I never thought about it.

IN THE FOLLIES

In January 1994, one of my lady dance students in Pasadena told me about "this great show in Palm Springs." She said I should be in it.

Mulling it over, I said to myself, *What am I going to do with the rest of my life? I love to dance.*

I was 70 years old and started at The Fabulous Palm Springs Follies. The show has everything that makes me happy— working with great people, from the dressers to the stage crew, all the way up to "Mr. W," Follies founder and producer Riff Markowitz. He has never missed a single performance.

At 5 feet, 5½ inches in height, I'm a "long-legged lovely," and at the age of 84, I was named "World's Oldest 'Still Performing' Showgirl" by *Guinness World Records.* The honor is all mine!

Entertaining the Troops

Recruiting Phyllis for Laugh Duty

From 1967 to '75, I covered most of the country doing TV and radio shows, community speeches and newspaper interviews as a Women's Army Corps recruiter.

From '65 to '67, I was the only WAC recruiting officer in Seattle. One of the funniest media stunts I was asked to do there was to make entertainer Phyllis Diller an honorary WAC recruiter.

All the news media—and even the City of Renton's mayor—were at the airport for the event. Wearing dress whites, I presented her with a WAC overseas hat with a recruiting logo on it, an "Honorary WAC Recruiter" banner and a bouquet of flowers. A male Army recruiter gave her a pair of combat boots with red-and-white laces, and she donned them and struck funny poses that later appeared in the news media.

A few years later in 1969, I was stationed in New York City, where I assisted women and men in joining Army Reserve units. A young man visited my office and asked for my help, explaining that he was playing the stand-in skier for Robert Redford in the movie *Downhill Racer*.

The man was staying with Redford and wrote down his phone number for me. Later, when I called the man, Redford answered, and we had a delightful and funny conversation based on his opening question, "What's a nice lady like you doing in the Army?"

Needless to say, that made my day!

—**Charlotte Kinney,** *Carlisle, Pennsylvania*

BOJANGLES STOPPED THE SHOW. "I'll never forget when Bill Robinson and his wife entertained at Camp Bradford, a Naval training base in Little Creek, Virginia," writes Hal Barnes of Concord, California. "In mid-program, Bill stopped and left the stage for a few minutes. When he came back, he announced that the Japanese had agreed to surrender. It was Aug. 14, 1945. You can imagine the roar that followed from the hundreds of sailors in the audience."

This Was No Act

When the war ended in Europe in 1945, my husband, Capt. Walter Damon, had been overseas for more than a year. As a Special Services officer, he was stationed in Bayreuth, Germany, and in charge of entertainment for the troops there. Walter arranged for the appearance of Paul Robeson and many others at the famous Wagner Opera House in Bayreuth.

His letters were infrequent and often delayed by weeks. But I did get one saying he was busy making arrangements for the appearance of Lynn Fontanne and Alfred Lunt, probably the most famous acting couple in the world.

I had just finished reading the letter when the phone rang. When I answered, a man said, "Mrs. Damon? This is Alfred Lunt. My wife, Lynn Fontanne, and I flew in from Bayreuth this morning, and I just wanted to tell you what a wonderful job your husband is doing. He's well, misses his family and hopes he will be coming home soon."

To this day, I can't get over the kindness of this famous man taking time from his busy schedule to call me with firsthand information about my husband. It surely was the nicest thing anyone ever did for me.

—Elinor Damon, Nashville, Tennessee

Now Cut That Out!

After I was wounded in Germany in 1945, I was returned to the States. Ultimately, I was sent to an R&R facility in Santa Barbara, California, where I was assigned to Special Services.

The unit put on two or three shows a week. We lived in the Biltmore Hotel, where the theater was located, and our group's job was to entertain the entertainers themselves.

I met and associated with such stars as George Burns, Ingrid Bergman, Edgar Bergen and Frances Langford. I even went golfing with Bing Crosby and Bob Hope, but as a host, not a golfer.

Many of the stars left tips for the men. I still remember the one left by Jack Benny, who always made jokes about his purported stinginess.

He gave me an envelope—inside I discovered a $20 bill and a note that said, "Thanks for a job well done. I would have left more for you, but the bank has all of my money."

—Glen Foster
Layton, Utah

KEEPSAKE. "This photo of my mother, Eula Kelly Horton, and me was autographed in Berlin in August 1945 by Bob Hope, Jack Benny, Mickey Rooney, Jerry Colonna, Martha Tilton and Ingrid Bergman," writes George Horton of Metaline Falls, Washington. "My father, Staff Sgt. George J. Horton, was running an Army mess hall, and Dad served the entertainers after a USO show. He asked them for their autographs, and the only paper he had on hand was this photograph."

Forever Young

LIKE TINKER BELL'S DUST, TV TRIPS TO NEVERLAND WERE MAGIC.

By Marilyn Gabriele, Newburgh, New York

On Mar. 7, 1955, a tradition was born in my family—one that would continue until the early 1960s.

It was on that date that *Peter Pan* aired on NBC's *Producers' Showcase*, becoming the first full-length Broadway production to be broadcast on color television.

The musical, staged by Jerome Robbins and based on a J.M. Barrie play, had enjoyed a successful run on Broadway. It came alive on TV with Mary Martin starring as Peter and Cyril Ritchard as Captain Hook.

It was special to me because it was my introduction to musical theater. My parents, who were children of Italian immigrants and of modest means, had not taken me to the theater in Bronx, New York.

The story of the Lost Boys led on their search for a mother by a boy who wouldn't grow up captured my heart and my 5-year-old imagination.

Mom Made It Extra-Special

On the evening of the show, Mom cooked dinner early and homework was completed right after school. She was a stickler about bedtime, so a nap was required for me to stay up late to watch.

Popcorn was popped, and my brothers and I set up the couch and chairs to mimic a theater. I was the "ticket-taker" for the 7 o'clock show.

Once the show began, we sat mesmerized, flying along with Peter Pan and the Darlings out the nursery window toward the second star to the right, straight on till morning, to Neverland. After, I'd go to sleep and dream about Indian princesses, pirates, fairies and crocodiles.

The tradition ended when the annual broadcasts stopped in 1962. NBC showed *Peter Pan* in 1988, but it somehow wasn't as powerful.

I've shared the video with my grandchildren and we enjoy it, but I can't help but miss the days when a simple pleasure could be such an event.

STARS OFF STAGE

Basil Rathbone Had Me Shaking

I held many odd jobs to help pay my room and board at Louisiana Tech during the 1950s. For one of them, I occasionally assisted backstage during theater performances.

On Halloween evening in 1955, the show featured Basil Rathbone doing a program of dramatic readings. With his delightful English accent, the actor had been cast onscreen as the brilliant Sherlock Holmes. But I better recalled his roles as dastardly villains: an evil pirate in *Captain Blood*, the lead role in *Son of Frankenstein*, and the threatening "Black Knight."

Though I knew that movies were make-believe, I was intensely intimidated when I first saw Mr. Rathbone in person. My fear only worsened as Halloween night progressed.

At intermission, I was to serve Mr. Rathbone coffee. Trying to keep the cup and saucer from rattling, I timidly knocked on the dressing room door, praying "Mr. Black Knight" wouldn't unsheathe his sword and run me through.

I was surprised when a pleasant voice said, "Come in." Holding my head high, I managed to enter without spilling the coffee.

After I'd walked in, the door mysteriously slammed shut behind me. Oh, no...I was trapped!

I saw a figure rise to greet me as if I were royalty. Setting down the coffee, I began my backward retreat to the closed door.

"Do you have other responsibilities demanding your attention?" the actor asked. I didn't.

"Then please have a seat and visit with me," Mr. Rathbone invited. When I discovered he was much different in person, I began to enjoy our visit.

I complimented him on his dramatic readings, which I really did enjoy, and our conversation swung around to the power of the spoken word.

"When you study in the evenings, do you read aloud?" Mr. Rathbone asked, and advised me to try it. (Later, I found he was right!)

Our conversation continued for 10 minutes, until the intermission was over. That brief time became permanently embossed in my memory.

My final assignment of the night was to drive Mr. Rathbone to the college president's home for a reception. Upon arrival, everyone left the station wagon for the short walk to the house. Everybody, that is, but me.

I'd just started home when I heard someone calling, "Jim! Jim!"

As I turned, I saw the actor coming back down the president's sidewalk, extending his hand as he approached. "I just want to thank you for a delightful visit," he said.

We never saw each other again. But not a Halloween passes without my thinking of that warm, pleasant gentleman.

—**James Vaughn**, *Conroe, Texas*

He Loved the Theater

More than 1,200 students were enrolled in the 1937 senior class at Tulsa Central High School.

A classmate who saw the obituary of one of them, Leonard Rosenberg, told me the quirky boy had been her first date. He and I were in a few high school plays together. Later, he moved to New York and changed his name to Tony Randall.

After he'd achieved stardom, he graciously spoke to a drama class I taught. Instead of telling stories about the glamour of Hollywood and famous stars he had worked with, Randall spoke of the importance of great plays, playwrights and actors in the history of Western culture.

Not only was he a fine comedian and actor—my friend really cared about good theater.

—**H. Rodman Jones**, *Tulsa, Oklahoma*

CELEBRATING THE BARD

A Shakespeare Lover 'Not-to-Be'

Miss Bess Marie Hoover loved Shakespeare. No, she adored, worshipped, *lived* Shakespeare.

And so, on an unseasonably hot day around 2 p.m., she sat—nay, she perched—on the edge of her desk, reading aloud the works of the Bard of Avon. When she read the words of a male character, she'd lower her tone to as deep a note as possible. When it was the part of a woman, she would add a lilt to her voice.

A few of her students actually liked Shakespeare. Most of my classmates tolerated him, because they knew their semester grade depended on it. Me? I not only disliked his writings, I couldn't even tolerate them. In fact, while she was reading, I fell asleep a few times.

Suddenly, I snapped awake as Miss Hoover closed her beloved volume of Shakespeare and placed it on her desk with a decisive thud.

Then she made an unexpected announcement. "Lovely, lovely, lovely!" she trilled. "I'm certain that all of you, even Edward Withrow"—that part was said with a malicious smirk—"have enjoyed these words for their beauty.

"Now for your assignment. Each of you will write an essay of 2,000 words detailing how and why you personally liked and enjoyed *As You Like It*. Since this is Friday, you will have the entire weekend to compose your words and have them on my desk Monday morning."

What a revolting development! I hadn't heard a single word of Miss Hoover's reading!

Monday morning arrived. Everyone turned in his or her assignment. All of the essays but mine

CLASSICS CLOWN. The anti-Shakespearean, Ed Withrow (left), mugs with buddy Bob Ryan in June 1938. "We were just acting silly for Bob's girlfriend," recalls Ed.

were several pages thick. My single-page paper looked like this:

Edward Withrow
Sophomore Class
English Literature

As You Like It
by William Shakespeare
I didn't. (Ditto it 1,000 times and it equals 2,000 words.)

Need I say, Miss Hoover completely failed to appreciate or enjoy the humor.

I got a huge red "F" on my "essay." And to escape failing for the semester, I had to read and report on the infernally long historical novel *Westward Ho!*—with absolutely no sophomoric humor included in the report, either!

— **Ed Withrow,** *Delray Beach, Florida*

Grandpas Can Surprise You

When my grandfather retired from his career as a bookbinder, he came to live with my parents, my brother and me, in Boston.

We had a wood-burning stove in the kitchen, and as he stood with his back toward it to warm up, he'd suddenly start speaking lines from a William Shakespeare play, such as *Romeo and Juliet* or *The Merchant of Venice*.

Apparently, while binding books, Grandfather had been reading some, too! This partly solved the puzzle of how someone with a fourth-grade

education, but a good memory, would be so familiar with Shakespeare's work.

My grandfather belonged to the Foresters lodge, and members would ask him to recite poems at meetings. He had a clear, strong speaking voice and used lots of expression.

He also read many books, especially romance novels. Sometimes he'd be reading and take his handkerchief out of his pocket to wipe away tears.

In fact, the day my new husband and I left for Michigan, Granddad was the only one who cried.
—*Agnes Pulling,* Williamstown, Michigan

To Party Perchance

My sister, who is 10 years my elder, used me for a sounding board when memorizing poetry and Shakespeare for her high school English class.

One day in 1938, I was invited to attend my girlfriend's seventh birthday party in the Willoughby Spit section of Norfolk, Virginia.

After refreshments were served and the presents opened, our hostess suggested we recite nursery rhymes. When my turn came, I broke into a cold sweat. I didn't know any.

I frantically searched my memory and came up with a quote my sister had taught me from Shakespeare's *As You Like It*: "Sweet are the uses of adversity, which, like the toad, ugly and venomous, wears yet a precious jewel in his head. And this our life exempt from public haunt finds tongues in trees, books in running brooks, sermons in stones, and good in everything."

No one, including me, had a clue as to what I'd said, and the party promptly broke up.
—*Kilby Hodges,* Capron, Virginia

The Duchess and the Frog

In 1934, when I attended Whitworth College in Brookhaven, Mississippi, new students were honored with a reception and given the title of "Duchess." We wore a formal dress and new shoes.

Money was scarce in those days. We always had plenty of food and warm clothes, but nothing fancy. So I was very proud of my pretty peach organdy dress, made by my dear, sweet aunt.

In the spring of 1935, the beautiful front lawn of the college was turned into a stage for Shakespeare's *A Midsummer Night's Dream*.

A small group had been selected to be frogs. I've always been on the "goofy" side. I loved to kid around, cut up and make people laugh. So I was one of the dancing frogs. We hopped out onto the lawn and did a little hippity-hoppity dance. We had the time of our lives, and everyone laughed and enjoyed the frog dance.

In just a few months, I had turned from a duchess into a frog!
—*Agnes Wilson Foster,* Natchez, Mississippi

And the Winner Is...

MOM WASN'T A WRITER BUT HAD FAITH SHE'D WIN THE PLAYWRITING CONTEST.

By Micky Johnson, Glenview, Illinois

Prairie Farmer magazine has been a longtime source of news for Illinois farmers, including my parents.

Back in 1935, when I was in high school, the magazine and radio station WLS launched a national playwriting contest to promote the Rural Electrification Act, which brought electricity to much of rural America for the first time. The prize was $100, a lot of money back then.

We had electricity in our farm home near Peoria, but my mother decided to enter the contest anyway. My dad, sister and I told Mom it would be fun to have her be a playwright. So even though she had never written anything before, Mom decided to try.

As she wrote, she became almost obsessed. Mom was incredibly focused and preoccupied when she was writing. One day my sis and I asked her if we could play with the neighbor kids a quarter-mile down the road. She said we could, but when we got back at suppertime, she asked, "Where have you kids been?" She had no memory of telling us we could go!

My dad asked Mom what she would do with her prize money, and she said she'd install a bathroom. Dad had always promised we'd have one, but whenever there was a little extra money, we always needed a new plow or planter or some other farm machinery. And those essentials were more important than a bathroom.

The three of us kidded Mom about becoming a writer. As she wrote, she would often talk about her bathroom. My sis and I would laugh and say, "Sure, Mom. Dream on!"

Mom Submits 'Country Lights'

The contest ran for many weeks, with lots of updates on WLS and in *Prairie Farmer*. Some issues even featured photos of the judges amid stacks and stacks of play submissions.

The entry deadline was finally at hand, and I accompanied Mom to the post office to mail her play, *Country Lights*, written in longhand.

Weeks passed as the judges read more than 1,000 entries from 14 states. While we waited for the results, Mom continued to talk about her bathroom, even taking me with her to Peoria to look at different bathroom fixtures.

Then one day, a woman came to the door asking for Mrs. Sam Johnson. My dad said, "Fern, there's a lady here to see you. I think she's trying to sell something."

The woman greeted Mom by saying, "Mrs. Johnson, both WLS Radio and *Prairie Farmer* are proud to present this check for $100 for your outstanding contribution to the betterment of rural families through your play, *Country Lights*."

Basking in the Spotlight

Needless to say, we were flabbergasted! That is, all of us but Mom. She said she always thought she would win. After all, her play included humor, romance, a happy ending and a new bathroom.

The play made history throughout the Midwest. It was broadcast live by WLS, printed in *Prairie Farmer* and produced in a number of rural areas. My sister and I even had roles in our community production of the play, and we were so proud to be part of Mom's great achievement.

Looking back, I realize that my dad, sis and I never meant to put Mom down for her incredible belief that she would win. We joked about it because we didn't want her to be too disappointed if she lost. I believe now that Mom's unswerving belief in herself rubbed off on us, and that deep down, we all believed she would earn first prize.

And yes, she did get her bathroom. In fact, the original fixtures that my mother selected are still in the bathroom and functioning well all these years later.

Country Lights

by
Mrs. Sam Johnson

CAST OF CHARACTERS

Mr. Gordon	A Farmer
Mrs. Gordon	His Wife
Bill Anderson	A Neighbor Boy
Phyllis Gordon	The Gordon's Daughter
Jack Travers	A College Graduate

COSTUMES: Overalls for Mr. Gordon and Bill until Bill changes his clothes, then to a neat, business suit. Mrs. Gordon, an attractive house dress. Phyllis, a dark travel dress. Jack, a business suit.

PLACE: The living room in the Gordon's farm home.

TIME: Half past three on a June afternoon.

SCENE and ARRANGEMENT OF STAGE: The living room in a better type country home. At upper center is a curtained opening. A comfortable chair sets just to the right of the opening. At right center is a radio of the floor type.

Page Three

There is a floor lamp at upper right midway between the easy chair and the radio, so that a person seated can read comfortably by its light. A library table at down right holds a desk-type telephone and an electric fan. At upper left, placed diagonally, is a settee or davenport. There is a straight chair at down left and a rocker at down center.

As the curtain rises, GORDON is seated by the radio, listening to a program and reading a newspaper. If there are

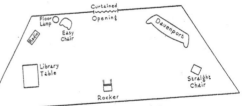

Suggested arrangement of stage.

windows in the set, the shades are drawn to keep out the hot sunlight. The reading lamp is turned on and the electric fan, focused on GORDON, is going full force. He is in overalls, and has a red handkerchief around his neck.

GORDON reads peacefully for a moment, tracing lines with his finger. Then he becomes suddenly alert, looking toward the opening as if he hears approaching footsteps. Bending over, he quickly shuts off both reading lamp and fan and sits, with an air of innocence, listening to the radio. (Enter MRS. GORDON. She is carrying a pitcher of lemonade and a glass. GORDON turns off radio.)

MRS. GORDON: I've fixed you a nice cold drink of lemonade, Henry. It must be terribly hot out in the alfalfa field this afternoon. How many more loads do you have to put up this afternoon? (*Pours glass of lemonade, and hands it to GORDON.*)

GORDON: (*taking glass.*) We just finished the last load. (*Sips lemonade.*) Bill's putting the team away while I cool off and listen for tomorrow's weather report. (*Finishes drinking lemonade. Sighs with satisfaction.*) My! That's a good drink.

Page Four

A CHILD OF THE ZIEGFELD FOLLIES

WHILE HER SHOW PARENTS WORKED IN THE '20S AND '30S, HER BABY-SITTER WAS ROGER...THE CHIMP!

By Stacia Gerow, Clearwater, Florida

My most vivid childhood memories were those of traveling with my parents, who were with the Ziegfeld Follies.

The Follies was the largest, most beautiful and most extravagant musical revue of all time. The 1920s and '30s were a memorable and unique period in the American theater, and while there were other famous, massive Broadway musicals, none had the glamour and grandeur of the Follies.

A typical production included huge sets with revolving stairways, glittering chandeliers and girls descending from the rafters on flower-decked swings. There were also leading men and ladies, comedians, acrobats, jugglers and animals. Behind the scenes were stagehands, carpenters, electricians, grips, musicians, dressers, wardrobe mistresses, advance men and publicity people.

Famous stars who were in the Follies at some point included Al Jolson, Will Rogers, Eddie Cantor, Fanny Brice, Jimmy Durante, Bert Lahr, Fred Allen and Billie Burke, Ziegfeld's wife and the good witch in *The Wizard of Oz*.

Started as a Carny

My dad's first taste of show business was when he joined a carnival as it came through his hometown of Nacogdoches, Texas. He eventually signed on with the Follies as a stage carpenter and stayed with the troupe for 35 years. My mother met my dad when she was a Follies chorus girl.

When the show was in New York, we lived in an apartment and I attended day care or kindergarten. On the road, we lived in hotels and I went where my parents did.

It was a lonely time for me because I had no friends my own age, unless you count Roger, the chimp. Chimpanzees are very intelligent, and after Roger's trainer instructed him to guard me against everyone except himself and my parents, he was my fierce protector.

When the chorus girls were on stage, we'd wander through their dressing rooms and put makeup on each other's faces. We also played jacks, and Roger won most of the games!

This kept us both out of trouble while my parents were working and saved them the cost of a baby sitter—Roger worked for peanuts!

Dinner in the Diner

When the show went on the road, the huge scenery and costumes called for up to 12 railroad cars, plus more for the cast and crew.

My favorite memory was of eating in the train's dining car. The superb service and food were almost outweighed by the fact that we were enjoying each course in a different town.

I doubt if today's astronauts like floating in space as much as I did when I slept in an upper berth. The wheels' clickety-clack as we raced through the dark was the best of all lullabies.

When I was 8, it was time for me to get a formal education. Mother gave up her career and rented an apartment in New York.

I enrolled in first grade and was mortified to discover I was the oldest pupil in the class. Determined to get through it as quickly as possible, I graduated eighth grade at 13.

When my senior year began, my mother decided she was tired of living apart from my dad. She packed our bags and my schoolbooks, and we boarded the Twentieth Century Limited for Chicago to link up with Dad.

I graduated from a Chicago high school at age 17 with an incredible childhood to look back upon.

FLO'S GIRLS. Florenz Ziegfeld, seen here with some of his famous chorus girls, headed up the Ziegfeld Follies, the most extravagant musical revue of the '20s and '30s.

TEENS TURNED THESPIANS. After World War II, these Buffalo, New York, youngsters transformed downtime into showtime, performing all over their community for grateful crowds that even gave them a standing ovation!

Let's Put on a Show!

In 1946, the world was once again at peace, but since returning veterans got first crack at scarce jobs, it was hard for us teens to find summer work in Buffalo, New York.

It looked like it was the destiny of the kids in our parish to gather beneath the giant elm tree in front of St. Margaret's Roman Catholic Church to glumly contemplate our fate.

"What do you want to do?"

"I dunno, what do you wanna do?" And so it went until the president of the men's guild at the church asked what the group could do for us kids.

It was my grandfather Ernie Clare, a member of the church men's guild, who came up with the answer: "We could stage a musical!"

It sounds like a Judy Garland-Mickey Rooney movie, doesn't it? But Grandfather had been a part-time entertainer who had sung and danced on Great Lakes cruise ships.

He opened his well-worn leather briefcase and pulled out his portfolio of songs, then proceeded to write the first of our way-way-off-Broadway musicals, *Down on the Levee*. My grandfather and various vaudeville friends collaborated on costumes and the large painted backdrop of a stern-wheeler under a full moon.

The show contained both old and current show tunes, including songs from *Oklahoma!* and *Show Boat*.

Grandfather was the captain and emcee in the cast of choir members, amateur musicians and actors.

The grassy lawn under the elm emptied of teenagers, as we had something more important to do with our time—we could sing and dance!

We sold out our performances, with profits going to the Catholic Youth Council, and took our show to the Batavia veterans' hospital, where we got a standing ovation.

The next year, my grandfather shifted gears and venue to prewar Europe for *Romany Lane*. Our cast remained largely intact, and we did two more shows in subsequent summers.

Our run came to an end in June 1950 with the outbreak of the Korean War. We had grown up during World War II and were still full of patriotic zeal. By year's end, every able-bodied male cast member was in a new costume—a uniform.

The shady lawn under the big elm tree was vacant; we had a new role to play.

—**Thomas Clare Owen,** *Port St. Lucie, Florida*

DANCING
Changed Our Lives

The Day I Danced With Arthur Murray

Back in the early '40s, pert and popular vocalist Betty Hutton sang the familiar lyrics "Arthur Murray taught me dancin' in a hurry!"

At that time, Arthur Murray Dance Studios were springing up all across the country. I'll never forget visiting one in New York City—not to learn the latest steps, but to look for work.

I was staying with a hometown friend in her Greenwich Village apartment. I could share the walk-up with her...if I could find a job.

After almost wearing out a pair of shoes pounding the pavement, I saw an ad that read, "Learn to dance and learn to teach dancing at the same time." I decided to give it a try.

I polished my one pair of high-heeled pumps, donned the slinkiest dress I could find in my roommate's closet, caught the subway and joined a group of young people at the studio.

About 20 of us were ushered into a large ballroom, handed numbered cards (I was No. 10) and told to sit in order along the wall. I was considering a quick exit when a door marked "Mr. Murray" opened. A tall, balding middle-aged man strode out to face us.

This must be Arthur Murray himself, I thought. The unsmiling man walked to the end of the row and began interviewing us.

Soon he was directly before me, staring into my eyes. "Miss Robb? Why do you think you can teach others to dance?"

"Because I've always loved to dance," I quavered, "and would like to teach others to enjoy the sport."

"The sport?" he echoed. "Why do you call dancing a sport?" He spat out the word.

I could feel a trickle of sweat down my back as I replied, "I think dancing is a very good form of exercise, as well as an art form." I was sure he'd crossed me off his list.

After what seemed like an hour, a secretary came out and read the names of the 10 who'd been selected to remain, including No. 10!

Soon we'd have to prove to Arthur Murray himself whether or not we could "trip the light fantastic." Would I be able to follow him or would I be too shaky to keep from stumbling over his feet? I wanted to run for my life!

Too late! He swooped down on me, graciously extending his hand and saying, "Miss Robb, may I have this dance?"

Suddenly I was enfolded in his arms, gliding across the room! I was "Ginger" to his "Fred," soaring on the softest of clouds as my feet seemed inches off the floor. I felt like I was floating as we swerved and swooped around the room.

The magic moment stopped abruptly with the music, and another number was called. After Mr. Murray had finished dancing with each candidate, he retreated to his office. Soon, the secretary walked out and read off the finalists...not No. 10.

"Well," I remarked, "I guess it's back to the pavement. Gotta find a job soon."

One of the other "rejects" gave me a curious look. "Didn't you know that you wouldn't have gotten any pay? They just give you meal tickets to Schrafft's Restaurant while you train. Later you get a chance to teach somewhere else in the country."

That was news to me...and I was glad I didn't get the job. Soon, I did find a paying job and spent several exciting years living in the Village, sharing the walk-up apartment with my friend.

Still, that wonderful dance with Arthur Murray is one of my cherished memories from those years.

—**Carol Anderson,** *Maple Springs, New York*

ARTHUR MILLER, ARCHIVE FILES

SCHINE'S **RIVIERA** THEATRE

1937 Feature OCTOBER Attractions 1937

SUN	MON	TUE	WED	THU	FRI	SAT
3 LORETTA YOUNG — DON AMECHE in "LOVE UNDER FIRE" FRED MacMURRAY — FRANCES FARMER in "EXCLUSIVE"	4	5	6 Jeanette MacDonald, Nelson Eddy in "NAUGHTY MARIETTA" CLARK GABLE, MYRNA LOY in "MANHATTAN MELODRAMA"	7	8 Jean Arthur, Edward Arnold in "EASY LIVING" PETER LORRE, VIRGINIA FIELD in "THINK FAST MR. MOTO"	9
10 PAUL MUNI — LOUISE RAINER in "THE GOOD EARTH" DAVID CARLYLE — CAROL HUGHES in "MEET THE BOY FRIEND"	11	12	13 MARX BROS. in "HORSE FEATHERS" Shirley Temple, Gary Cooper in "NOW AND FOREVER"	14	15 JOE E. BROWN, GUY KIBBEE in "RIDING ON AIR" DONALD WOODS IN "TALENT SCOUT"	16
17 SONJA HENIE — TYRON POWER in "THIN ICE" WILLIAM GARGAN — JEAN ROGERS in "REPORTED MISSING"	18	19	20 Edward Arnold, Frances Farmer in "TOAST OF NEW YORK" LYLE TALBOT, POLLY ROWLES in "WEST BOUND LIMITED"	21	22 EDWARD G. ROBINSON in "THUNDER IN THE CITY" GUY KIBBEE in "BIG SHOT"	23
24 ELEANOR POWELL — ROBERT TAYLOR in "Broadway Melody of 1938" JANE WYMAN — DICK PURCELL in "PUBLIC WEDDING"	25	26	27 Frances Farmer, Ian Hunter in "CONFESSION" MARY BOLAND, HUGH HERBERT in "MARRY THE GIRL"	28	29 RICHARD DIX, JOAN PERRY in "DEVIL IS DRIVING" Kenny Baker, Gertrude Michael in "MR. DODD TAKES THE AIR"	30
31 LORETTA YOUNG — WARNER BAXTER in "Wife, Doctor and Nurse" SECOND FEATURE ANNOUNCED LATER—	NOV. 1	2				

—Added Attractions—
Wed. Nite GIANT BANGO Fri. BANK NITE
Thur. Play Ten—O—Win Sat. Nite BANGO

Ballet, Spanish Acrobatic

Alean Academy of Dance Arts
NEXT TO RIVIERA THEATRE

Toe, Ballroom, Character Dancing

IT PAYS TO ADVERTISE. When Alean Charles was 18, in 1937 (left), she opened a dancing school. To promote her business, she advertised in the monthly calendar of the theater next door (above).

Theater Drew Them In

When I was 18 in 1937, I opened my own dancing school. It was on Lake Avenue in Rochester, New York, next to the Riviera Theatre.

I placed an advertisement in the theater's monthly calendar (above). In those days before television, you could attend as many as six movies a week, and many people did.

Notice, also, under "Added Attractions" the drawings the theater routinely held. I remember winning a baseball when I was 10 and my number was picked. I'd really wanted a pair of roller skates.

—*Alean Charles,* Largo, Florida

Dancing up Romance

In 1954, I was a geologist with the U.S. Atomic Energy Commission in Grand Junction, Colorado, usually working in northeast Arizona.

One noon hour, I was walking down Main Street in Grand Junction with my childhood friend Jack and a third geologist when we noticed a very attractive young lady window-shopping. Jack went up to her and made a rather sophomoric attempt to get a date, a proposition she firmly rejected in no uncertain terms.

Later, I found out this young lady, Kay, was the manager and an instructor at an Arthur Murray dance studio in the same building where I was attending our annual technical conference. One day, seeing Kay in the coffee shop, I introduced myself and apologized for the poor behavior of the man who had accosted her on the street. She accepted the apology, and I found her to be very personable and friendly.

Right then, I knew I had to see this lovely woman again, and what better way than to enroll in dance lessons at Arthur Murray?

As my lessons progressed, I found that Kay, who grew up in New Mexico and Texas, and I, raised in suburban Chicago, shared many other interests.

Soon, the dance studio was urging Kay to sign me up for a lifetime course in dance lessons. I did sign a lifetime contract, but not quite in the way the dance instructors had hoped. Kay and I were married the next year.

—*Raymond Kosatka,* Conroe, Texas

Eager 'Tex' Had Lots of Hope

It was 1950, and it was the biggest event in my first 17 years—Bob Hope's radio show was coming to my hometown, Kerrville, Texas!

He was arriving early in the evening at our small airport, so I decided to go watch for his arrival.

The plane with his troupe of entertainers, including actress Marilyn Maxwell and Les Brown and His Band of Renown, was probably the largest to land there at that time. When they all headed for town, five miles away, I followed in my 1934 Ford to the Blue Bonnet Hotel. When I got there, I ran into Bob Hill, president of the Chamber of Commerce, and asked him if he could introduce me to Bob Hope.

He took me into a private dining room where Mr. Hope was enjoying a steak.

"This is Ken Klein," Mr. Hill said. "He rides bulls."

"Ever ridden this one?" Mr. Hope asked, cutting into his meat.

He took my green Stetson hat and wore it around the hotel lobby while visiting and making people laugh.

I couldn't afford a ticket to the show, so I followed them to the high school stadium. When they got out and walked in, I entered with the group. The most expensive seats were folding chairs on the playing field. Seeing a chair on the ground, I unfolded it and sat down.

Shortly after the show started, to my surprise, Bob Hope shouted, "Hey, Tex, come on up here!"

He wore my hat again and told some jokes that I no longer recall.

I do remember whispering in his ear, "Hey, Bob, call me back when Marilyn Maxwell comes out."

He repeated that to the audience, of course, for another laugh.

I wish I knew who took the picture of Mr. Hope and me, but I will always treasure it—Bob Hope himself and the memories.

—**K.K. Klein,** *Boerne, Texas*

Blond Bombshell's Boys

On Aug. 28, 1944, when I was 15, my friend Jim and I went to the RKO Theatre in Boston, eager to see Betty Hutton onstage.

After straining to see her from the top balcony, we decided to go down the main aisle and see her up close as she sang. Then, she bent over and said, "Can't you boys find some girl's lap to sit on?" I replied, "I just wanted to get one good look at you before we left."

She asked us to come up onstage and have a better look. I hesitated for a minute, then figured, since we'd gone this far, why not? The audience laughed as Jim and I fumbled, finally boosting ourselves up onto the stage with the help of a band member.

He and I sat in front of Boyd Raeburn's orchestra as Betty dedicated her next song by saying, "For the benefit of our guests up here and all the servicemen in the audience, I want to dedicate my next number to them—*I'm Doin' It for Defense.*"

While she sang, Betty pulled the mic over and settled in on my lap as the audience roared. I put my arm around her waist and she started running her free hand all over my face and hair. She was beautiful with her blue eyes and blue ribbons in her hair.

COMPLIMENTS OF

BETTY HUTTON

•

APPEARING IN

PARAMOUNT PICTURES

After the number, she stepped backstage, asked us if we'd enjoyed ourselves and gave us her autograph. We were both so excited, we went home and wrote down the whole event.

A day later, two girls who'd been in the audience came into the drugstore where I worked. They thought the whole thing was planned and were shocked when they heard that it would not have happened except for Betty's being so considerate.

I later wrote Betty a letter telling her how much we both enjoyed and appreciated the event, and we received a photo from her Los Angeles studios in return.

—**Frank Maloney,** *Waltham, Massachusetts*

Hilarious Heckler

In the late '40s, I was assistant manager at Minsky's Rialto Theatre in Chicago. As part of the job, one of my duties was to sit in the back of the house and heckle the comedian.

I couldn't do this very often, as the audience would get wise that I was a plant. But it was my chance to get a big laugh.

When the comic had been on stage for about five minutes, I would yell out, "Get off the stage! You're terrible!"

The comic would ignore me and continue.

"You heard me," I'd yell again. "Get off the stage. You're terrible."

The comic would stop the show and yell back, "One more word out of you, fella, and I'm calling the manager."

I'd reply, to much laughter, "I am the manager."

—**Dennis Leslie,** *Garden Grove, California*

Minnie Pearl's Hat

In 1943, a beautiful blind lady whose name was Ophelia Bauers lived in the apartment across the hall from my family.

She convinced me to take her to hear Minnie Pearl perform at the Missouri State Fair, where she and Rod Brasfield were being featured in a Nashville radio program.

So there I was, a blind woman on my left arm and a 15-month-old baby girl in my right arm. I was also expecting my second child, so I was a "monster" in the very front row.

Later, when the performers were taking a last call, Minnie and Rod stopped to give a bow and I said in a loud voice, "Minnie, a blind lady wants to see you." Minnie stood at the steps and took Ophelia up on the stage.

Ophelia touched her face and said, "Oh, Minnie, I'm so glad to see you." Minnie asked her name. When Ophelia answered, Minnie said, "That's my name, too, and my mother is also blind." She gave Ophelia her trademark hat.

I later visited Minnie's museum and saw the yellow dress and flat slippers she had been wearing that night, but no hat. I wrote Minnie Pearl, telling her where the hat was and thanking her for her kindness, and she called me and said, "I could never remember where my hat went!"

—**Maxine Griggs,** *Sedalia, Missouri*

HELD OVER in New York

A BROADWAY STAR SHOWED THE AUTHOR A GOOD TIME IN THE BIG APPLE.

By Rex Anderson, Englewood, Florida

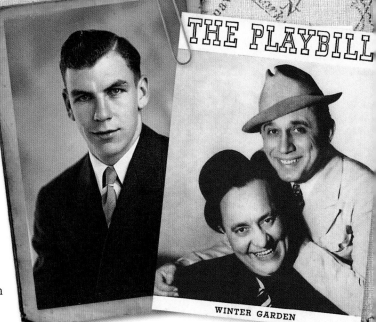

THE PLAYBILL

WINTER GARDEN

In June of 1939, a few days after my high school graduation in Wabash, Indiana, a school official asked if I'd be interested in an all-expenses-paid trip to New York City and the World's Fair.

Would I! He explained that the offer had been made by alumnus John "Ole" Olsen, producer and star of the Broadway hit *Hellzapoppin'*.

Olsen had apparently decided to show a couple of boys from his hometown around the big city. Although a good student and active in sports and extra-curricular activities, I was never sure why I'd been picked.

Neither of us boys had ever been on a train, so the trip to New York was an adventure. After arriving at Grand Central Station, we took a taxi to our hotel, where we waited for Mr. Olsen.

When he arrived, I liked him right away. He gave us a short tour of New York City before driving us out to Malverne, Long Island, where he lived with his family.

That night, we saw *Hellzapoppin'*, and I about flipped when, during a skit, a guy was asked his name and replied, "Rex Anderson from Wabash, Indiana." (I found out later they did this often.)

Another highlight of the week was a visit to the World's Fair. I was thoroughly impressed by a demonstration of television, the "entertainment of the future."

We also went to Yankee Stadium for the All-Star Game, the first major league game I'd seen. From our box seats, we saw many future Hall of Famers. Joe DiMaggio even hit a home run!

Another day, Mr. Olsen's daughter, Moya, arranged for us to fly with her pilot boyfriend, Bill (Bill Lear of Lear Jet fame!).

We were pleased when Mr. Olsen extended our visit for another week. That meant more sight-seeing, shows and trips to Jones Beach.

After the show one night, he arranged for two New York detectives to pick us up. We rode around with them answering calls until 4 a.m. At one point, we went down Broadway at 60 miles an hour with sirens screaming!

Our stay was extended again when Mr. Olsen's three nephews arrived from Fort Wayne. Being the oldest, I was now "tour guide" for the group. When Mr. Olsen learned I could drive, he bought a new Ford for his mother, who lived in Fort Wayne, and asked me to drive the five of us back to Indiana!

He insisted that we visit Washington, D.C., on the way home and called ahead to an FBI friend who had an escort ready when we arrived. Two days later, five tired boys finally made it back home to Indiana.

Four years later, I was in Navy Midshipman School at Columbia University. When the show *Sons O' Fun* came to town, a friend and I went to the theater and had a nice visit with Mr. Olsen and his partner, "Chic" Johnson. They were about to leave for Hollywood to work on the film version of *Hellzapoppin'*.

Mr. Olsen gave me tickets to a show and told me to raise my hand when volunteers were requested. I did so and was called to the stage and given a case of beer.

Then my name was called again...and again. Each time I went to the stage, my load of pretzels, candy and other goodies increased. On my final trip, I received a wristwatch and a pass for two to the Latin Quarter.

That was my last contact with "Ole" Olsen, a man who brought a lot of joy into a lot of lives.

turn around!

This handsome young man is my husband, Harry A. Mincarelli, performing in his junior class play, *Swamp House*, at Upper Moreland High School in Willow Grove, Pennsylvania, in 1949. He played a detective, and in this scene, a "ghost" is behind him, ready to perform some dastardly deed. We've been married for 46 years, and Harry is still quite the ham—and has the initials to prove it!

—**June Mincarelli,** *St. Petersburg, Florida*

HOT OFF THE PRESS

So many of us had childhood friends we never met, from the Bobbsey Twins to Pinocchio. For us, a good book was an alternate reality that we could be part of wherever we were.

"During my preteen years in the early 1950s, I lived in the remote Allegheny Mountains of rural northern Pennsylvania," says David Harford of Emporium. "Our television reception was poor at best, so I spent many enjoyable hours reading mystery novels.

"Nancy Drew, the Hardy Boys and early issues of *Alfred Hitchcock's Mystery Magazine* were all favorites, but I especially liked reading the Judy Bolton series by Margaret Sutton.

"Against a backdrop of unpaved mountain roads, clapboard houses with coal stoves, some horse-and-buggy travel, precious few phones and mom-and-pop country stores, plucky Judy Bolton tracked down the solution to one mystery after another."

On the following pages, recall some of the many publications that kept us riveted, informed and in style.

MY HEROES HAVE ALWAYS BEEN COLLIES

BELOVED BOOKS BY ALBERT PAYSON TERHUNE THRILLED GENERATIONS OF KIDS.

By Rick Van Etten, Des Moines, Iowa

When I was a youngster, the hero I most admired didn't ride a white stallion or leap tall buildings in a single bound. He didn't wear a mask or a cape, either.

Instead, he wore a shaggy brown and white coat of "mahogany and snow," as the author described it. My favorite hero was a collie named Lad.

Lad's adventures—and those of other courageous collies—were written by Albert Payson Terhune. Penned during the 1920s and '30s, those books made the author and his canine heroes internationally famous.

I discovered Terhune's books in the late 1950s, when our next-door neighbor read to me from her son's copy of *Lad: A Dog*.

I was enthralled. Later, when I was old enough to read the stories on my own, I spent much of my allowance on Terhune's books.

I saved for weeks until I'd amassed the $1.50 price. Then it was off to Dunsworth's Bookstore on the town square in Macomb, Illinois, where I'd linger over the selections, each with its colorful dust jacket. Eventually I'd make my choice and carry my precious purchase to the cashier.

All of my friends in the neighborhood were also Terhune fans. We'd share our copies, and each of us selected one of Terhune's dogs as our personal favorite. Mine was Lad...my best friend, Kerry Nielsen, chose Mars...Kerry's older brother, Jeff, picked Gray Dawn...and their sister Mardeen chose Wolf.

A TRUE FAN

I still have my Terhune books, and I've added biographies about him to my collection.

The author was born in Newark, New Jersey, in 1872. His father, Dr. Edward Payson Terhune, was a member of the clergy, and his mother, Mary Virginia Terhune, was a prolific writer who published a variety of works, including a best-selling cookbook.

Terhune graduated from Columbia University and in 1894 took a job as a cub reporter with the *Evening World* in New York City. A prolific writer himself, he remained at the newspaper for more than 20 years, during which time he published hundreds of short stories and dozens of novels.

His home was a wooded estate called Sunnybank, near Pompton Lakes in northern New Jersey. There, Terhune and his wife, Anice, bred and raised collies. Many of Terhune's stories took place at Sunnybank and were based on the real deeds of his dogs.

Millions of readers across generations thrilled to those stories, and decades later, Terhune fans still recall them in vivid detail.

LAD AND LASS. A young Rick Van Etten cuddles his collie, Lassie, a gift from parents who knew of their son's love of the Albert Payson Terhune stories. His books featured Lad (Rick's favorite) plus numerous other heroic collies, seen on the right in cover photos. Lad taught Rick courage, and the books continue to give him reading pleasure.

DELIGHTFUL DESCRIPTIONS

Almost anyone who read the stories about Lad, for example, will remember Terhune's description of the dog's "absurdly tiny white forepaws," his "snowy ruff" and his coat of "burnished mahogany."

Much of the stories' appeal came from Terhune's description of his home, idyllic life and, of course, the dogs themselves.

The majority of the stories were told from a dog's point of view. Terhune referred to himself and his wife as the Master and the Mistress. Sunnybank was simply called the Place.

Besides Lad and the other dogs already mentioned, Terhune wrote about Bruce, Buff, Jean, Sandy, Fair Ellen and more.

In nearly every story, a collie performed some act of heroism, often rescuing a human from extreme peril—a charging bull, an armed robber, a poisonous snake or a burning building.

But the dogs were more than heroic. They were sympathetic and understanding, possessing a noble character that was downright inspiring.

When I finally faced up to a classroom bully in junior high school, I was at least partially motivated by having read that Lad had never run from a fight.

Like hundreds of other kids who read Terhune's stories, I hoped for a collie of my own. After our family's old cocker spaniel died, my parents surprised me on a rainy November afternoon with a female collie puppy to whom I gave the none-too-original name, Lassie.

Luckily, I never had the opportunity to see if she'd save me in a life-threatening situation. But Terhune's powerful stories make me certain that if the occasion had ever arisen, Lassie would have done just that.

THE SECRET OF
NANCY DREW

READER FOLLOWED IN HER HEROINE'S FOOTSTEPS.

By Annemarie Henny, Torrington, Connecticut

SUPER SLEUTH. Armed with a magnifying glass, a flashlight and a clue box, the author (at age 8) was set to solve.

Nancy Drew, girl detective—what pleasant memories this familiar phrase brings back! I was 8 or 9 years old back in the 1930s when I read *The Bungalow Mystery*, the third book in the series by Carolyn Keene.

I was immediately hooked and decided I would become Nancy Drew. This would be no easy feat, but an active imagination helped.

Nancy, you see, is a tall, willowy blonde who lives in a beautiful house in River Heights. She drives a snappy blue roadster and is the only child of well-to-do lawyer Carson Drew.

Hannah Gruen keeps house for the Drew family and plies Nancy with hot cocoa and chicken salad sandwiches. Nancy has two good friends, Bess Marvin and George Fayne, and there's also the handsome Ned Nickerson, Nancy's boyfriend.

I, on the other hand, lived with my parents in a first-floor, cold-water railroad flat in Queens, New York. I had a Buster Brown haircut and scooted around the neighborhood on a red and white two-wheeler.

Papa worked 10 to 12 hours a day maintaining a fleet of coal trucks. Mama was a housefrau

who plied me with sandwiches of liverwurst on thick rye bread and a mouthwatering sour pickle (my favorite).

I didn't have a boyfriend (boys...ugh), but, like my sleuthing heroine, I did have two loyal friends, Ruth and Marian Rosenthal.

Being an only child was basically the only other thing I had in common with Nancy! But beyond that, what Nancy and I shared

was a ready sympathy for people in need, as well as a natural inquisitiveness.

Then one Christmas, I received a gigantic magnifying glass, a flashlight and an empty cigar box to store clues in. I knew I was ready to go into the sleuthing business.

DECIPHERING THE CODE

On the first warm spring day, I set up a small table and a chair in front of the house. On it were stacks of paper and an inkpad. It was time to fingerprint all the kids on our street! The turnout was heartwarming: "Name? Age? Address? OK, now put your thumb on the ink pad..."

By the time my mother called me for lunch, everyone was squared away.

Marian and Ruth and I also devised a secret code. This really was a must! Flipping the alphabet, the letter "A" equaled "Z," "B" equaled "Y" and so on. A typical message read: *Roo yv levi gl kozb zugvi hxsllo.**

We had one problem, though. There weren't too many real mysteries to solve. At the Saturday matinees, besides watching movies about cowboys and Indians, we learned about Chinese Tong wars and opium dens. So, if you were sent to the local Chinese laundry, you took a bunch of your friends with you.

A REAL-LIFE SLEUTH

And what do you do when you're a girl detective and don't have a mystery to investigate? You create one!

When a family moved in the 1930s, it was the custom for the landlord to have the vacant apartment painted.

Why did this particular family move away so suddenly? Armed with my magnifying glass, flashlight and clue box, I arrived at the scene, hastily introduced myself to the bemused painters and explained my mission.

I examined the closets and found dead flies (highly significant). I carefully speared them on a straight pin and, together with chewing gum wrappers (also highly significant) and pieces of cloth, deposited them in my clue box. I also found a smear of a mysterious red substance on the windowsill—dried blood, of course.

The pinnacle of our investigation occurred

later that evening, when a group of neighborhood kids sat on the front steps hashing over the clues. Soon, the tall-tales storytelling began. We shivered and shuddered, eventually arriving at the certain conclusion that the mild-mannered family had been counterfeiters. To this day, I wonder how we came up with that!

As the years went by, I passed down my Nancy Drew books to my children, grandchildren and now great-grandchildren. Taking their inspiration from Nancy Drew, they are more interested in becoming bona fide detectives than they are in watching television.

Oh, yes. I still have the magnifying glass, flashlight and clue box.

Code solution: I'll be over to play after school.

Our Favorite Books Were No Mystery

Remember the first "real" book you read on your own? For many of us, it was from a series like Nancy Drew, the Hardy Boys, Tom Swift Jr., the Lone Ranger or the Bobbsey Twins.

Long before the days of television and afternoon radio shows, stories such as these helped young readers travel to foreign lands and imagine adventures involving scary and unusual villains.

The dustcover illustration was

the first thing to pique your interest, since you knew that scene would appear somewhere in the book. If you were like me, you couldn't help but wonder, "What does it mean?"

To find out, you had to buy the book. So, during the '30s and '40s, saving the 35 or 50 cents for a new purchase became a goal for many kids.

My favorite series was the Hardy Boys. *The Shore Road Mystery, The Tower Treasure* and *The Mystery of Cabin Island* have remained locked in my memory for decades.

For both my brother Stephen and me, the unforgettable character of that series was Aunt Gertrude. She'd visit the Hardy household just as each mystery began, and her cantankerous antics and lectures lent comic relief to many of the books. Of course, she often stumbled upon a clue for Frank and Joe's benefit.

Whenever I visited a friend's house, I'd keep an eye out for books I hadn't read yet. Trades were fun because both parties could begin new adventures.

—*Doug Allcock,* Cranford, New Jersey

LITTLE BOOKS,
BIG WELCOME

UNEXPECTED GIFT EASES NEW STUDENT'S FIRST DAY IN CLASS.

By Birney Dibble, Eau Claire, Wisconsin

I wonder how many people remember Big Little Books? I have very fond memories of these little wonders.

In January 1935, when I was 10 and in fourth grade, my family moved from New Lenox, Illinois, to Rochelle. On my first day at my new school, I was assigned a desk that had a hinged top, which you could lift to keep your school supplies inside. My new teacher, Miss Eden, introduced me to the class and said, "Now, Birney, open your desk!"

Touched by Kindness

I did—and was thrilled to find it jam-packed with Big Little Books!

Now, there may be some people who have never heard of these marvelous little books, which originally sold for a dime each.

Most of the popular cartoons of the day were reprinted in these small hardcover books. Their pages measured 3⅝ inches by 4½ inches, with cartoon drawings on the right-hand page and text on the left. But the books made up for their tiny pages by being more than 1½ inches thick.

Every student in class had donated one of his or her Big Little Books to me, the new kid on the block. Among the books, I discovered Little Orphan Annie, Sandy and Daddy Warbucks. There was Dick Tracy (wearing a tiny radio on his wrist—nobody will ever make a radio that small!) with Tess Trueheart.

I found Terry and the Pirates and the Dragon Lady; Gasoline Alley stars Skeezix and Uncle Walt; Andy Gump; Barney Google; Li'l Abner and Daisy Mae; Brenda Starr; the Katzenjammer Kids and the salty captain; and Maggie and Jiggs and the everlasting smell of corned beef and cabbage.

Although we weren't allowed to read Big Little Books in class, I did look through some of them at the first recess. The next day, I brought in a laundry bag to carry them home, where I read each and every one of them.

Even now, after many years, that moment replays itself in my mind and I can see that little kid in knickers and boots staring in wonder at his treasure trove. I've often wondered what happened to those great little books. Guess they were left behind in Rochelle when our family moved during my sophomore year and I was too old and too busy to bother with Big Little Books anymore.

BOOKWORMS. The author and his sister, Elsie, were avid readers back in 1934, before they moved to their new town.

A Real Page-Turner

When I was a child in the 1930s, I bought Big Little Books for 10 cents apiece. Those tiny adventure books had pictures in the upper right-hand corner of each page. By quickly flipping the pages, you could watch an animated action scene!

My favorite Big Little Book was titled *Perry Winkle and the Rinky Dinks*. How I wish that and my other Big Little Books were still around. They'd sure bring back memories!

—*Beverly Finstad, River Falls, Wisconsin*

WRITERS of RENOWN

When Ogden Nash Lost His Stash

"You know Ogden Nash, don't you?" the editor of the *Boston Globe*, Laurence L. Winship, asked me one day in 1964.

I was working on the rewrite battery then, and Winship handed me a letter from the famous poet.

A week before, Ogden Nash and his wife had stayed at the Ritz Carlton in downtown Boston. Their car had been rifled and their luggage and personal property stolen.

His letter to the paper said, in part, "Since I am sure there are no thieves among your readers, I make this appeal to whoever found three suitcases and two dress bags in my station wagon.

"The loss of the contents is far more crushing to my wife and me, than rewarding to the finder, as some of them are impossible to dispose of for a fraction of their worth."

Fortunately I was able to contact Nash at his New York flat. "How about writing a short poem about the robbery?" I suggested. I could put it at the top of the story. The robbers might see it and decide to return some of the stuff."

Then I had the nerve to add, "You'll have to write it in a hurry, though. My deadline's in 15 minutes."

But Nash was up for it. "Call me back in exactly 10 minutes, Dick," he replied.

I did, and Nash dictated to me the now-famous *Robbed in Boston*:

I'd expect to be robbed in Chicago,
But not in the home of the cod,
So I hope that the Cabots and Lowells
Will mention the matter to God.

The Associated Press picked up the poem and story and circulated it across the nation. It was front-page news everywhere.

But, alas, the clever verse failed to inspire the robbers, and the property was never recovered.

Not surprisingly, the poem did have an effect in Chicago, where the city fathers were not smiling. Nash quickly and graciously made a written public apology to the citizens of the Windy City.

Editor's note: Nash's impromptu poem was inspired by a toast made by John Collins Bossidy at a Holy Cross reunion dinner in 1910:

And this to the good old Boston,
The home of the bean and the cod,
Where the Lowells talk only to the Cabots,
And the Cabots talk only to God.

—Richard O'Donnell, *Port Richey, Florida*

POETIC LICENSE. Richard O'Donnell (above) had the nerve to ask writer Ogden Nash (right) to write a poem in just 15 minutes.

Meeting 'Papa' in Cuba

My mother, then known as Arlene Engelmeyer, was a photojournalist filming a documentary on Cuba in 1954, when Ernest Hemingway and his fourth wife, Mary, arrived from Africa, where they'd been on safari for 10 months.

Mom was invited to meet the famous couple, and she filmed some of the first color footage of Cuba and Hemingway. She was captured in this photo with the writer (above). We even have reel-to-reel footage of her with Ernest and Mary in Cuba, where the Hemingways had a home.

—**Lisa Wyninger,** *Gig Harbor, Washington*

Gals Doubly Talented

When I was on the nursing staff at an Eau Claire, Wisconsin, hospital in 1949 and 1950, we had a group of volunteers called the "Gray Ladies," named for the color of their uniforms.

Two of those volunteers, in particular, had personalities that were anything but gray. They were twins, and their outgoing attitudes and happy dispositions, tempered with compassion, were just what our patients needed.

The twins later used those personalities and became the famous advice columnists Ann Landers and Abigail Van Buren.

—**Alma Rosenau,** *Eau Claire, Wisconsin*

Enhancing the Good Earth

Whenever I reminisce about my one-room schoolhouse days in rural Pennsylvania around 1948, one of my teachers goes to the head of the class. Mrs. Hunsberger (pictured above in the frame, below my own class photo) introduced us to the arts not just through our studies, but also through her own dress and demeanor.

After getting parental permission, she would occasionally take one of the girls home for the evening. When my turn arrived, I was nervous. But on the short walk to the trolley, she found lots of things to talk about.

Before I knew it, I was sitting comfortably at her living room desk doing my homework. Classical music played softly, while the aroma of supper filled the apartment. Later, I curled up on the daybed and was lulled to sleep by her voice as she read.

The next day at school, a book titled *The Good Earth* was passed around, and we learned that Mrs. Hunsberger was a friend of the author, Pearl Buck, who was visiting us that day.

I was struck by the similarities between the two women, right down to the pencils stuck precariously in their hair. Pearl Buck read from her book and spoke to us about writing.

Years later, while browsing through my high school library, I came across *The Good Earth*, and it brought back memories of that day when grace and style merged with education.

—**Dorothy Rothrock,** *Quakertown, Pennsylvania*

Beloved Storybooks

Butcher Paper Is a Fond Reminder

I grew up in a house with few books. While my dad read the comics to my younger sister and me most Sunday mornings, books were nonexistent at our home in Milwaukee, Wisconsin.

I didn't really notice this until I entered first grade when I was 6. It was the year I learned to read. How I looked forward to each morning when my teacher, Mrs. Haas, set up a large wooden easel at the front of our classroom.

After carefully draping a sheet of brown butcher paper over the top of the easel, she would dip her paintbrush into fruit jars full of different colors of poster paint. Using bold strokes, Mrs. Haas painted letters with a corresponding picture on the paper for all of us to see.

My classmates and I learned to read phonetically. *Dick and Jane* was one of the first real books I read. Soon *Weekly Reader* was introduced to us, then *Scholastic News*.

The more I read, the more I wanted to read. My house now seemed empty without any books. I longed for a book of my own that I could read whenever I felt like it.

The Christmas that I was 8, my sister and I went to see Santa Claus at Schuster's, a local department store. A 25-cent ticket guaranteed me the opportunity to tell Santa my secret wishes. After our chat, Santa handed me a large, flat package. My fingers trembled slightly as I tore off the wrapping. It was *Black Beauty*—and became the first book I ever owned.

I filled out my first library card application when I was 10. With card in hand, I walked into my neighborhood library almost daily during the summer months.

I especially liked reading stories about Greek and Roman mythology, as well as animal tales. *Beautiful Joe* was one of my favorites.

My parents both worked, so after I finished my chores, I would settle down on our front porch and read the day away. It wasn't unusual for me to read a book a day. Soon, I had read most of the books in

Once Upon a Time...

My daughter, Vicki, was almost 2 and my son, Michael, was 3 months old when this slide was taken in 1957. Those were the days when the kids often enjoyed a quiet time in the easy chair with their Mother Goose book. Who needed television?

—**Doris LaMarr,** *Magnolia, Texas*

the children's section of the library and, at 13, I got an adult library card.

After I married and we had children, my husband and I purchased a set of encyclopedias and a set of children's books. I read to my children almost nightly when they were small and encouraged them to read phonetically. A son and daughter were able to read before kindergarten, and all five of my children are avid readers as adults.

I'm sure I'll never forget my first-grade teacher. To this day, whenever I see brown butcher paper, I remember Mrs. Haas and the precious gift she gave me the year I turned 6—the year I learned to read.

—**Bernadine Grutza,** *South Milwaukee, Wisconsin, as told to Gail Safranski*

Kindness Helped Her Recovery

Christmas of 1946 was a very strange and lonely time for me in my hometown of Corvallis, Oregon. I was 9 and had contracted viral pneumonia two weeks earlier. I was admitted to the hospital on December 21 for what turned out to be a 10-day stay.

Christmas carolers visited our floor every evening to cheer the patients. I really enjoyed their music and even sang along with the songs I knew.

After dinner each night, my father would arrive with a Bobbsey Twins book. He'd sit by my bed and read it to me until I fell asleep.

How I loved to have him read to me! During the stories, I imagined the twins were about my age so I could relate to their experiences.

These storybook readings were very special because when I returned home, my father didn't have time to read the stories to me. He was helping my mother with my 2-year-old twin sisters.

Our family doctor, who had delivered me, heard about my illness. He visited me and discovered that my medication was making me sicker. He intervened, and I began to improve quickly.

When I returned to school three weeks later, I was very lonely because I couldn't play with my classmates outside.

From January through March, Mrs. Owens, my teacher with a heart of gold, became more like a grandmother. During recess, she helped me sew doll clothes. We became very good friends.

At the end of the school year, all of the students who attended our old school were transferred to a new building across the street, and Mrs. Owens retired.

My father and Mrs. Owens each helped make a terrible illness much less unpleasant for me.

—*Judith Hanson, Seattle, Washington*

Truth Be Told

Pinocchio was always a favorite book of mine when I was growing up. I was going through some boxes in my mother's basement recently and found it. I was even happier when I found a photograph of me reading the book, when I was about 5 years old! My mother made the rag doll that is sitting by my side in the photo.

—*Joan Dickson, San Diego, California*

Commemorating the Classics

Code Name: Barby

We moved from Bemidji, Minnesota, to Los Angeles and then Long Beach, California, when Pa was called to duty in 1943.

Mom took in washing and ironing because Pa's allowance didn't cover expenses, and she had a victory garden, in which we raised a lot of our food. Rent was $19 a month for half of a bungalow, with two bedrooms.

During air-raid drills, Mom read *The Wind in the Willows*, *Heidi* and *The Adventures of Tom Sawyer*, while we sat under the tipped-over sofa. I held the flashlight and loved the drills.

The mail was censored when Pa went overseas, so no one knew where the troops were, but my parents worked out a system. On her bedroom wall, Mom had a big map crisscrossed with lines and names in boxes drawn on specific areas. Pa would write and say to tell a person something, and she would know by the person's name where he was. I felt bad—my name wasn't on the map.

In December 1945, Mom came out to our playground waving a paper and calling, "He's coming home; your daddy's coming home!"

Pa's letter said, "Tell Barby I saw a whale alongside the ship today."

It turned out my code name was the best one of all; it meant Pa was coming home.

—*Barbara Schmeling, Rhinelander, Wisconsin*

A WHALE OF A TALE. Barbara Schmeling's nickname was the most important code word of all in her dad's letters home from World War II. Here they are in 1942.

TV or Not TV?

As a young boy growing up in Los Alamos, New Mexico, during the 1950s, books were a fixture at our house. And when I was old enough, I rode my bike to the corner drugstore, where they had racks of comic books on display.

Fortunately for me, the public library also was within biking distance. My aunt was the children's librarian. She suggested many books for me to check out, like *Robin Hood*, *Treasure Island* and *Robinson Crusoe*. I read everything!

Saturday mornings meant no school, sleeping in and reading before breakfast. I still remember the happiness I felt on waking up and realizing it was Saturday. During the day, of course, I kept busy playing with friends, but later, it was back to those wonderful books.

At night, I read by flashlight in secret hiding places like the closet, beneath the covers in bed or under the bed. The floor-length bedspread framed a perfect spot for reading Hardy Boys, Black Stallion and Sherlock Holmes books.

Then we got a television.

I was about 10 but still clearly remember the impact. Evenings spent putting puzzles together were a thing of the past. Dinners at the table were replaced by TV trays. Our nights were filled with *I Love Lucy*, *The Honeymooners*, *Maverick* and *The Adventures of Ozzie and Harriet*.

The habit of reading slipped away, and I hadn't even noticed. Fortunately, my mother came to the rescue. She had nothing against those wonderful shows of the '50s, but, as she said, "Everything must be done in moderation, and reading is too important to give up."

A new rule required that I read for an hour before watching TV each night. For the first few nights, I would watch the clock. About the fourth evening, I began looking around for something to do and grudgingly picked up a book and began to read. At first, I didn't hear the knock on the door.

Another knock, and my mom opened the door. I looked up from my book and she smiled and said, "Your hour's up. In fact, it was up half an hour ago." I had lost track of time.

The lifeguard had rescued the reader, and I've never stopped reading since. Sure, I've managed to catch a few good shows on TV, too...but always in moderation.

—*Paul Reed, Santa Fe, New Mexico*

The 12-inch Schoolhouse

HERE'S a new kind of schoolhouse . . . where nobody tries to learn and everyone learns without trying . . . where great artists become teachers too.

Here, on Decca Records, are enchanting excursions into storyland . . . those trips we promised you through the wonder world of poetry, drama and literature. Behind us lies a break with tradition . . . ahead lie still more frontiers. For other classics America loves are yet awaiting the magic of sound.

We shall record these classics for you and your children. The familiar voices of beloved personalities will bring to life all the story-book characters who lived in your childhood. They'll live again . . . on Decca Records.

Listen and learn . . . and love it . . . with

Decca Records

THE PIED PIPER OF HAMELIN. The enchantment of Ingrid Bergman recreates the spell of this moving legend. 4 sides. 10 inch. No. DA-450 . . . $2.50

Prices do not include federal, state or local taxes.

CINDERELLA. New fascination in the verse of Alice Duer Miller and narration of Edna Best. 6 sides. 10 inch. No. DA-391 . . . $2.75

All with full musical accompaniment

THE HAPPY PRINCE. Bing Crosby as the Happy Prince in ageless fairy tale narrated by Orson Welles. 4 sides. 10 inch. No. DA-420 . . . $2.50

TALES OF THE OLYMPIAN GODS. Adventures of Apollo and other heroes brought vividly to life by Ronald Colman. 6 sides. 10 inch. No. A-475 . . . $3.50

TREASURE ISLAND. Swashbuckling tale of high adventure. Stars Thomas Mitchell as Long John Silver. 6 sides. 12 inch. No. DA-409 . . . $3.85

"Decca" Reg. U. S. Pat. Off. © 1946, Decca Records, Inc.

Mad for Magazines

Couldn't Wait for 'Life'

I loved reading *Life* magazine, which my parents got when I was a little girl in the mid-'60s. Even better were the photographs!

The time between issues seemed to last forever. But when it came, I'd race back to the house from the mailbox, jump onto the old daybed in the breezeway and spread the magazine on my lap.

The size of that magazine seemed to make the stories more dramatic. It was so big, it went past my knees.

—**Peggy Scott**, *Richmond, Virginia*

Monthly Musical Joy

There was always a lot of wonderful music in my family's home while I was growing up in the 1940s and '50s.

Dad, a Methodist minister, played the cornet; Mother studied the piano and later learned the pipe organ to help out at church; my brother also played piano and then the organ; and I played the violin and piano, but enjoyed singing most of all—and still do.

The arrival of *The Etude* music magazine was greatly anticipated. Its covers were attractive and fun, and the articles were very interesting and even included music to play and sing. What a joy!

—**Kay Huffman**, *Williamsport, Pennsylvania*

Pop Hits at Your Fingertips

I was 12 just years old when I started taking piano lessons and learning all the latest hits. These 1940s *Song Hits* featured stars "direct from Hollywood," including Doris Day, Mary Martin, Dick Powell and Bing Crosby. For less than a quarter, you could learn all of the lyrics to the "latest popular songs of stage, screen and radio."

—**Donna Stanton**, *Pierre, South Dakota*

Met Her Pen Pal
I subscribed to *Playmate* from 1939 through the early '40s. The magazine's stories, articles and puzzles were aimed at early teens.

My favorite part was the pen pals section. I corresponded with Julia Curtis until we each married. One summer Julia and her mother came from Ohio to visit us in Pennsylvania. What a thrill to meet my pen pal in person!

—**Marjorie Brumbaugh,** *Parkersburg, West Virginia*

Hot-House LEGS
IN A COLD OUTDOOR

· FOOTBALL GAMES
· COLD WEATHER
  GOLF
· FISHING
· HUNTING
· RIDING
· HIKING
· SKATING

PROTECT THEM WITH
Jockey LONGS
BY
Coopers

· SKIING
· SLEDDING
· SAILING

BOY NEXT DOOR. At left, the author shows off the good looks that got him into modeling. The former physical education teacher posed for a bevy of advertisements.

WHEN REGULAR
FOLKS WERE MODELS

Modeling Wasn't All Glamour

In October 1937, at age 25, I landed my first job teaching elementary school physical education in Highland Park, Illinois. I was only paid $1 an hour, but it was better than the IOUs many teachers were collecting from their board of education.

To earn extra money, I agreed to supervise an adult volleyball class. One of the guys in it said I had a good build and suggested I try modeling at a studio in nearby Chicago.

A lot of young men were trying to get into this business, but the studio took a shine to me because I didn't *look* like a model. They said I had a friendly, boy-next-door kind of appeal.

Soon, I was contacted for my first shoot. I expected my modeling career might *be* brief, but I never expected to model a brief by Jockey!

My wife kept a scrapbook of my ads, which eventually numbered more than 100.

—**Don Slutz,** *San Jose, California*

My Days as a Breck Girl

When I graduated from high school in Springfield, Massachusetts, in 1947, I faced a decision. Should I accept a scholarship to Boston University, or take an office job with a local company, Charles Sheldon Advertising?

It was no contest when I learned that Mr. Sheldon was the artist behind the popular Breck shampoo ads. This was my chance to become a "Breck Girl!"

Through the Breck ad campaign, Mr. Sheldon gave many of us in the office our "15 minutes of fame." He often changed hair color and styles and minor facial features to disguise the fact that some models posed more than once, including me. It was fascinating to see myself not only with my natural brown hair, but also as a redhead and as a blonde.

For one portrait, Mr. Sheldon gave me blond hair. It had a 1930s quality and reminded me more of Jean Harlow than myself. In 1977, my husband, Russ, and I toured the Breck plant in West Springfield and came across the original of the pastel on the left below. I hadn't seen it for 25 years, but kept thinking, *I should know who this woman is!* Then suddenly I realized...*It's me!*

Before such famous Breck Girls as Cheryl Tiegs and Brooke Shields, we were an anonymous group earning about $35 a week plus a $35 weekly bonus at month's end and a $50 bonus each time we posed for an ad.

But we received much more from Mr. Sheldon. Besides doing wonders for our self-esteem, he inspired us with his kindly philosophy of life and introduced us to far more culture than most of us had ever known.

—**Jean Ivory Stevens,** *San Diego, California, submitted by Roberta Sandler, Wellington, Florida*

Picture-Perfect

This cover on the February 1943 issue of *Parents' Magazine* shows my wife, then Miss Veronica (Bonnie) Larkin and 20 years young, with her niece Virginia McCartan, known as Baby Gin.

Baby Gin was a child model registered with Walter Thornton Model Agency, New York City, and had an appointment for a magazine cover photo shoot. Her mother, Mary McCartan, was a wartime "Rosie the Riveter" and asked Bonnie to take Baby Gin to the photo studio.

While waiting for Gin's call-up, Bonnie was assumed to be a model, and the receptionist asked for her portfolio. Upon being advised

of the situation, the Thornton people quickly registered Bonnie and told her she was in the photo shoot!

The result was a tribute to the professional skill of the Thornton agency and Constance Bannister, who took the picture. Bonnie and I married the month after the cover appeared.

—**Joseph Loughran,** *Hampton, Virginia*

PARENTS' MAGAZINE

The Family Home
Feeding The Family
Family Fashions
Family Fun

Two Thirds-Million Paid Circulation

FEBRUARY 1943
25¢

WAR JOBS FOR MOTHERS?
Uncle Sam needs women workers. This article will help you decide where your duty lies.

Patrons of 'The Post'

William Randolph Hearst Was a Nice Guy

Back in 1939, when I was 8 years old, my older brother, Glen, and I decided to try selling the *Saturday Evening Post*. When selling door-to-door didn't work out, we pedaled our bikes to downtown San Francisco, about three miles from our neighborhood, where we planned to try our luck in the office buildings.

One of the pearls was the Hearst Building at Third and Market Streets. Like most of the office buildings in the area, it had a strict policy against peddlers. I got caught a few times by the elevator bell captain—and he'd always throw me out. But I was able to evade him with enough frequency to develop a client base by trying every door in the 12-story building.

One day I was on the fifth floor, where I opened the door and asked the elderly man inside my usual question, "Would you like to buy the *Saturday Evening Post*?"

The secretary quickly said she would take care of me. But the man interrupted and said, "I'd like to speak to the boy."

The two of us talked for 10 or 15 minutes. I don't remember today what we discussed, but I do recall the shock I felt when the secretary addressed the man as "Mr. Hearst."

Oh, no! I had been caught by the owner of the building, the publisher of the *San Francisco Examiner*...selling a competitor's publication in his building where peddling was strictly prohibited and enforced.

I hurried with the rest of my clients and left the building before the bell captain had the chance to throw me out.

It turned out I had nothing to worry about. When I came back the following week, fearing I'd get thrown out, I was informed by the bell captain that I could use the elevator. What a relief! Eventually, I discovered that I was the only peddler allowed in the building!

One day I was riding my bike downtown with about 150 magazines in newspaper bags on the back. I lost control, fell and suffered a serious head injury. I spent a month in the hospital and another month recuperating at home. During that time, my brother, who also had his own routes downtown, took care of my clients.

When I was ready to go back to work, I got another surprise. I was informed by the *Post* distributor that I would no longer have to carry my magazines downtown. They would be left for me at the Hearst Building!

Once again, I realized that my few minutes of conversation with Mr. Hearst had gained me a friend and a protector.

I tried Mr. Hearst's office door weekly, but it was always locked, so I never got to thank him.

—*George Smith, Austin, Texas*

The Race to the Mailbox

Every week when we were girls, my three sisters and I always ran to check the mail for the newest issue of the *Saturday Evening Post*. Each of us wanted to be the first to see the latest Norman Rockwell cover.

But no matter who spied the cover first, we all had to wait our turns to read the latest installment of *Captain Horatio Hornblower*. That was the grown-ups' privilege.

The four of us thought this was terribly unfair. After all, Horatio was such a dashing young hero.

—*Elinor Damon, Nashville, Tennessee*

SATURDAY EVENING POST, APIC/GETTY IMAGES

Reading in the Kitchen

Like a Good Neighbor

Step into Leanna Driftmier's kitchen and enjoy her recipes for cookies or casseroles, or read her stories about family and local events in Shenandoah, Iowa.

Thousands of readers did just that through a magazine published by this ambitious woman and her family once a month from 1937 to 1986. It was called *Kitchen-Klatter*.

This little 20-page magazine on newsprint—12 pages during World War II—was started in the '30s, when Leanna suffered a car accident that put her into a wheelchair for the rest of her life.

Together with Leanna, we soldiered on, through war and other tribulations, raising our children, cooking and gardening. The magazine, which reached 90,000 subscribers in its heyday, was comforting and informative.

Need a program for church? Planning a bridal shower? You could find ideas for these on the pages of *Kitchen-Klatter*.

There were also tips for frugal home decorating. My favorite involved boxing in old automobile seats and upholstering them for use in your living room. Another idea gave explicit directions for using burlap to cover your wall.

The Driftmier family also pitched their own brand of cleaning products and flavoring extracts for baking.

Snippets of poetry, hints for gardening and health and updates on Leanna's family made everyone feel like close friends of the Driftmiers.

The "Klatter in the Kitchen" included letters from Leanna's children: Frederick, a minister in New England; Dorothy, a farm wife in southwestern Iowa; and Margery and Lucile, daughters in Shenandoah.

Regular features were Leanna's columns "From My Letter Basket" (similar to "Dear Abby") and "Recipes Tested in the *Kitchen-Klatter* Kitchen."

Leanna's December 1944 column talked of family members absent due to the war and other circumstances. She ended so poignantly with this:

"And so it is time to say goodbye for now. To you and yours we send our warmest wishes for a Christmas in which all Faith and Love is renewed. Lovingly yours, Leanna."

—**Jane Weno**, *Iowa City, Iowa*

A Cook Book for Children

A Cookbook of My Own

On my eighth birthday, I received this cookbook—and, boy, did I put it to use! *Kitchen Fun* was written especially for children with simple language and pictured ingredients. Learning to cook made me feel so grown-up, though I did call on Mother for help. Every now and then, I take it down, pull an apron from the drawer and stir up a batch of penuche. The taste of that brown sugar fudge transports me right back to those days!

—**Janice Mitchell**, *Colorado Springs, Colorado*

PULP FICTION

THE HEROES IN THOSE ADVENTURE MAGAZINES INSPIRED MANY A KID DURING THE DRAB DAYS OF THE DEPRESSION.

By Wooda Carr, Fort Wayne, Indiana

Doc Savage...The Shadow...The Spider... some of those early superheroes are still around today. But do you recall their humble beginnings? Those characters—and many more—first came to life during the 1930s in 10-cent adventure magazines called "pulps," which dominated magazine racks throughout the Depression era.

Named for the cheap paper on which they were printed, pulps weren't exactly high-quality literature, but as a kid, I loved them! Back before television, all you needed was a pulp and a good imagination to share the adventures of Doc Savage, The Man of Bronze, or ride the Western trails with saddle buddies such as The Lone Ranger, Pete Rice and The Pecos Kid.

'UNDERCOVER' READING

The very act of reading pulps was often an adventure. Since many parents didn't approve of the lurid books, kids had to smuggle them home to read night, under the bed covers with a flashlight. (I know I did!)

I clearly recall carrying a copy of *The Spider* home from school in my violin case. It was the March 1936 issue, and was titled *The Green Globes of Death*. Mother would have been horrified had she known!

By today's standards, pulp stories may seem tame. The common theme running through them all was of good triumphing over evil. The story lines were rather similar, and they all seemed to run (and sound) something like this: Threatened by a mad genius, the forces of law and order have collapsed! This threat is too gigantic to be handled by ordinary means! Against the weak resistance of good men, criminal hordes are striding ever forward and...

At the climax of the story, the hero would

enter with fists flying and guns blazing and somehow save the day. Next month, he'd have to do it all over again.

Where are these great old magazines today? Most remaining copies belong to collectors, who believe pulps are a part of America's rich literary heritage and should be preserved for future generations to enjoy.

If you should be so lucky as to find an old pulp magazine in your attic, hang on to it: Pulps are highly collectible. But, please, don't just store that wonderful old magazine away! Instead, open its pages and let it give you a chuckle or two as you read your way back into the past. And, just for fun, why not do your reading in bed, under the covers, by flashlight?

million-dollar dog

Have you ever seen a million-dollar dog? Well, Terry Briscoe and his brother, Gerald, are posing with one—their dog, Janie.

The boys are sitting with Janie in front of the magazine rack of their parents' drugstore in Ottawa, Kansas, in the summer of 1948. One day, a man came into the store, saw Janie and offered to buy her.

"Heck, no," said Gerald. "Not for a million dollars."

"Someone from the *Ottawa Herald* heard the story," explains Terry, now of Pueblo, Colorado.

"They sent over a photographer, and this picture appeared in the paper labeled, 'Million Dollar Dog.'"

There are some neat magazines behind the boys. In fact, Terry was able to read a date off one. That's how he remembered the picture was taken in June or July of 1948. Terry was 9 at the time and Gerald, 15.

Janie's age isn't listed. But she still looks a little nervous about the prospect of being sold for $1 million.

OUT & ABOUT

A change of scenery—whether an evening at a nightclub, an afternoon at the amusement park or a jaunt to the big city—is often a special, unforgettable treat.

"Back in 1944, when I was 19, a friend and I saved enough money to take the train to New York City," writes Evelyn Kolb, who lives in Canton, Ohio. "We stayed in a hotel that was close to Times Square.

"We tried to see it all and were in awe of everything, from the subway to the skyscrapers. We rode the subway to Coney Island, took the elevator to the top of the Empire State Building and got blisters climbing the Statue of Liberty stairs. We walked everywhere!

"Years later, my husband and I went on some exciting trips, but none ever equaled the rush of this venture to New York."

Turn the page to read others' prized recollections—and savor your own—of being out and about.

IT'S ALL ABOUT THE MOUSE. Sporting the famous ears, this little girl was ready to become a Mouseketeer at Disneyland, which hosted 50 million visitors in its first 10 years, starting in 1955.

TRIP TO WALT DISNEY WAS
OUT OF THIS WORLD

AT DISNEYLAND'S OPENING, ONE 5-YEAR-OLD FAN MET WALT DISNEY HIMSELF!
By Larry Williams, Tomball, Texas

As a 5-year-old boy, I lived for *Walt Disney's Wonderful World of Color* on Sunday nights. Walt was everything to kids my age: the man who brought us *20,000 Leagues Under the Sea* and those spectacular nature films. His talents were beyond comprehension.

And to top it all off, he was building an amusement park in California! But as terrific as it sounded, a trip to Disneyland from our town of Denison, Texas, seemed out of the question.

To my shock and disbelief, however, my father announced that we were going to Disneyland for the opening! It was almost too much for me

to process, but one morning in late June, we were up before the sun and headed west. It was memorable; we even stopped on the side of the road in California and picked fresh oranges. I had never seen orange trees before, and they fascinated me.

THE PLACE WAS MOBBED

The week after the publicity opening for VIPs found us sitting in a vast parking lot with about a dozen other cars. The facade of Main Street just behind the sloping hill was all manicured, set off by a huge clock made out of flowers. As 8 o'clock came and went, those of us in the parking lot

QUITE THE CROWD-PLEASER. Walt Disney speaks to the crowd (above, left) and poses with the author and his mom at the 1955 opening of his theme park in Anaheim, California.

kept looking around. Nothing was happening. We couldn't see any movement on the hill.

Finally, someone came out and waved us in. From the minute our group entered, I was living a fantasy. No one had ever seen anything like this. We were right in the middle of a living, breathing movie set! We walked down a lane with a river on our left and saw the big riverboat pull away. Just ahead was the Sleeping Beauty Castle.

Now, Dad was no photographer, but I begged him to shoot everything with our Kodak Brownie, and he tried to oblige me as best he could. While he was shooting the castle, I was looking around for other surprises—and lo and behold, I saw my idol! Now, maybe parents wouldn't have recognized him at the time, but little kids knew Walt Disney on sight! He was sitting on a bench, puffing on his pipe and looking around with a big grin on his face.

SHOOK HANDS WITH THE VISIONARY

I couldn't approach *the* Walt Disney, so I begged Dad to ask him. Dad finally walked over and said, "Excuse me, but my son seems to think you're Walt Disney."

The man stood up, smiling, and stretched out his hand. "Well, he's right. I am. How do you like my park?"

From then on it was a blur. I shook his hand and he said hello to my mother and older sister. There was some small talk, and then he strolled away. I was too dazed to remember anything else for a while. I still couldn't believe it.

We made the rounds from one spectacle to another, and we were all impressed. Though Frontierland and some other exhibits were still unfinished, I could hardly take it in.

Later that day, we got in line to ride the steam train around the park. It was a real steam engine, and Dad and I both liked that. But then, to my amazement, up walked Walt Disney and asked Dad if it would be all right if I rode up in the engine cab with him! Dad said sure, so up we went. Mr. Disney slowly pushed the throttle forward, and the steam engine began to puff, slowly at first, then faster as we gained steam.

I sat on Mr. Disney's lap, my hand on the throttle, as he pointed out things in the park that he was particularly proud of having finished before the park's opening. We made one complete circuit and pulled in where we had boarded. Dad came over to get me, and we said our goodbyes to Walt Disney.

What a wonderful memory!

NEW YORK, NEW YORK

FIFTY-SEVENTH STREET and SIXTH AVENUE, NEW YORK

Our Favorite Field Trip

In the '50s, I attended a NYC public school, so a visit to the Statue of Liberty was a favorite field trip. I remember how incredible the inside of the statue and the staircase looked to a little kid! I still have the "bronze" Statue of Liberty that I bought as a souvenir on one of those long-ago trips.

I also remember how much fun it was to take the ferry to Liberty Island. Although I've visited many times since then, nothing compares to the first time you see Miss Liberty greeting you in New York Harbor.

—Joan Farruggio Chicchetti,
via Facebook

Didn't Sour the Experience

When I was a kid, my family traveled to New York City from Boston twice a year in the late 1940s. We'd take in a Broadway show, see the Radio City Rockettes and watch some live television shows being filmed at the NBC and DuMont studios.

My family always ate at the Horn & Hardart Automat. The lemon meringue pie was my favorite and had to be eaten with a glass of cold milk.

I went to the window to order a "bottle of milk" from the attendant and he gave me a glass filled to the top.

Back at the table, I took a sip and exclaimed that it was sour. My dad took a sip and laughed. I learned that when a Bostonian says "bottle of milk," running the words together quickly with a Boston accent, a New Yorker hears "buttermilk." And that's what I got.

These truly are cherished memories of New York City from a "youngsta from Bahston."

—Russ Butler, *Fresno, California*

LUNCH AT THE WALDORF. New Yorker Hastie Lowther (left) shared this photo of three co-workers from the city's housing department and herself at a Benjamin Banner Society luncheon in 1962 at the Waldorf-Astoria Hotel in New York. "There was a time when women wouldn't think of stepping out without wearing gloves and a hat," she remembers.

Quite the Climb!

I remember being about 6 years old when our parents took my sister (then 3) and me to visit the Empire State Building. It was absolutely amazing! I still recall traipsing up the many, many steps to reach the top. Back in those days, we could climb all that way! If I recall correctly, the elevator was broken the day we visited.

—Norma Redin-Garcia, *via Facebook*

Destination: Brown Derby

Stellar Service With a Smile

The Brown Derby restaurant opened in 1926, during Hollywood's golden age, and quickly became the place to dine, meet and be seen.

Florence Knapp recalled seeing an ad, "Waitress Wanted," in the newspaper. She joined 263 other hopefuls to apply for the position at the Brown Derby in 1936. Florence was one of a dozen women hired. By the end of six months, she was the only one still on the job.

It was hard work, 5½ days a week. Florence got paid $2 a day. Tips were great, sometimes as much as $12.50 a night, more than a week's wages.

The staff frequently saw celebrities, including Bing Crosby, Gary Cooper, George Burns, Barbara Stanwyck and others. Here is Florence, serving actress Irene Hervey and actor and singer Allan Jones (right).

Cary Grant lived just around the corner and was a regular. Ed Sullivan came in almost every day for breakfast. He always left a $5 tip, covering himself and whoever might join him.

Clark Gable and his wife liked Scotch on the rocks. "One time, with the manager's OK, I filled an ice cream container with ice and Scotch for them to take to an Ice Follies premiere," Florence said.

Jimmy Stewart's legs were so long that she "had to be careful not to trip over them" in the aisle.

Florence enjoyed the fun she had while she worked there. It all came to an end in 1945, when World War II ended. The troops came home, and the restaurant wanted only male waiters.

—**Gaël Mustapha,** Coos Bay, Oregon

Livin' High on the Hat

When I was a high school senior, in 1953, my parents sent me from the New York City suburbs to California as an early graduation gift. My flight took 11½ hours, with a fuel stop in Chicago, and I was met by my aunt and uncle, Cynthia and Dan Glazer, and cousins Richard and Gere.

One of the highlights of my weeklong visit was lunch at the famous Brown Derby in Hollywood. Uncle Dan said it was likely I would see celebrities. A cold lobster half salad was $2.25; the "Spaghetti Derby," a house specialty, was $1.60; and my favorite, the Brown Derby layer cake, was 50 cents. I have kept the menu (top left), autographed by Art Linkletter, Edgar Bergen and others.

—**John Citron,** South Harwich, Massachusetts

We Looked Forward to Our Day at the Zoo

FREE PASSES IN THE '40S LEFT THIS READER WITH A LIFETIME OF PRICELESS MEMORIES.

By Dorothy Stanaitis, Gloucester, New Jersey

When *Let's Visit the Zoo* aired on Philadelphia radio during the 1940s, kids like me always paid attention.

It was a 15-minute weekly program, and Philadelphia Zoo curator Roger Conant never failed to amuse, entertain and educate us. But the real reason we were glued to the radio was the quiz that ended each episode.

Roger asked three to five questions per week, based on information he discussed on the program. If you mailed in the correct answers on a penny postcard, you would win two free passes to the zoo.

Since there were seven in our family, it took three weeks' worth of perfect answers to earn enough passes. Baby Nancy could get in free.

It seemed like an eternity before the postman delivered those last two passes. And as our big day at the zoo approached, Mother was busy. Since she sewed most of our clothes, she made all of us special outfits for the outing. In fact, those clothes became our "special outfits" for the entire summer.

Mom Packed a Picnic

On the morning of "Zoo day," Mother packed a huge box of sandwiches, homemade cookies and the juiciest fruit she could find. By then, she'd run out of room to pack any drinks.

The lunch box fit into baby Nancy's carriage, along with sweaters, a diaper bag and, of course, Nancy.

Like everyone else on our street, our family didn't have a car. Wartime gasoline rationing made driving a luxury.

But that didn't matter to us. In spite of fine public transportation, we saved money and walked the 15 blocks to 34th and Girard, home of the Philadelphia Zoo.

Father pushed the carriage while my mother walked behind, holding our little brothers' hands. They sang nursery songs as they walked along.

We girls had a different, more grown-up diversion. Father helped make the long walk pass quickly as he quizzed us on the state capitals and the presidents of the United States.

When we neared the gate, crowds of vendors offered caramel corn, peanuts, balloons and toy monkeys on a stick.

A BANNER DAY. Chicagoland's Brookfield Zoo was a fun place to visit in 1958, says Pauline Ball of Bella Vista, Arkansas. That's Pauline at far right behind two of her children, with friends and their kids. Husband Don snapped the photo.

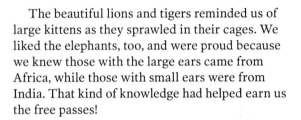

ZOOLOGICAL TRANSPORTATION. When it came time to ride, author Dorothy Stanaitis sometimes chose the camel (she's the girl in the camel chair). Other days, she rode an elephant, as the unidentified boys at right did.

Father bought us a package of five caramel corn cakes to share, and we were each allowed to buy our own bag of peanuts.

I had the honor of proudly presenting the free passes and hoped the ticket-taker would be impressed with my cleverness. But he merely nodded and waved us through the wide gate.

Visited Monkey Island

We wanted to go through the revolving wrought-iron door like the other kids, but the baby carriage wouldn't fit, so we stayed with Father.

Inside the gate, an exotic green parrot gave us a raucous and cheery greeting. From there we hurried down the path to our favorite spot, Monkey Island. The little animals put on a hilarious show.

Then we had to visit Massa, the huge gorilla that seemed so menacing as he sat sullenly behind his bars. And no visit to the zoo was complete until Mother saw her favorites, the giraffes.

It was important to watch the clock so we wouldn't miss the zookeepers feeding the seals. And if we had any peanuts left, we'd feed them to the bears.

The beautiful lions and tigers reminded us of large kittens as they sprawled in their cages. We liked the elephants, too, and were proud because we knew those with the large ears came from Africa, while those with small ears were from India. That kind of knowledge had helped earn us the free passes!

Highlight Still to Come

We walked past the colorful flamingos to the picnic grounds. Lunch was good, but the highlight of the day came after we were done eating.

That was when we got to choose a ride on a slow, stately elephant or on a grouchy camel. It was hard to decide.

But once we were riding high above the ground on the back of one of those exotic animals, we were happy. Father captured our joy with his old black camera.

My family loved the zoo, and it seemed our perfect day had ended all too soon. But as we strolled home, filled with wonderful memories, we were determined to tune in to the next episode of *Let's Visit the Zoo* and win some more free passes.

Amusement Parks Lived up to the Name

Chicago's Riverview Park Was Big Fun for All

As a girl growing up on Chicago's South Side during the early '50s, I treasured our family's summertime outings to what was billed as "the world's largest amusement park."

In my younger years, the merry-go-round, with its hand-carved horses and chariot seats, was my favorite attraction. I liked the Ferris wheel, too, although it seemed enormous to me. I enjoyed riding up there—as long as the seat didn't rock—and the view was the best!

I wasn't very daring, so I'd wait while my brother, Larry, rode the roller coaster and the Pair-o-Chutes, which dropped riders from above. For an adventuresome water trip, we climbed aboard the popular Shoot-the-Chutes. And we took the leisurely Tunnel of Love boat ride, enjoyed by all ages—not just young lovers.

Wandering around, stopping occasionally for refreshments, playing a few games and perhaps winning a stuffed animal—a trip to the amusement park was a fun-filled and inexpensive way for a family to spend a summer day.

I'll always have fond memories of the time we enjoyed at Riverview.

—**Carole Bolster,** *Oak Lawn, Illinois*

Wild About Coney Island

A day at Coney Island and Steeplechase Park was the ultimate summer adventure for my friend Helen and me.

As we got off the trolley with my parents, we heard a calliope in the distance. "Freak shows" of sword swallowers, fire eaters, the alligator man and tattooed lady lined the main streets, and the concessionaires boasted of their own favorites.

The air was filled with the aroma of Nathan's hot dogs, Shatzkin's knishes, hot buttered corn and french fries. We always bought Willie's custard for dessert: vanilla, chocolate, strawberry, banana or pistachio with juicy green nuts.

My parents waited patiently on the boardwalk while Helen and I entered Steeplechase Park through the spinning barrel rides.

Shaking with fright, trying to keep our balance, we'd tumble and fall. We were carried up the sides of the barrel and dropped down again before finally tumbling out the other side, where we'd look up woozily to see a giant cutout of a red-haired clown with a huge red mouth and a toothy grin. We also enjoyed the steeplechase ride, six mechanical horses on metal rails.

All too soon, the wonderful day was drawing to a close. The salty sea air mingled with the coconut scent of suntan oil as people pushed and shoved to get home before dark. The mechanical laughing lady giggled goodbye to us, signaling the end of a magical day.

—*Judith Heller*, *Brooklyn, New York*

COUPLE OF DREAMERS. A Coney Island photo studio captured these two lovebirds in 1910. In her story (below, left), daughter Julia McGlinchy recalls the special memory behind "their song."

Dreaming of Dreamland

Sometimes it seems I can still hear Pop singing *Meet Me Tonight in Dreamland*. That song had special meaning for him and Mom.

When they were young, the two of them often went to the Dreamland Ballroom at Coney Island. In 1910, they posed at a Coney Island photo studio near Dreamland.

I love to think of them in that big, warmly lit ballroom, doors open to the sea breezes, waltzing to the gentle music of their day. It must have been a special treat for them to spend an enchanted evening at Dreamland.

—*Julia McGlinchy*, *Wappingers Falls, New York*

Pier Was a Jump-Off Point

In 1951, when I was a senior in high school, I sang in a variety show on the famous Steel Pier in Atlantic City, New Jersey. (That's me below!)

Back in those days, the Steel Pier hosted the big bands and famous singers. Its most famous act was the horse that ran down a passageway onto a diving board and jumped into a large swimming pool, carrying a lovely young lady all the way.

For years after, I sang for fun around the area—even on the radio and TV, where I met my wife!

—*James Shockley*, *Atco, New Jersey*

LET THE GOOD TIMES ROLL!

In the winter of 1952, the late Bill Stear and two of his buddies from Rochester, New York, set out on a trip to the sunny South. They drove to Florida, then made their way over to New Orleans to experience the excitement of Mardi Gras.

Bill's wife, Ann (still of Rochester), felt *Reminisce* readers might enjoy seeing what Mardi Gras looked like nearly 50 years ago.

Larry Howe, who joined Bill (in the gray jacket below) on the trip, says they had a great time. "We stayed in a hotel suite on Canal Street and could watch the parades from our room," he recalls. "When the biggest floats came by, we'd venture down into the street with everyone else and try to pick up candy and trinkets thrown from the floats."

During their stay, the three young men (all in their 20s) sampled plenty of New Orleans food and nightlife. Larry notes that Mardi Gras was still "small" enough then that they even ran into some people they knew from Rochester!

PRICELESS VIEW.
From the window of their New Orleans hotel, Bill Stear and his two friends had a bird's-eye view of the 1952 Mardi Gras parade floats and all the people who came to enjoy the storied spectacle.

'64 WORLD'S FAIR WAS A WORLD-CLASS EVENT

HE WENT TO QUEENS FOR A CUTTING-EDGE EXPERIENCE.

By Adrian Nader, River Edge, New Jersey

In early 1964, advance tickets to the New York World's Fair were advertised at half price, so my wife, Martha, and I emptied our piggy bank and bought 40 tickets.

Since we lived only 25 miles away from the fair, this was a perfect chance to make up for previous world's fairs we had missed. We arrived at the fair early each morning, chose what to see, then rode the auto-trams to our destinations throughout the fair's 643 acres.

The Flushing Meadows Park fairgrounds, also the site of the 1939-'40 World's Fair, boasted 200 buildings with 50 nations and many U.S. states and industries represented.

The Space Park displayed full-size rockets. Entertainment events were staged all over the grounds. There were even a number of ride-through exhibits.

On our first day at the fair, I bought a camera at the Kodak building—my first good-quality camera—and enjoyed taking slides, a few of which are shown here.

At the Vatican exhibit, my wife and I saw Michelangelo's renowned Pieta sculpture. And at the Atomic Energy Commission exhibit, I got a souvenir Roosevelt dime that had been harmlessly irradiated and encased in a good-luck horseshoe token.

Mac in Wood

I was very interested in the Philippines exhibit because I had served there in World War II. We saw a large multipaneled wooden carving commemorating Gen. Douglas MacArthur.

Some days at the fair were designated as national days. On Denmark Day, we invited two Danish-American friends and their family to come with us. We even got to meet Princess Margrethe, who went on to be Denmark's Queen Margrethe II.

Every day at the fair always ended with the spectacular "Dancing Waters" show at the main fountain, followed by fireworks.

We used most of our tickets during the first year of the fair, but we saved two for the final day in 1965, when we were part of an immense crowd.

I'm sure we're not alone in thinking this international exposition was an experience that will not be surpassed.

WORLD CAME TO NEW YORK. Some 50 nations were represented at the New York World's Fair in 1964. The symbol of the fair, the Unisphere, represented the theme, "One World: Peace Through Understanding." The multitiered building in the background above was Taiwan's exhibit. That's Adrian on the right side of the photo, in the blue jacket, waving.

THE CROWNING TOUCH

WHEN BAD LUCK SHADOWED THEIR VIEW OF QUEEN ELIZABETH'S 1953 CORONATION, A SUNNY SURPRISE SAVED THE DAY.

By Audrey Harris, San Luis Obispo, California

June 2, 1953, was coronation day for Queen Elizabeth II, and an unforgettable day for much of the world. It was for me, as well—although part of the thrill was meeting a queen of a different sort.

A year earlier, my mother-in-law had arranged for the two of us and my 10-year-old daughter, Claudia, to travel to England with a tour group from Santa Cruz, California. We eagerly anticipated seeing the coronation day parade from bleacher seats near Buckingham Palace.

Leaving our accommodations in nearby Hastings, we'd gotten up before dawn to head to London since all roads would soon be closed. Upon our arrival, we learned our seats had been sold out from under us—no doubt at a much higher price than we'd paid!

A SUDDEN CHANGE IN PLANS

We were given the alternative of watching the parade from bleachers erected on the third floor of an office building.

Disenchanted, the three of us decided to leave the tour group for the day. We discovered a restaurant had its own large television screen where we could watch the parade.

Soon we were seated on red velvet benches along the wall, eating a hearty English breakfast, when I looked up and saw Audrey Hepburn and Gregory Peck walk in! They'd just returned to London after filming *Roman Holiday*.

The restaurant began to fill up, and everyone was free to move about as parade pictures appeared on the screen. The pomp and ceremony included marching bands, military personnel, elephants and thousands of horses.

Later, I found myself looking in the plush ladies' room's mirror next to Miss Hepburn. We smiled at each other, and I mentioned that we shared a common first name.

I complimented her darling hat, and she asked me how I'd come all the way from California for the occasion. After explaining, I mentioned that my daughter had accompanied us.

"How wonderful!" she remarked. "She'll never forget this occasion."

SIGN OF A TRUE LADY

Finally the time came for us to view the queen as she entered her golden coach. The cameras caught her placing a delicate purse on the seat.

A few rows away, Miss Hepburn chuckled and said to Gregory Peck, "Look at her lovely bag. A real lady goes nowhere without one."

I suggested to Claudia that she might want to take her menu card and ask the two movie stars for an autograph.

"But, Mother," she protested, "they look just like ordinary people." After an entire day viewing royalty attired in crown jewels and silks, her reaction was understandable, although now she wishes she'd asked.

Still, we all carried away the vision of this lovely and personable young woman. In her own way, Audrey Hepburn was royalty, too.

DRESSED TO IMPRESS

We Wore Our Sunday Best

I'm positive my mother would faint at the sight of the sloppy clothes many shoppers wear today.

When our family went downtown to San Antonio in the '40s, we dressed up because it was a major event. For my father it meant a suit, white shirt and tie. My mother dressed in her Sunday best, with high heels, hose and gloves. I usually wore my best dress, patent leather shoes with buckles and sometimes a flower in my hair.

Many times a street photographer, with his reflex camera held at waist level, would look down into his viewfinder and snap a photo of us.

The photographer would hand my father a card with the name of his studio and the telephone number. Later, if my parents liked the photo, they'd buy it. I still have several of them like this one (left).

When we got downtown, we'd window shop along Houston Street. After that, we'd often see a movie at the famous Majestic Theatre. Afterward, a visit to the candy shop next door was in order.

Houston Street changed after World War II. The postwar building boom created suburbs some distance from downtown, and the first malls, built in the '50s, lured shoppers away from the old Houston Street shops.

With fewer dressed-up shoppers downtown, the street photographers also began to fade away. By 1965, the last of them, Mosher and Zintgraff, had retired and become part of Texas history.

I'm glad I still have several of those old street photos to remind me of the excitement of dressing up and going downtown.

—**Dot Hatfield,** *Medina, Texas*

Saturday Surprise

On a Saturday morning in 1945, a friend and I took the "El" train to the Chicago Loop to see a movie.

We got there early and decided to stop off at The Fair, a large department store that had a club room called the Fairteen Club, where girls could gather to sip Cokes, read magazines and find out about the latest fashions.

We were surprised to find an unusually large crowd there. Tryouts were under way for models to show teenage fashions in the store's tearoom.

Just for fun, Marge and I decided to line up behind the hundred or more aspiring models on the runway. We figured it wouldn't take long and then we'd head out to the movie.

Well, girl after girl was eliminated, and we were surprised to find ourselves still in the running. As we awaited the final results, my heart raced, and— *yes!*—we both were winners (see us above right)!

In the following weeks it was great fun and so exciting to sashay among the tables of shoppers in the tearoom, showing off the latest teen fashions.

Our only "pay" was a bracelet engraved with "Fairteen Model." I wore that bracelet with pride. The memory of that surprise ending to a casual Saturday outing will remain with me always.

—**Elaine Tonnesen,** *Prospect Heights, Illinois*

The Ballyhoo of Broadway

I will never forget the fun we had at the parties we attended at the Broadway Department Store at Hollywood and Vine in Hollywood, California, in the mid- to late '40s.

There was a party called the "Coke Sesh" every Saturday afternoon. They held a fashion show of the latest in clothing for girls ages 10 to 17. But the best part was when they played the latest songs.

CHICAGO'S FAIREST. Above, Elaine Tonnesen (second from left) and her friend Marge were teen models at The Fair, a downtown department store. At right, Kate Wells modeled at Marshall Field & Company. Read their stories below.

We jitterbugged and drank all the free Cokes we could handle. My partner and I won the jitterbug contest once.

There was also live entertainment, including the Andrews Sisters, Peggy Lee and Helen O'Connell.

Those Saturday afternoons were a highlight of my teens, and I will never forget the fun we had.

—*Nancy Kirkham*, *Vista, California*

Marshall Field's Style Maven

The picture taken in an F.W. Woolworth store's photo booth tells the story of how I started a 12-year modeling career with Marshall Field & Company of Chicago.

Louise Levitas, who ran the models' room at the Marshall Field's store in downtown Chicago, told me at a March 1944 audition for models that she was looking for a blonde.

My background as a newspaper reporter for *The Indianapolis Times* had taught me the lesson "Never give up." Accordingly, just before the April audition, I invested in a big bottle of hydrogen peroxide and some ammonia, poured them in a bucket and dunked my head in it. Wow! She wanted a blonde, and she was going to get one!

It worked, and I was hired by Marshall Field & Company, then the premier fashion headquarters of the Midwest.

Each girl chosen was given a little talk, advising that she was now a "face" for Marshall Field's and that if she wanted to stay, no scandal must ever be associated with her name—ever! She was also expected to dress well, even while out in public on non-working days, but we were aided by a 20 percent discount.

The models' room was behind one of the six tearooms and grill rooms that occupied most of the seventh floor. Fashion shows were held almost daily. We models appeared in so many that customers would tell us, "I feel like I know you."

Marshall Field's sponsored a lot of early Chicago TV. Among the many TV commercials I did was one on the *Don McNeill TV Club* show introducing the Barca chair, a full-length lounger shaped like a dental chair. I was supposed to approach the chair and position myself on it elegantly, but when I sat down, the chair flipped over backward. There I was, legs skyward, my feet flailing to get upright.

Cameras for the show, broadcast live from Chicago, were hastily shifted. I was rescued and had to crawl on all fours to stay out of camera range. I remember thinking, *Well, so ends this career!* But my boss, Larry Sizer, the promotions director, laughed and said, "Katie, promise me you'll do that every week!"

My modeling career ended when my husband was transferred to San Francisco, but I'll always remember Marshall Field's as a nice place to work.

—*Kate Wells*, *Delray Beach, Florida*

A Scene to Be Seen

Stars Came out at Cocoanut Grove

I was so pleased the day Mama announced that, in honor of my high school graduation, she was taking me and my sisters to the Cocoanut Grove in Los Angeles for a Saturday afternoon tea dance!

The Grove, which showcased the day's most popular orchestras and entertainers, was a famous rendezvous point for national and international dignitaries, society folk, film stars and social climbers. And it was expensive.

Entering the glamorous room with Mama and my sisters on that special Saturday was like walking into a fantasy. Flowing chiffon dresses, hats and white gloves were all part of the '30s style, and we saw it all in this fabulous place!

Well-lit and spacious, The Grove had half-circled tiers facing the dance floor and bandstand. Silken pastel drapes enhanced the luxurious decor, and tables sparkled with crystal goblets and fresh flowers. White-gloved waiters wheeled about ornate tea carts of pastries and miniature sandwiches deftly arranged on silver trays.

Gus Arnheim's famous band was featured that day. The star performers, who'd been heralded for weeks, were the Rhythm Boys and Bing Crosby, who was just beginning to create a furor among young women at that time.

I pinched myself. Imagine! The Cocoanut Grove and Bing Crosby all in one day!

But there was more. Perhaps the most memorable part was the appearance of a small dark-haired girl about 10 years old.

After trying to adjust the microphone for her, Gus Arnheim finally just stood her up on a chair. "I'm sure you'll all love this little lady and remember her name," he announced. "Meet Miss Frances Gumm!"

I stood to get a better look. The girl was tiny but not at all shy—she belted out her song like a true professional. The audience gave her a standing ovation. Years later, this talented young singer became known as Judy Garland. I'd seen it all at the Grove!

—*Georgie Brooks*
San Lorenzo, California

I Was the Main Attraction At the Copacabana

I moved from the Midwest to New York City in the mid-'40s. I was a very young woman, filled with excitement and in awe of the big city.

One of my first dinner dates was at the famed Copacabana, and I trembled with the thrill of it all. I was wide-eyed during dinner, looking for movie stars and hoping to be noticed myself.

After we finished our food, my date asked me to dance. I happily accepted and glided to the dance floor in my platform-soled, very high-heeled ankle-strap shoes.

We danced ever so smoothly on the elevated dance floor, and it seemed everyone in the restaurant was watching. With all that attention, I executed steps that had never been in my repertoire.

Then I noticed my audience was not only watching—they were laughing. I soon discovered why.

On my way to the dance floor, one of my 4-inch heels had impaled a dinner roll!

—*Pearl Wahler*
Loveland, Colorado

TEENAGERS IN PARADISE

IT WAS A SUMMER TO REMEMBER ON SANTA CATALINA ISLAND.

By Jeannine Praschma Landreau, Granada Hills, California

CATALINA CUTIES. Author (right) and her pal "Teep" (left) took in the sun and fun on Santa Catalina Island in 1947 (below left).

When I graduated from high school in 1947, Mother gave me the best gift ever—a summerlong trip to stay with my aunt in California.

In Los Angeles, Aunt Ruth met me and my best friend, "Teep" (short for her last name, Teeple), at the train. She was surprised when, after dropping off our bags, we were ready to go out on the town!

We'd learned that the love of our young lives, singer Frankie Laine, was appearing at the El Morocco in Hollywood. We pleaded until Ruth's gentleman friend finally convinced her to go. We even got Frankie's autograph! Ruth was mortified.

IN LOVE WITH CATALINA

One day, Ruth suggested we see Santa Catalina Island while she was at work. We went to appease her—but once there, we knew that's where we wanted to spend the summer. For two Midwestern girls, it was paradise. We even saw quite a few movie stars, including Edward G. Robinson, June Haver and Cornel Wilde. Plus, there were lots of kids our age working odd jobs. That's what we'd do, Teep and I agreed.

We rented a room and were delighted to learn our landlady knew someone who needed a nanny.

The next day, we went back to L.A., packed our bags and gave poor Ruth the news—another shock in her unsettling summer.

When the nanny job didn't work out. Teep and I went back to the rooming house, and the landlady let us stay in a small room in exchange for some daily cleaning.

All we needed was money for food! After unpacking, we went to the beach and found the answer to our food-money problems.

Two boats came to the island each day, and the passengers would throw money over the side to kids in the water. Teep and I just had to join in. The first week we caught almost nothing, but we eventually got the hang of it.

Luckily, we met a boy who worked at a bakery. He'd leave us a bag of rolls each day at 4 a.m., signaling the drop with a tap on the door.

TIME TO THINK FAST

Life was perfect until Ruth said she was coming to check on us on the island. You see, we'd assured her we had plenty of money.

When we met her boat, she was appalled by the kids diving for coins. (We agreed, of course.) She was also unnerved by the rap on our door before dawn. We told her it was a special bakery service.

Things went well after that, and we convinced Ruth to take the early boat, saying we'd heard the late boat had problems. We waved goodbye, then dashed home for our swimsuits so we could meet the late boat and dive for our dinner money!

That summer passed all too quickly. Now, years later, Teep and I are still the best of friends, and we savor memories of our Catalina adventure.

Aunt Ruth and I have also had many laughs about her experiences with a couple of exuberant teenagers. She admits she's awfully glad she never knew the whole story back then!

FUN AT
THE CIRCUS!

Circus Train Trickster

My father and his 10 siblings were raised in the mountains of eastern Kentucky. Times were tough, and even if they'd had any money, they didn't have anyplace to spend it.

One day they saw a colorful poster announcing that a circus was coming to the nearby town of Barbourville. Admission was 50 cents, and Dad's parents could only afford to send one child. Straws were drawn, and my father was the lucky winner!

When the great day arrived, Dad and the mule set out for Barbourville long before dawn. As he neared the small town, he noticed people lining both sides of the road.

He tied the mule to a tree and worked his way to where he could see what was going on. Later, he said it was the greatest thing he'd ever seen. There were elephants, horses, camels, clowns and all kinds of wagons with strange animals inside.

After everything had passed by, my wide-eyed father turned to the man standing next to him and asked, "Who do I give my money to?"

The man said he'd take it, so Dad handed over the 50 cents, untied the mule and rode most of the day back into the mountains, eager to tell his family of the wondrous things he'd seen.

It wasn't until years later that Dad realized he hadn't seen the circus—only the parade!

—**Tom Baird Jr.,** Middletown, Ohio

they loved a parade

This picture of the Great Circus Parade was taken in 1964 from a truck parked on the corner of Water and Mason streets in Milwaukee, Wisconsin. Our three kids were enchanted to see the beautiful circus wagons and hear the bands. This was back in the early days of the circus parade, a promotion of Circus World Museum on the streets of Milwaukee, Chicago and Baraboo, Wisconsin, where the museum is still located today.

—**Bill Barr,** *Cincinnati, Ohio*

CHAPTER 8

HAVIN' ⚾ A BALL

As the home of America's pastime, the baseball park was the place to be! Kids used to clamor to fill the seats and meet the athletes they idolized.

"During the Depression, someone came up with the idea to issue free 'Knothole Gang' passes to kids to help fill the ballparks," says Frank Mueller from Mesa, Arizona, of the cards that were good for any weekday game.

"Using that card, I saw most of the day's great ballplayers, including Babe Ruth, Lou Gehrig, Jimmie Foxx, Al Simmons and Lefty Grove. We kids not only got to see games in both major leagues, we also got to talk with the players.

"After the games, my friends and I would pick up discarded scorecards and ask the players to autograph them. I'll never trade in my memories of being an official card-carrying member of the Knothole Gang!"

From baseball and football to golf and figure skating, there was a sport—and a star athlete—for everyone, as the following collection of memories shows.

BEING A
BATBOY WAS THE BEST

WHAT KID DIDN'T DREAM OF BEING A BATBOY? MEET ONE WHO GOT THE JOB DURING THOSE GOLDEN DAYS OF THE '50S.

By Richard McCabe, North Babylon, New York

D ad was a Yankees fan, so it was with some reluctance that he took me to a springtime game between the New York Giants and the Cincinnati Reds at the Polo Grounds in 1951.

That's the exact moment when I fell head over heels for the Giants. My father was understanding, though...after all, not everyone can be a Yankees fan, he supposed.

I got a part-time job so I could save up fare to take the D train to the Polo Grounds from our home in the Tremont section of the Bronx. Lucky for us, buying tickets wasn't a problem—most of the gate personnel understood and let us in for free around the seventh inning.

There were also times when I wanted to see the game so much that I climbed the 30-foot-high left-field wall outside the park in order to sit in the grandstands.

A few years later in September 1953, with only 13 days left in the season, I was at the Polo Grounds and happened to find myself in the right place at the right time.

I was milling around outside the stadium when a man came out of the Giants' clubhouse and asked me to run over to the lunch counter and order him a sandwich. When I returned, he offered me the change for a tip. I refused, saying I was happy to help.

Four days later, the same thing happened. This time the man asked my name, where I lived and where I went to school. When I told him, he introduced himself as Ed Logan, the Giants' clubhouse manager. Then he asked me if I wanted to work for the Giants. Of course, I said yes!

I had to show up at 5 the next morning. Ed took me into the clubhouse and explained that the Cincinnati Reds were coming to town to play the Giants, and their equipment would be arriving early, about 6 a.m. He said I should have a seat until it came.

TOO GOOD TO BELIEVE

I couldn't believe I was in the Giants' clubhouse, along with all their equipment. I walked over to Willie Mays' locker and touched his glove and uniform. I was in seventh heaven!

Ed came back in to tell me the Reds' equipment had arrived. He introduced me to Little Pete, the Yankees' assistant clubhouse manager, who worked the visiting clubhouse at the Polo Grounds when the Yankees were on the road.

As we were unloading the Reds' gear, I asked Little Pete what my job would be. He looked at me with mock aggravation and said, "You're the batboy. Is that all right with you?"

I nearly fainted! I'd thought I was going to be a vendor or something else much less exciting...but batboy was the best!

For the rest of that season and all of the '54 and '55 seasons, I was the batboy for the visiting teams at the Polo Grounds. I got to meet such great ballplayers as Roy Campanella, Stan Musial, Robin Roberts and Warren Spahn.

One day Reds slugger Ted Kluszewski, who had the biggest arms in baseball, grabbed me with both hands and lifted me like a set of barbells. It seemed like he did a thousand repetitions!

I enjoyed it when winning teams—including the Brooklyn Dodgers and Milwaukee Braves— came to town. The players were always laughing and joking. There was none of that on the losing teams.

THE WORK WAS WORTH IT

Before each game, I put the bats in their proper slots according to the batting order and got out towels and the water bucket.

That done, I could get my glove and join the players on the field during batting practice. I learned that major league ballplayers hit and throw the ball very hard!

Playing catch with Reds starting catcher Ed Bailey soon had my hand killing me from the balls he was throwing back. But I wouldn't quit. When we finished and Ed saw my puffy, red hand, he had a good-natured laugh at my determination not to give in.

When the game started, I made sure there were two towels in the on-deck circle to kneel on, one for the next batter and one for me. I also brought out the weighted bat for practice swings and carried a pine tar rag in my pocket.

During the game, I retrieved the bats and shagged foul balls off the screen. When the visiting team was on the field, I could sit in the dugout and watch the game. If there was a pitching change, I'd run out and get the new pitcher's jacket.

It was a wonderful and exciting time. My friends also shared in my luck—I usually had an armload of broken bats for the neighborhood kids.

My final two visits to the Polo Grounds on the D train were to watch its demolition several years after the Giants moved to San Francisco. Each time the wrecking ball hit—especially that left-field wall I'd scaled so many years earlier—it felt like part of me was being torn down.

I still feel privileged to have been a batboy at the Polo Grounds. And, I might add, I'm still a Giants fan.

Pigtailed Player Struck It Big This Time

For one special night in July of 1966, freckle-faced Nancy Lotsey was almost an honorary batboy for the New York Yankees.

She sure was qualified. That summer, 11-year-old Nancy had led the Orioles to the Morristown Small Fry League championship with a 10-0 record on the mound. She had struck out 62 boys and never struck out herself. With an amazing .692 batting average and 54 hits in 72 at bats and 28 RBIs, Nancy was the first girl in New Jersey to participate in an organized boys' league; perhaps the first in the nation.

Nancy's interest in the sport wasn't limited to the field where she played, however. Once she wrote a letter to Casey Stengel, offering a few ideas about his lagging New York Mets. He invited her to the Polo Grounds for a chat.

Her biggest baseball feat came after she entered a contest to become an honorary Yankee batboy and won! The rules clearly stated the contest was limited to boys, though, so she gave the honor to her brother Alexander.

Still, the sponsor was so impressed with Nancy's attempt that she was invited to attend a Yankees-Detroit Tigers game along with Alexander, her brother Harold and her dad, Harold. The team gave her a Yankees warm-up jacket.

That's where I came in. As sports editor for the Morris County, New Jersey, *Daily Record*, I had written about Nancy for my paper and *Life* magazine's "New York Extra" section.

Using my field pass, I asked Mickey Mantle to meet Nancy and her brothers and dad. He agreed and even gave her one of his bats, which he autographed. (In years since, she's been offered $10,000 for that bat, but she's hanging on to it.)

After they got their photo taken, Nancy gave him a thank-you kiss and asked a favor—a homer just for her. He obliged in the ninth inning.

Recently, I asked her about that special night at Yankee Stadium.

"Even though it was years ago, I recall all the events as if they happened yesterday," she said.

—*Ray Goin, Boonton, New Jersey*

HUDDLING UP. Coach Curly Lambeau finalizes plays with (left to right) Tony Canadeo, Irv Comp and Don Huston, members of his 1943 Green Bay Packers team.

Curly Crashed the Party

In the early '40s, I lived in Green Bay, Wisconsin, and delivered my hometown newspaper, the *Green Bay Press-Gazette*. If all my 60 customers paid their weekly bills, I made more than $3 a week.

The big treat of the year came each June, when the paper threw a picnic for all of the carriers. At the 1941 party, we played ball, hiked around the park, and generally had a wonderful time.

At lunch, we were helping ourselves to hot dogs and root beer when a red Cadillac convertible made its way down the long gravel road.

Everybody gathered around. Behind the wheel was Earl L. "Curly" Lambeau, our local hero and longtime coach of the Green Bay Packers.

Curly unfolded himself from the convertible with a big grin, shook a few hands, tousled a few heads and answered a lot of eager questions. Then, he walked back to the Caddy, opened the trunk, and tossed a few beat-up footballs to the guys.

It was a big moment in time for a bunch of very proud kids.

Less than six months later, the Japanese bombed Pearl Harbor, and a lot of those paper peddlers went off to fight in World War II. But most came back home to cheer on the Green Bay Packers at Lambeau Field, the stadium named in Curly's honor.

—*Donald Gordon, Rochester, New York*

Beacon on the Track

My husband, Bernie Miller, drove in the Hardtops, a division of NASCAR auto racing, in southern California and southern Oregon.

In this 1953 photograph (above), Bernie had just won the Trophy Dash in Medford, Oregon, and was puckered up to kiss the Trophy Girl, who had presented him with his award. On the back of the picture, he wrote, "I'm ready!"

The car number on top of his car was in neon lights. His sponsor was Johnny's Signs in Medford, and owner John Eads thought the lit number would command attention. He was right!

When the announcer would introduce "Bernie Miller in car No. 6," my husband would hit a switch and turn on the neon light. The crowd would roar.

The other drivers made bets among themselves as to who would be the first to hit and roll No. 6 to put out that light, and people in the grandstands did the same thing. It never happened. Bernie finished the 1953 season with the neon light intact and the season championship in his pocket!

—**Gladys Miller,** Grants Pass, Oregon

Corn Dog Memories

On warm Saturday nights in the summer, while I was growing up, my parents would take me to a place where the combination of sights, sounds and aromas was known only to race fans. That special spot was Hickory Motor Speedway in Hickory, North Carolina.

The best part about it was having time with my dad, who was my hero. He couldn't spend much time with me during the week because he worked so many hours to make ends meet.

Dad would buy delicious, deep-fried golden corn dogs, holding the mustard pack and putting just the right amount of mustard on my corn dog between bites.

Sitting beside Dad while watching those car races, I had the happiest times of my life.

Though he worked hard, my father couldn't afford to buy mego-karts, dirt bikes or other things that my friends had, but he was giving me the greatest gifts in the world—himself...and those wonderful corn dog memories.

—**Richard Auton Jr.,** Newton, North Carolina

BOYHOOD HERO. Author Richard Auton Jr., standing beside the family's 1968 Dodge Charger with his dad (above), made memories meeting race car drivers Buck Baker in 1968 (right) and Richard Petty in 1974 (top right).

MODIFIED MOTORING. "These 1940s roadsters were customized and painted in bright colors for dirt-track racing in the 1950s," writes Marsha Tursso of Fargo, North Dakota. "This picture was taken at the state fair in Syracuse, New York, around 1955. These were known as 'crazy cars.'"

Skating Was Slick With Sonja

THIS READER FONDLY REMEMBERS GLIDING
ALONGSIDE FIGURE SKATING'S FIRST SUPERSTAR.

By Buff McCusker, Valencia, California

I first met Sonja Henie in May of 1936. She was making her California debut at the Polar Palace, a Hollywood ice rink owned by my dad and uncle. Sonja's own dad paid me $5 a day to hand her flowers after each performance.

I'd begun skating when I was 8, getting free ice time at the rink. Although I never got any formal training, the pros gave me tips now and then. After years of practice—and many falls!—I was invited to join the Ice Follies.

That was in 1939. Remember the ice skating comedians Frick and Frack? They were in the show then, too. I not only met them at the Ice Follies, it was there that I met my wife, Joanne.

Like me, Joanne had no formal skating training. She grew up in St. Cloud, Minnesota, where she learned to skate by studying newspaper photos of Sonja, the Norwegian Olympic champion. One day in 1941, she went to Minneapolis to try out for the Follies.

To her surprise, she was asked to join. The two of us soon met and married in 1944. We skated together for 23 years (top right). During that time, we choreographed all our moves, designed our own costumes and never had a coach.

What an Offer!

Not long after I met Joanne, Sonja Henie called. She'd seen me perform in the Ice Follies and asked if I'd like to be her partner in the movie *Wintertime*. I was in the Army Air Corps at the time but was given leave to do the picture.

Some of you may recall the scene from the movie where we skated together on a rink of black ice (top left). The ice was actually coated with a thin layer of black ink that made a stunning reflection as we glided around the rink.

Working with Sonja was wonderful. I had to watch her closely because our movements needed to match perfectly. I had a tendency to lift my legs higher than hers, so I had to watch that. And when we did the jumps called axels, I had a tendency to spin a little more, so I had to tone that down a bit, too.

Still, it was a great experience. Not only was she the world's greatest ice skater (with three Olympic medals and 10 world championships), but that famous Norwegian smile and her bright eyes were real crowd-pleasers.

She Had It Together

A smart businesswoman, Sonja started the profession of traveling ice shows. Even as an amateur skater, she was an innovator, being the first to wear silk stockings and fancy costumes. By the late '40s, she'd become one of the wealthiest women in Hollywood.

Once, before a performance at Madison Square Garden, Sonja noticed that a row of seats had been added at rinkside, shrinking the size of the ice sheet. She was particular about the rink's size, and no one had told her about this change.

I couldn't see a difference—but she could. She spoke to the manager and threatened to leave if the offending seats were not removed. They were.

After the war, Joanne and I appeared in another Sonja Henie movie called *It's a Pleasure*. As the years passed, Sonja sometimes called and reminisced with us, saying how much she enjoyed the show. And we were often invited to her home in Beverly Hills to visit with her and her mother and, of course, talk ice skating.

Looking back on our long career, Joanne and I realize it was difficult to juggle touring, rehearsal schedules and raising four children. But we'd do it all again in an instant! It's been a wonderful 51 years of marriage...and we'll always treasure the memories of our friend Sonja Henie.

THE OLYMPICS
INSPIRED

One-on-One With Jesse Owens

It was spring of 1936 and almost everyone was looking forward to the Olympic Games that would be held that summer in Berlin. And, of course, one of the greatest track athletes of all time, Jesse Owens, was going to represent the United States there. At the time, I was a high school junior in Chester, Pennsylvania, and a member of the track team—needless to say, I was very interested in the Olympics.

This particular spring, Jesse Owens was visiting several cities around the country to promote the Olympics, I believe. At any rate, when he came to Philadelphia, he stayed at the home of Mr. Bert Reading, who worked with my father, in Chester. For me, this was a bit of luck.

Naturally, I called Mr. Reading and he arranged for me and a friend to come to his house to meet Mr. Owens. I will always remember the thrill of talking to him one-on-one. We must have talked for a good hour or more, and he was as interested in my progress as an athlete as I was in his. He was a most gracious person.

—**William McClenachan,** *New Hope, Pennsylvania*

My Mom Was a National Hero

My mother, Helene Madison, just plain wanted to win—and win she did! This picture of Mother and me is my favorite. I was just 2 and an only child.

At age 19, in 1932, she was the first woman to win three gold medals in one Olympics—the 100-meter freestyle, the 400-meter freestyle and as part of the team for the 4x100-meter relay. When she returned to her home in Seattle, she enjoyed a tickertape parade.

Records? My mother held them all—her list was practically a mile long. At one time, she held all the women's swimming records between 40 meters and 1 mile.

She turned professional in 1934. Many people wanted to be on her swim team in Seattle. I was on the team and later taught for her. She pushed me a lot, just as her mother had encouraged her. Unfortunately, I wasn't as good a swimmer and had a lot to live up to.

She was inducted into the International Swimming Hall of Fame in Ft. Lauderdale, Florida, in 1966.

In 1968, she became seriously ill, and the city of Seattle put on a fundraiser to help with her extensive medical bills. It was a memorable evening with friends, admirers and celebrities.

At this time, the Washington Athletic Club named their pool after her, and in 1972, the Seattle Parks Department built a new pool in her honor.

My wonderful mother died in 1970. I'm so proud to be her daughter.

—**Helene Madison Ware,** *Marysville, Washington*

CHAMPION TICKET PRICES. Compare today's thousand-dollar Olympic ticket prices with the Summer Games during the Depression! The 10th Olympiad was held in August '32. Despite the economy and the then-remote location of Los Angeles, the Games drew record crowds. Among the 100,000 people at the opening cermonies was the father of Joann Schueller Cooke of Reseda, California. His ticket cost a mere $3. He also saw a swimming event.

Hole-in-One MEMORIES

Lawn Ornament Was No Duffer

My wife and I were passing through Ohio in 1952 and stopped at The Pines motel located on the outskirts of Mansfield.

As we were registering, the clerk asked if we'd noticed the gentleman who was practicing golf shots on the front lawn. We had, but had paid him little attention.

When the clerk told us the man was Bob Hope, I grabbed my camera and ventured out to introduce myself and hopefully get a picture or two of the famous entertainer.

After a brief conversation and a few quips about golf, Bob gave me permission to take some photos, but not before noting, "Maybe I should check first with Paramount."

He also said golf was his real passion; entertainment was just a sideline.

"I tell jokes just to pay my green fees," he said.

We never learned why he was at The Pines that day, but when we went to dinner at the motel restaurant that night, Bob and his family were there celebrating one of the children's birthdays.

We enjoyed seeing them have such fun, and didn't interfere in any way. It was a brief encounter that I cherish.

—**Ralph Fuller,** *Pensacola, Florida*

The Other 'Babe'

Throughout the summer of 1950, I was the swimming pool manager at Skycrest Country Club in Libertyville, Illinois.

At the same time, the famed Olympian Mildred "Babe" Didrikson Zaharias was the club's golf pro, though she also excelled in many sports—track and field and basketball among them. The pool overlooked the practice tee, so it was my pleasure to watch Babe, who usually wore a silk dress, show her pupils how to hit golf balls.

I also considered it a red-letter day when Babe came to the pool. She was an expert diver, and she always drew a crowd as she churned up and down the pool with easy, strong strokes.

I remember Babe not only as a great athletic champion, but also as a champion person.

—**Bob Tannehill,** *Amherst, New York*

Gloves Up!

TV Boxing Was Fun
Family Viewing in the '50s

The clang of the bell, the thud of punches, the crowd noise and the announcer yelling out the split decision—those were the sounds of boxing in the 1950s.

Boxing was big in our family. We listened to radio broadcasts and later, watched on television. While my dad served in the Marine Corps during World War II, he learned jujitsu and boxing. He was so enthusiastic that he bought my brothers and me boxing gloves for our own Sunday night fights in the dining room.

We also listened to the Wednesday night fights sponsored by Mennen Skin Bracer and the Friday night fights sponsored by Gillette Safety Razors, with their slogan offered up between every round.

Grandfather Brookhart loved listening to the radio accounts of the championship boxing matches. He never missed a Joe Louis bout, although he claimed Louis always worked over the opponent's eyes before going for the knockout.

We listened to bouts featuring all the famous fighters of the time. And who could forget the third man in the ring, referee Ruby Goldstein?

For the Friday night fights, Mom popped a large pan of white popcorn and we'd drink Dad's Old Fashioned Root Beer. What memories!

In 1951, the Topps Bubble Gum Company came out with small cardboard boxing cards—excellent renditions of the famous boxers, usually the champions. We collected and traded these and learned a lot about the combatants from the backs of those cards.

Boxing continued to be a spectator sport for Dad, my brothers and me as we watched the newer fighters on TV. But the '50s remain my best memories of boxing—the taste of freshly popped popcorn, the flickering black-and-white screen, and Grandpa, Dad and my brothers all rooting, booing and yelling for their favorite boxers.

—**J.D. Brookhart,** St. Marys, Ohio

PINT-SIZE PUGILIST. Author J.D. Brookhart with his dukes up back in the '50s, when he and his brother Gary sparred under the tutelage of their father.

Knuckle Sandwich

During World War II, I was a U.S. Navy cook in the Royal Hotel in Weymouth, England.

One of the officers' stewards came into the galley one day in May of 1944 and told me to make coffee and sandwiches for Lt. Cmdrs. Jack Dempsey and Gene Tunney. I couldn't believe he was referring to the famous boxers, so I jokingly asked the steward to tell them to get in the galley and make their own food.

All of a sudden, two of the biggest men I had ever seen walked through the door. I was dumbfounded and embarrassed. They really were there!

First, they wanted to know who the wise guy was. I made what they ordered as they joked. Then, they invited the steward and me for a drink in their quarters.

Never again have I ever doubted anyone.

—**Syd "Wahoo" Anderson**
Sanborn, New York

THE DAY WE
PICKED UP 'THE MICK'

IN 1951, TWO YOUNG BASEBALL FANS GOT THE SURPRISE OF THEIR LIVES WHEN THE FAMED YANKEES SLUGGER CLIMBED INTO THEIR CAR.

By Don Smith, Martinsburg, West Virginia

I'll never forget July 4, 1951. I was in Hagerstown, Maryland, that day visiting my best buddy, Jerry Nuckles. For weeks, we'd planned on attending the holiday doubleheader between the Washington Senators and the New York Yankees.

Jerry and I planned to hitchhike the 70 miles into Washington, D.C., to watch the games. Although 70 miles doesn't seem far these days, such a trip was a major undertaking before the interstate highway system.

But at 17 and 16, Jerry and I were adventurous teens who saw no obstacles in our path. Besides, we wanted to see the Yankees rookie sensation, Mickey Mantle, the young slugger who would replace Yankee legend Joe DiMaggio.

Early that morning, Jerry and I hiked out to Route 40 on the east side of Hagerstown and began our unforgettable adventure.

No sooner had we stuck out our thumbs than a late-model car braked and stopped about 100 yards down the highway. After climbing in, we discovered our benefactor was also headed for Griffith Stadium—what luck!

"In fact," said the driver, after introducing himself and his little brother in the front seat, "I'm an FBI agent assigned to major league baseball."

He then told us about some of the big leaguers he knew. Jerry and I rolled our eyes skeptically at this unlikely tale, but we were careful not to let our disbelief show.

COULD IT BE?

When we arrived at the edge of Washington, the driver said we could hop out there and seek a quicker ride to the stadium, or take the long way across town with him. "I've got to pick up a couple of guys first," he explained.

Thinking it best to stick with a sure thing, we agreed to go the whole way with him. About a half hour later, we pulled up in front of the most majestic building we'd ever seen. (Today it's the

Washington Sheraton Hotel. I'm not sure what it was called then.)

When the driver went inside, we backseaters—still incredulous—asked his brother, almost in unison, "Hey, is he really in the FBI?"

"Yeah," the brother responded.

"Does he really know all those ballplayers?" we persisted.

"Yeah!" the brother repeated emphatically. We still rolled our eyes...but those eyes nearly popped out when two familiar figures walked out of the lobby with our driver.

"Hey, that looks like Jim Brideweser," I murmured to Jerry.

"Yeah," he gasped. "And the other one looks like Mickey Mantle!"

The little brother up front just shrugged. "What are you two so surprised about?" he asked. "That's what he's been telling you the whole trip!"

When they got into the car and our FBI agent (now we knew it was true!) introduced us, we were dumbfounded. I was sitting right beside Mickey, and what I remember most vividly are his arms. They looked as big and solid as the branches of an oak tree.

A HUMBLE HERO

Mickey was one of the most humble people I'd ever met—he was obviously embarrassed that we teenagers were so awestruck. Getting him to talk was like pulling teeth. But after much prodding, he reluctantly agreed to hit a homer for us.

When we got to the stadium, Mickey apologized over and over for already having given away his allotment of free tickets.

Stunned by our experience, we made our way to the ticket window, took our seats and excitedly related our story to the fans around us (who rolled their eyes the same way Jerry and I had earlier).

Looking back now, I don't remember many details of that day. I don't recall what the weather was like or even who won the games. But I do remember one thing—sometime that afternoon, Mickey stepped to the plate and belted one over the right center field wall!

There was never any doubt in my mind (or Jerry's) that he'd done it for us. Mickey Mantle had promised us... and he'd delivered!

NUTTY FOR THE NATIONALS

When I was in high school during the '50s, my sister, Rose Marie, and our two friends, Sharon Allen and Gloria Buske, were big fans of the Syracuse Nationals professional basketball team. My favorite player was Dolph Schayes (then one of the tallest players in the league at 6-foot-7).

The four of us formed a singing group we called the Nats' Brats. We took popular songs and changed the lyrics to fit the Nationals. One night at a preseason benefit game, we stood behind the team and sang one of our songs.

Their manager heard us and asked if we'd like to sing at halftime during their home games. Of course, we were thrilled to accept!

We got into every home game at Syracuse War Memorial Stadium for free and were given excellent seats right behind the Nats.

Those wonderful two years with the Nationals were the highlight of our high school days.

—Marilyn Furman Kinnison, *Urbana, Ohio*

SUPER SINGERS. Author Marilyn Furman held the mic as the Nats' Brats pumped up the crowd at professional basketball games in Syracuse, New York.

> *I wanted to be good. I wanted to get everything out of it that I could... so I don't have any regrets.*
>
> —George Mikan

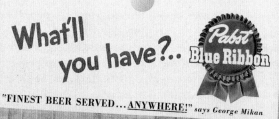

What'll you have?.. Pabst Blue Ribbon

"FINEST BEER SERVED...ANYWHERE!" *says George Mikan*

GEORGE MIKAN—Top scorer of the Basketball Association of America, 1948-1949-1950.

Harry's Magic Show

IN 1948, A LUCKY STUDENT WITNESSED BASEBALL BROADCASTER HARRY CARAY CREATE A GAME OUT OF THIN AIR!

By Stephen Raymond, Lecanto, Florida

Today Harry Caray is as much a part of baseball history as Abner Doubleday, Babe Ruth or Hank Aaron. But I remember a time—before TV—when he made the game come alive sitting 1,200 miles from home plate!

I first heard announcer Harry Caray over the radio one night in 1948, while studying at the University of Missouri. I wrote him a fan letter, and Caray invited me to observe his broadcast!

Of course, I gladly accepted his invitation to come to St. Louis and watch him in action—broadcasting a game between the Cardinals and Braves that was being played in Boston.

My knock on the door at KMOX brought a hearty "Come in!" Five men sat in the drab room. Caray introduced me to early 1900s catcher Gabby Street, engineer Fred Beeler, Dave Brilliant from Western Union and someone called "Stretch."

The notes I took on that captivating night are recorded on yellow sheets, now spotted with age. They tell how Caray took a bare-bones report from a Morse code telegrapher's key, dressed it in baseball jargon and "made up" a game for his St. Louis radio audience.

We're On!

The action began as soon as Beeler shouted, "Hold it—we're on the air!"

"Hello, everyone," said Caray, all business now. "This is Harry Caray and the Old Sarge..." (That was Street's nickname.) Stretch sat at Caray's left, meantime, and made strange signs in Beeler's direction while Caray talked.

Also to Caray's left was Brilliant, the Western Union tech. He had a phone cup in one ear, a telegrapher's "bug" or "key" to his right, and a typewriter in front of him to convert Morse code into English.

"Stretch keeps statistics for every player in the league," Caray had explained before going on the air. "It's a simple matter for me to flip those pages with the tabs on them to the man I want."

After describing a player's "at bat" from a sheet of paper, Caray placed it in a wire basket. Here's how the commentary sounded: "Ball one, low and inside. The Braves catcher looks back at umpire George Barr and comments on it. No, Masi is asking for another baseball.

"You know, Gabby, it's a funny thing," Caray ad-libbed. "The pitcher can ask for a baseball and he'll get it. Same with the catcher. But let the batter ask for one, and the umpire thinks he's nuts! Ball two. Masi walks out to the mound to confer with Sain. The whole Braves infield has gathered. Now they go back to their positions...

"Now Sain has the signal. He stretches, delivers—and it's a sweeping sidearm curve over the outside corner for a swinging strike two. Marty liked the looks of that one, but couldn't seem to find it."

Street spoke up. "There's nothing harder to hit than them sidearm pitchers when they're good. I used to have trouble getting my young batters to hit that stuff when I was managing the Cards."

"Here's the pitch," Harry continued. "*He struck him out swinging* on a knee-high curve that nipped the outside corner of the plate!"

At that point, I wandered over to the wire basket and picked up the sheet of paper Caray had used. What I saw made me do a double take—it was almost blank, reading, "B1/B2/S1, swinging/S2, swinging/S3, swinging."

Obviously, Caray was already honing the tools of imagination and knowledge of the game needed for a fabulous broadcasting career.

HARRY CARAY, BERNSTEIN ASSOCIATES / GETTY IMAGES

HAVIN' A BALL ● 183

BABE RUTH
Came to Our Block

A BIT OF BAD LUCK FOR THE BABE WAS
THE BEGINNING OF THE MOST MEMORABLE DAY
IN A YOUNG FAN'S LIFE.

By John Vergara, Scarsdale, New York

It happened many decades ago, but I've never forgotten the day I met the great Babe Ruth. We lived in the north end of New Rochelle, New York.

I was playing stickball in the street with seven of my buddies. The sky was beginning to get dark, and we were just about ready to quit and go inside for supper.

Suddenly, another friend came running up and announced breathlessly that Babe Ruth was in our neighborhood! Doc Painter, trainer for the New York Yankees, had a home nearby, and that's where the Babe had been spotted. We dropped our stickball gear and took off at a run.

By the time we reached Doc's house, our excited group numbered an even dozen kids, ranging in age from 11 to 13. Doc's house had a huge screened porch, and we immediately saw the Bambino himself sitting there.

Doc came to the screen and waved us away. "The Babe was hit on the hand by a pitch this afternoon. It is badly swollen, so he won't be able to sign any autographs. I hate to disappoint you boys, but I suggest you head on home before it gets dark."

"Can't we at least talk to him?" I pleaded.

"Sorry, guys—the Babe isn't feeling well."

BABE WAS BRUISED

None of us made a move to leave. After a moment, the Babe got up from his chair and walked over to the screen.

"Look, fellas," Babe explained, "Doc is right. My hand is swollen, and I probably won't be able to play for a couple of days...maybe even a week. But I'll tell you what: If you boys come on the porch and line up against the wall, I'll give each of you one autograph.

"I don't want anybody getting an autograph and then going to the back of a line trying to get another one, understand?"

No army sergeant ever got his troops lined up as quickly as the Babe did with us. Doc went inside and came back with a pad and pencil. The Babe started at the front of the line and worked his way back.

I was next to last. When he asked my name, I stammered, "Johnny."

"Are you a good boy, Johnny?" he asked.

"Yes. Yes, I'm sure I am."

With that, the Babe handed me his autograph, patted me on the head and said, "That's good. Always be a good boy, Johnny."

HE WAS 'FLOHRED'

I couldn't believe the great man actually touched me! And true to his word, the most talented slugger of all time gave each of us his autograph. We kept our word, too, and no one tried to get his signature twice.

The next day in the *Daily News*, I read that Babe Ruth had been hit by a wild young left-hander from the Philadelphia Athletics named Mort Flohr.

In his short career during 1934, Flohr wound up compiling a record of no wins and two losses. In 14 games, he pitched 30.2 innings, allowing 34 hits and 33 walks.

I certainly won't forget Babe Ruth, but I'll never forget Mort Flohr, either. If Flohr hadn't made it into the major leagues—no small feat, if even for a short time—I probably would never have been able to brag that the immortal Babe Ruth once touched me!

dad and the babe

It was April 23, 1935, opening day of the baseball season, and Babe Ruth had returned to New York. However, this time the game was at the Polo Grounds, and Babe was with the Boston Braves. My dad, Ted Holmes, was 14 then and got the great slugger to autograph his 1933 edition of *Who's Who in Baseball*. The photo ran in the *New York Daily News*. The following year, when Babe attended the Yankees' opening game, Dad was able to get him to sign the photo as well.

—**Don Holmes,** *Bergenfield, New Jersey*

CHILD'S PLAY

When we were young, a new adventure seemed to wait around every corner. We were always having fun, often with lots of help from our favorite heroes—on screen, in the comics or straight from the history books.

"In the summer of 1959, my three brothers and I set out on a two-part adventure in our town of Washington, Indiana," writes William Barbrick, who still lives there. "Jerry was 9, I was 8, Fred was 7 and Larry was 6.

"We scoured the town and the nearby countryside, along roadsides and alleys, on our bicycles. We even waded, with boots, into the lake and then with bare feet in the river, feeling for treasure with our toes.

"The loot was in the form of pop bottles worth 3 cents each. With this cash, we accomplished the second half of our adventure: buying a Davy Crockett tent so we could camp out in our backyard. What a glorious time to grow up!"

Inspired by television, toys and even cereal boxes, we had the time of our lives just being kids. Turn the page, where many more fond memories of youth await.

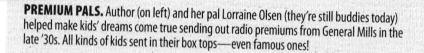

I WAS A
'BOX TOP GIRL'
FOR GENERAL MILLS

REMEMBER SENDING AWAY FOR ALL THOSE SWELL RADIO PREMIUMS? SHE WAS ON THE "OTHER SIDE OF THE MAILBOX" IN 1938, MAKING SURE THEY WENT OUT.

By Shirley Holt Pitman, Fort Dodge, Iowa

If you used to rush home from school each day to check your mailbox for a radio premium, chances are that I mailed it!

In 1938, my friend Lorraine and I typed the labels for those treasured packages, which were sent out all across the country.

As recent graduates of Washburn High School in Minneapolis, Minnesota, we found jobs in short supply. So Lorraine and I both felt lucky to land work with the Universal Letter Co.

The company, which did the mailing labels for General Mills, was in the Corn Exchange Building in the mill district of Minneapolis. This was just half a block from the Grain Exchange Building, General Mills' onetime headquarters.

Making a fabulous 30 cents an hour, we thought we'd really arrived! We were able to meet all of our needs on those wages—plus save a little

and still give our parents a couple dollars a week for room and board.

Most radio premium offers ran for about three months. The mail started off light, but soon letters were coming by the thousands! Sometimes there were a dozen girls typing labels.

The "Hike-O-Meter" was an especially popular premium, as were pencils shaped like baseball bats. Ladies sent in for items such as lace doilies.

Lorraine and I proved ourselves to be good typists and were usually called in early and stayed until the end of an offer. We were expected to do 200 to 250 labels an hour, so there was no time for fooling around!

LETTER CAUSED A STIR

We used manual typewriters, of course, and we didn't work from printed lists of names—we had

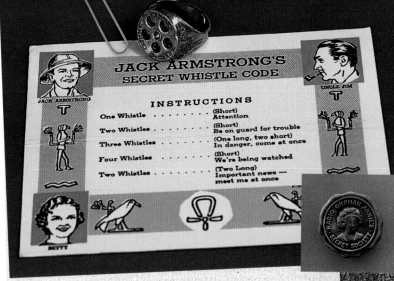

to decipher the handwriting on each order and, once in a while, consult the Postal Guide for the correct spelling of a town.

Although the work was tedious, occasionally something happened to give us a lift. One time, one of the girls in the "opening room" came across a letter from Shirley Temple, complete with coin and box top! That neatly written letter was passed around for all to see, but the girl who handled it first was allowed to keep it. (I wonder if she still has it.)

Sometimes Lorraine and I got to work on special labels that required a code. One might indicate an order for more than one item; another meant the letter arrived without money or the required box top. But General Mills never disappointed a child who was waiting for a parcel. A premium was always sent—along with a note reminding the recipient to mail back the coins or box top.

When the mail ran out on a particular premium, Lorraine and I both had other temporary jobs we went to between label-typing stints. I also managed to attend business college. We worked at the Universal Letter Co. on and off for 18 months until we both found full-time employment.

It was fun while it lasted, though. I just hope some of you "former kids" who sent for premiums now know what special care your orders received.

An Official Junior Detective

I'll never forget when I became a member of Inspector Post's Junior Detective Corps. To qualify, I'd saved enough box tops from Post Toasties cereal and sent them in.

My "official certification papers" came in the mail, along with a badge that signified my rank. By sending in more box tops, I was promoted to higher ranks. First I was a patrolman, then a sergeant, a lieutenant and finally, after many, many box tops, a captain!

Included with each mailing were instructions on how to solve crimes. Once I even received a fingerprint kit with a magnifying glass and other official gadgets needed to carry out my duties as a "junior detective."

But the best packages of all were those that carried new badges—bronze for sergeant, silver for lieutenant and gold for captain. Waiting for the mail has never been as much fun since!
—**Robert Moreland**, Norfolk, Nebraska

Still Owes for the Hike-O-Meter

As a radio promotional, Wheaties offered a Jack Armstrong Hike-O-Meter for one box top and a dime. I didn't have a dime, but since I really wanted that Hike-O-Meter, I tried sending in two box tops.

Several weeks later, I received a blue Hike-O-Meter from our postman. There was also a note from Wheaties saying I still needed to send them a dime.

For weeks, every time the postman came, I was sure he was going to take back my Hike-O-Meter. Of course, he didn't. In fact, I still have it—and it still works!
—**Taylor Goodrick**, Carlsbad, California

Breakfast and A Show

In the mid-1950s, you could turn boxes of Nabisco Shredded Wheat into finger-puppet theaters. After the cereal was gone, it was time for the curtain to go up at the breakfast table of my childhood home in South Bound Brook, New Jersey.

The Shredded Wheat biscuits were stacked in three rows of three each, with cardboard dividers between them. The puppets were part of one divider; they were character faces you slipped over your fingers. If I remember correctly, the other divider had dialogue printed on it so you could put on a play.

The back of the box was colorfully printed with either a theater stage or what looked like a television set, complete with dials and a screen. All you had to do was cut out the stage area or television screen. Then you placed the box over your hand with the finger puppets showing through the opening.

Toys like this are just one of many reasons the 1950s were so fabulous.

—**Ian Rose**, *San Diego, California*

More PEP, Please!

When I was growing up, I collected everything from butterflies to baseball cards. But what really caught my fancy were PEP pins. Do you remember them?

These small metal buttons appeared inside each box of Kellogg's PEP Cereal. In the early years, each button depicted a well-known comic character from the pages of the Sunday funnies.

Brenda Starr, Andy Gump, The Little King, Henry, Blondie and Dagwood, The Phantom and Popeye were a few of the colorful characters I collected.

Mickey Finn was one of my favorites from the funny pages, and as I munched my way to the bottom of each box of cereal, I was always hopeful that I'd find a button with Mickey's face on it. I never did.

Later, during World War II, Kellogg's put out a second series of buttons bearing the emblems of a variety of military units.

When I heard that a few boxes carried a button twice the normal size, I got mighty excited—I ate twice as much PEP as usual. That way, of course, I'd get to open a new box even quicker.

When I finally found a super-sized button with a World War II fighter on it, I was ecstatic.

At the time, I thought that eating PEP every morning gave me just as much energy as Jack Armstrong, "The All-American Boy," got from starting his day with Wheaties. Maybe there really was something to the idea that PEP gave you lots of energy. After all, today I eat toast and coffee and don't have anywhere near the pep I had in the '40s.

And, although I never did find that Mickey Finn, my quest wasn't a total loss. Recently I've become friends with Morris Weiss, the man who created Mickey Finn. Whenever we go to a restaurant that has paper tablecloths, Morris is kind enough to make a few sketches of Mickey for me.

Still...it would be great to have that button!

—**Donald Stoltz**, *Philadelphia, Pennsylvania*

PEP PIN PALS. When Donald Stoltz (here at age 12) was a kid back in the '40s, popular pins from PEP cereal put his priorities on comic-page people.

WE TOOK TO THE SKIES

When Wheaties Gave Us Wings
Cereal sales soared as boys exchanged box tops for model planes that really flew!

The biggest box-top promotion of all came in the summer of 1944, when Wheaties offered a series of model airplanes that really flew! For a nickel and two box tops, you received a pair of warplanes printed on heavy cardboard, ready to cut, fold and then glue into three-dimensional model planes.

The assembly process included gluing a penny to the nose cowling for proper weight distribution. Then, with a good toss, your completed fighter plane flew like a son-of-a-gun! Fourteen different models were offered in the series, including a Japanese Zero, British Spitfire, German Focke-Wulf and a whole squadron of assorted American planes including the Mustang, Thunderbolt and Hellcat.

Each week, my pack of friends and I rushed to the market to rummage through the Wheaties boxes on the cereal shelves after hearing that a new model fighter plane was being offered.

Who could blame us? With each commercial message, announcer Frank McCormack warned, "When they are gone, they'll be gone forever."

Our folks wondered if we'd ever tire of eating "The Breakfast of Champions." On market day, Mom would ask, "Why don't we get Cheerios or Rice Krispies this time?"

"We can't," I'd bleat. "I promise I'll eat my Wheaties...I'll eat 'em all!"

Of course, I was already putting away bushels of the stuff. But I seemed to be enjoying it, so my mom always bought more.

After the war, the model airplane mania was finally grounded. Wheaties began offering baseball cards and other premiums...and I started eating other cereals. But I never got over those model planes.

—**Robert Fudold,** *Roseville, Michigan*

Kits Were the Cat's Pajamas
Model airplane building was a favorite pastime for most boys back in the early 1930s. I'll always remember the thrill of opening a cardboard box containing a new model airplane kit!

The kits could be purchased for a dime, but a bottle of glue cost two cents more. After amassing that wealth, I'd hurry 12 blocks through the Brooklyn streets to buy the newest World War I model airplane.

The kits included a slab or two of balsa wood, bamboo struts, wheels, a propeller, a two-inch square of sandpaper and plans. There were no die-cast pieces to merely assemble like today's models—you had to cut out the individual pieces. I'd carefully trace the plane's fuselage from the plan onto the balsa wood with carbon paper. Then I'd cut the wood to shape, sand it into finished form and proudly paint it.

What I'd give to make another World War I balsa wood flyer. I wish old model airplane kits were still around!

—**Paul Jensen,** *Little River, South Carolina*

TRADING WAS TOPS

Tradin' and Tossin'

I grew up in the 1930s, the golden age of sports card collecting.

Back then, my source for cards was the local candy store. Packages of gum cards were always in a box on the back counter. If I were lucky, I might get a chance to peek inside the wrapper and check out the card (usually, though, the store owner's eagle eyes would put a stop to such tactics).

I still recall the excitement of trying to collect all 240 players in the Big League set. The fun was greatly enhanced by after-school trading sessions with my friends. More than once, I was late for dinner because I was pitching cards against someone's garage door.

That was a real pressure game, because the one whose card ended up closest to the door got to pick up all the others. My favorite pitching card was always well-worn with nice rounded edges. That kept it from bouncing off the door like a crisp new card would.

Luckily, when I left home for college and then the military, my mother saved my collection. It could have ended up in a World War II paper drive.

Thanks to Mom, I still have my collection of top cards to look back on and reminisce about—and I'm pleased to share some examples below.

—*William Evans, Grand Rapids, Michigan*

Collect All 12!

In the '30s, when my brother was 11, my sister was 8 and I was 5, a confectionery stood on the corner of our block. We were all excited when the store started carrying a new bubble gum (I think it was Fleer) that came in a flat package.

In the package was a picture card similar to today's baseball cards, only bigger. The colorful pictures came in series—the first was the Circus Series. There were bareback riders, trapeze artists, a clown and a ringmaster. The rarest card of all was the strongman.

"Collect all 12," the wrapper proclaimed, "and you win a wristwatch!" My brother and his friends traded back and forth, praying their next purchase would include the strongman.

It was fun, but never so much as the day when my brother bought the lucky package. Oh, boy! No one would believe this—the strongman at last!

The prize was ordered, and that magnificent Ingersoll watch finally arrived in the mail. My brother was so proud of the watch, he wore it all through grade school, high school and even into the Air Force in World War II!

—*Von Stuckemeyer, Wintersville, Ohio*

I'll Swap You...

Back in Detroit in the 1940s, collecting pictures of movie stars was a passion for young girls.

Summer would find us sitting on front porches, working on our collections. Clipping, sorting, saving—there was no end to our labors.

In one box were male stars; my favorites were Van Johnson, Lon McCallister and my hero, Alan Ladd. Two other boxes rounded out my collection, one for female stars and one for couples.

Don't think this was a simple pastime; I was a crazed collector. Remember that movies back

then played a significant role in our lives. The way we talked, wore our hair and dressed were all influenced by Sunday matinees.

My movie-star mania took up most of my summer days. If it wasn't cataloguing or trading with other little-girl fanatics, I collected.

If the alleys didn't reap a harvest of stars, I had another tactic. I canvassed all the small beauty shops within walking distance, where some saved their old copies of magazines for me.

When it came time for trading, however, I turned into a cold-eyed, 11-year-old collector driving a hard bargain. Shrewd deals were made beneath that old striped awning.

On a lucky day, I'd trade two Sonja Henies and an Esther Williams for one Alan Ladd, a marvelous transaction indeed. Trading continued all along the street until cool weather and school made their unwelcome appearance.

Then Mother would make me stash my movie-star collection in the back of the closet and get out the schoolbooks.

Since those years, I don't think any other collection I've ever had can match the pure joy of discovering a stack of movie magazines in an alley on a warm summer afternoon in Detroit.

—*Patti Ross*, *Kerrville, Texas*

Davy Crockett Cards Made My Summer
When school let out during the 1950s, our family packed up and moved from our suburban house in Dallas, Pennsylvania, to an unheated two-room cottage on Harvey's Lake.

Dad was a high school art teacher, and during summer, he and Mom ran a picnic area and beach called "Mayer's Grove." To me, it was a magical world. And there, during my eighth summer, I collected Davy Crockett trading cards.

Back home, my friends and I, fans of the popular television show, sported rabbit-fur "coon skin" caps and plastic-fringed buckskin jackets.

I'd walk down to a tiny neighborhood store where Jim, the owner, would fill my order: the usual supply of licorice whips, candy dots on paper and jawbreakers. Then Jim would reach under the counter, tap the packs and ask, "Which one today?"

Each pack contained one card along with a pink slab of gum. I can still recall the sweet scent as I peeled open the waxed wrapper to check my treasure. I think there were 72 cards, each with a scene from the television show.

All summer, my collection increased. From the Tennessee mountaintop to the Alamo, I filled in the gaps. But as the end of August neared, one card remained stubbornly unattainable—Card 68, titled "A Bullet Finds Its Mark."

The last week of summer arrived, and I walked to Jim's store for the last time. I slapped my nickel down on the counter. Jim reached toward the box of cards, as he always did. But this time he tapped one pack and said, "Try this one."

As I walked back to the cabin, I opened that last pack. Even before I lifted the gum to check the card underneath, I knew I had it!

There was a narrow strip of an unfamiliar picture visible around the pink slab. I also noticed the picture wasn't covered with the usual white powder. But there it was, Card 68. My set (and summer) was complete.

Long after that, I learned Jim had spent hours rifling through packs until he found the card.

I don't have my Davy Crockett cards anymore. But I wish I did...so I could feel their weight in my hands once more, just to reassure myself that that perfect summer was real.

—*Eric Mayer*, *Rochester, New York*

LOOPY FOR THE HOOP. "Lots of readers must recall when the Hula-Hoop fad hit," notes Maxine Champlin of Battle Creek, Michigan. "This is my oldest son, Ray, trying his skill at the Hula-Hoop in the '50s. We lived in Kalamazoo at the time."

Toys We Treasured

Great, but What Is It?

My father's job as a salesman for an aluminum company had him on the road often during the '50s. Each time he returned home, Dad invariably brought me some small gift.

In theory, these gifts were to reward me for my good behavior while he was away. In fact (since I probably wasn't all that good), I think they were more likely his way of showing that he had missed me.

Following one trip, Mom and I met him at the airport, and I noticed right away that he was carrying something unusual—something that resembled an orange barrel hoop. After kissing Mom, he handed it to me. It was made of plastic, and was light and smooth to the touch.

"You just might be the first boy in America to have one of these," my father said, beaming. (This kind of ear-to-ear grin was reserved for special occasions...like when Mom served creamed onions for supper.)

"Great!" I responded, trying my best to sound pleased. "But, well...what is it?"

"They call it a Hula-Hoop," Dad explained. "While I was on the road last week, I met a man who works for the company that makes them. The hoops will be released nationally in a couple weeks, so you'll be a real trendsetter, way ahead of the pack!"

I smiled back, but it wasn't ear-to-ear. Frankly, I didn't have the faintest idea what to do with the thing. It seemed like a hoop, nothing more.

Later, when I asked Dad why it was called a Hula-Hoop, he demonstrated for me—or at least tried to. I'd never seen anything quite as ridiculous as the sight of my usually dignified dad trying to keep that hoop around his midsection.

Right then I decided this was sissy stuff—nothing a boy worth his Davy Crockett plastic powder horn wanted any part of. Still, I kept the hoop and even brought it out when Dad was around, so he could see me with it. I felt foolish.

Salvation came not long afterward when our dog ruined the Hula-Hoop. It would be nice to say that was that. But as everyone over the age of 50 knows, the Hula-Hoop quickly became the hottest toy in America.

Realizing I'd made a horrible blunder allowing mine to be destroyed, I bought a replacement with my allowance.

I'd had my chance to be a trendsetter and I'd blown it. Instead, I was just one among the hip-swinging millions.

—**Bruce Dettman,** *San Francisco, California*

Matchbox Mania

As a kid, I had just a few Matchbox Cars, but always loved getting a new one (when they were sold in a box)! My local toy store had an awesome showcase on display.

—*David Hendrix, via Facebook*

Practical Jokester

Between Tinkertoys and Lincoln Logs, my little brother became an expert booby-trapper. If I stepped on one, I stepped on a thousand!

—*Kim Gentry Pittard, via Facebook*

Batman Was Snatched!

In 1964, I was in second grade. Mrs. Perkins warned me not to bring my $5 Batman troll to school, but when I did, it was taken away and never returned! I've never forgotten that. I also had a troll mask for Halloween. I think they had just come out then.

—*Sharon Kollmann, via Facebook*

Miniature Matchmaker

When I was little, I asked my mom and dad for Barbies so my GI Joe could go out on dates. One Christmas, they gave a couple Barbies to my cousins, and I got into trouble for opening the package. GI Joe was now able to go the movies with dates, where they watched the blue screen TV. All innocent!

—*Scott Rickhoff, via Facebook*

She Had the First Barbie

I had an original Barbie before they even went into the stores, because I worked for the PR firm that promoted it. I wish I still had that doll. It would be worth a fortune!

—*Lynne Wright, via Facebook*

Simple Fun With Slinky

I used to love my Slinky. I remember playing with it for hours on the steps of my parents' house. And if you weren't near steps, you could play with it from one hand to the other, back and forth. They just don't make toys like that anymore...no batteries, no instructions, just good fun.

—*Julie Hartstein*
via Facebook

Restoring a Friendship

Back in 1941, when I was 5 years old, Aunt Bess gave me a Shirley Temple doll, which was almost as big as I was.

Many years later, after I'd lived many places and married and raised a family of my own, I had not seen or thought about my beloved Shirley Temple doll.

One day, I found her in our attic, wrapped in newspaper, with her face, arms and legs cracked. Sixty years later, her body was slowly disintegrating. I heard about a lady who restored old dolls, so off to the doll hospital we went.

When I picked up my doll, I could not believe my eyes. On her head was a beautiful curly mohair wig, her eyes were changed from green to brown, like the real Shirley's, and her face, arms and legs were like new. Her fingers and toenails were polished bright red, she had a new snow-white cloth body and her dress was hand-sewn.

Every time I look at her, I remember how happy we were when I was 5 years old.

—*Pat Waldron, Joppa, Maryland*

A TERRIBLE TRIO. Far left, Don, Big Frankie and author Roger Hill enjoy some time in the Monster Den in 1962.

Monster-Sized Scare

BIG FRANKIE GUARDED THE MONSTER DEN UNTIL ONE FATEFUL NIGHT.

By Roger Hill, Wichita, Kansas

I discovered monsters around 1958, when I was 10 years old, in Wichita, Kansas, which has been my home nearly all of my life.

It started when the local TV station began showing Universal horror movies on Friday nights, movies like *Frankenstein* and *The Mummy* with Boris Karloff, *Dracula* starring Bela Lugosi and *The Wolf Man* with Lon Chaney Jr.

Dad would turn off all the lights in our living room, and we kids would lie on the floor with our pillows and popcorn and watch the monsters come to life on Channel 10.

My brother Don and I used to hang out at the local drugstore before and after school, playing the jukebox, drinking cherry Cokes and looking over the toys, model kits and comic books.

The Fascination Begins

One fall day in 1959, we spied a copy of *Famous Monsters of Filmland* magazine. It just jumped out at us and said, "Take me home!" Unable to resist, we plunked down our hard-earned allowance money of 35 cents and off we went. That was the real beginning of our monster memorabilia collecting. Eventually, Don and I began collecting monster movie posters, trading cards, comic books, model kits, photos, autographs and so on.

Halloween soon became our favorite holiday, and in the back pages of *Famous Monsters* we found cool monster stuff for sale: shrunken heads, rubber bats, giant flies and all kinds of monster masks, hands and feet.

Then, one day, we noticed something new for sale. The ad read, "Giant Life Size Frankenstein Pin-Up Over 6 Feet Tall!" The drawing, it said, was a "masterpiece of reproduction that will startle anyone who sees it."

The ad also noted that the pin-up was done by "America's greatest cartoonist-artist," Jack Davis, and would "supply 100 hours of laughs and thrills: Have your picture taken alongside your favorite ghoul; Scotch-tape it to the inside of your bedroom or den door; put it between someone's bedsheets, or just pin it on the wall. A million dollars worth of value for a low, low price!...only $2." This sounded good to Don and me, so we sent our money.

Fair Warning

Two weeks later, our Frankenstein pin-up arrived, rolled in a tube. We immediately hung it on the outside of the door to our bedroom, which we called our Monster Den. We put a little sign up next to Frankie saying, "Beware, Enter at Your Own Risk."

By then, all kinds of monster movie posters, photos, artwork and Aurora models decorated our Monster Den. Some of our neighborhood buddies freaked out at the thought of walking past the 6-foot Frankenstein pin-up for the first time.

We had a lot of fun with Big Frankie until one night a couple of weeks later. My parents' bedroom was located just across the hall from our Monster Den. My mom woke up at some point during the night and caught a glimpse of what appeared to be a towering figure of a man standing across the hall staring at her. She let out a scream that woke up the whole household.

We usually kept our bedroom door closed at night, but on that night, we had left it open a bit, allowing moonlight to lightly illuminate the Frankenstein pin-up.

The next morning, Mom strongly suggested that we move Big Frankie to the inside of our door. Our parents were very supportive of our collection and we loved them for their understanding, so naturally, Don and I complied right away.

About 10 years ago, an art-dealer friend of mine in New York got in touch to inform me that he had acquired several original paintings done for monster magazine covers. I wound up buying the original pen-and-ink art done by Jack Davis for the Frankenstein pin-up.

Today, Big Frankie is framed and hanging on the wall next to the front door of our house. Every time I walk past him, I am transported back to those childhood days of collecting monster items and hearing my mother scream from across the hall.

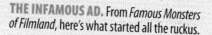

THE INFAMOUS AD. From *Famous Monsters of Filmland*, here's what started all the ruckus.

No Batteries Required

A SIMPLE CARD GAME MADE FOR AN EVENING OF SUPERCHARGED FUN!

By Cecil McClain, Elverta, California

A stay with our grandparents was an event my sister and I still cherish, and one of the most memorable took place in the late '40s. I was 8 and my sister was 11 when Mom and Dad left us for a two-week visit with Grandma and Grandpa. We lived in the small town of Rio Linda, California, and they were 300 miles south, in Bakersfield.

Our grandparents had a cupboard with puzzles and several games. On this visit, the cupboard held a new game, still in its wrapper, called Pit.

After dinner, it was a tradition for Grandpa to ask, "What shall we play this evening?" Sometimes we would put a puzzle together or play dominoes or Chinese checkers. There was little conversation so we could concentrate on our next moves. That was about to change when Grandpa pulled out the game of Pit.

"Now," he said, looking down at me over the top of his glasses, "the idea is to collect all of the same type of cards. In other words, try to get all nine of the wheat cards, or try for the oats or one of the other grains, whichever kind you have the most of in your hand, until you get all nine alike. Got it?"

With a big smile, I replied, "I think so, Grandpa." Then I asked, "What about the card with the bull and the one with the bear?"

"The bull," he said, "can be used in place of one of the other cards. It's a wild card. You can't go out with the bear in your hand, and you don't want to get caught with it. If someone goes out and you have it, it will cost you 20 points. It's a hot potato you want to get rid of."

By this time, the instructions seemed a little muddy, yet one thing was clear: I didn't want to be caught with the bear. Grandpa dealt the cards, and when I checked my hand, I had the dreaded bear.

"OK," said Grandpa, "you can trade as many as four cards at a time, but keep them face down. For example, if you have three you want to trade, extend them out and holler, 'Three-three-three!' If someone wants to trade with you, they can. If not, they don't have to." Pretty simple, right? Well, I just wanted to get rid of the dreaded bear.

"When I say, 'Pit's open' the game begins," said Grandpa. "If you get a full set, yell, 'Corner!'" Grandpa made sure we were ready before yelling, "Pit's open!"

Let the Game Begin!

Pulling the bear from my hand, I extended it, hoping another bidder would fall prey as I hollered, "One-one-one!" Across the table my sister yelled for three, while Grandma yelled for four. Grandpa, looking down at me, pulled a single card from his hand and yelled, "One-one-one!" Elated, I exchanged cards and looked at Grandpa's expression.

"Pshaw!" he said, with a sort of curled smile, then pulled three cards from his hand and traded with my sister. Desperately, I tried not to laugh, knowing Sis had just been slipped the bear. I watched as her eyes widened. Grandpa chuckled and placed two cards on the table, sputtering, "Two-two-two?"

By now the tears were running down my cheeks. I could no longer hold back the laughter, watching Sis take four cards from her hand, hollering, "Four-four-four," and trading with Grandma, who looked at her hand and blurted out the second new word I heard that evening, "Balderdash!" By this time Grandpa's eyes were tearing up from laughter and my sister was grinning from ear to ear.

As the game continued, the bear was lost in the shuffle as it went from one player to another. Finally, Grandma exclaimed, "Land o' Goshen!" and then shouted triumphantly, "Corner!" The first hand had ended with not a dry eye at the table.

Every time I hear "pshaw," "balderdash" and "land o' Goshen," I can't help but laugh, remembering that first evening of many spent playing the great game of Pit.

Pass Go! Collect $200!

My brother, John, taught me how to play Monopoly during the 1960s when I was very young.

As we set up the game on the floor in John's room, the two of us would sit cross-legged on opposite sides of the board. He'd tell me which properties were good and which were not-so-good.

He was always the race car—and I was the top hat, the dog or sometimes the thimble. When John rolled the dice, he never had to count spaces like I did. Instead, he would make little race car noises as he zoomed the car down the exact number of spaces, then brought it to a dramatic screeching stop.

John bought everything he landed on, even properties he didn't like. And he knew the rental prices by heart. Meanwhile, my own game piece

skipped merrily around the Monopoly board, with little or no strategy.

Sometimes we departed from the rules. Once, when John held both Boardwalk and Park Place, he proposed that I allow him to put two hotels on each property, thereby collecting double rent.

In return, I'd get a few properties and a generous financial boost. Feeling smug about the five or six colorful little piles of money sitting by my side, I thought a passerby might think I was winning! It never lasted long.

At the end of the game, all the money would be returned to the appropriate slots. Then John would fold the board and pour all the houses and hotels back into the box. Last of all, before the lid was closed, in went the race car—just another pit stop before the next time.

—*Martha Bartels*, Wayne, Pennsylvania

Paper Wardrobe

This photograph was taken around 1953, when I was 10, in my bedroom on our farm in White Lake, South Dakota. My cousin Carol and I are playing with paper dolls. On the bed is my last doll, a walking doll I named Susan. You can really tell, from the furniture and flowered wallpaper, that this photo is from a time in the '50s.

—**Kathy Bogenhagen Ostrem**
Rochester, Minnesota

PLAYING WITH PAPER DOLLS

Cutouts Kept Us Busy

The '50s were back in the days when parents did not entertain their children. Either we made our own fun, or it just didn't happen.

Summer vacation of 1956 started with excitement. My sisters and I played with our vast collection of cutout dolls. We fitted Debbie Reynolds with the more glamorous wardrobe of Elizabeth Taylor, and we bent the arms of Debra Paget to fit into gowns made for June Allyson. Such simple pleasures!

—**Catherine Kerman Anderson,** *Mt. Clemens, Michigan*

'Tillie the Toiler' a Treasure

When I run across an old *Tillie the Toiler* comic strip, I enjoy it just as much now as I did when I was a child.

Growing up during the Depression, although it was a difficult time for many, in our home, we children always had the Sunday paper to look forward to and were able to laugh at the comics.

I don't know how my parents afforded the luxury of buying the paper when so many other needs were not being met.

One treasure I have from that time period is my little box of paper dolls that I faithfully cut out of the funnies each Sunday. They were the only paper dolls that I had and, although they were played with day after day, they are still remarkably preserved.

Here is one of my dolls, including her wardrobe, in the hopes that other *Reminisce* readers will identify with that time and enjoy sharing them with their grandchildren.

—**Martha Lindquist,** *Seattle, Washington*

Growing up, I didn't have a lot of toys...entertainment depended on individual ingenuity and imagination.

—**Terry Brooks**, *American novelist*

RIDE 'EM, COWPOKES! "My father, Delbert Walker, took this 1950 photo of my older brother and sister with their prized Christmas presents on our family farm south of Hanford, California," writes John Walker of Clovis. "Bob, age 8, was in his Roy Rogers outfit with his gleaming J.C. Higgins bike. Carolyn, 5, was in her cowgirl outfit with her Donald Duck bike. My sister regretted selling her Donald bike at a yard sale in the 1980s, as she later discovered it became a rare collectible."

WESTERNS WERE THE RAGE

Earned His Spurs

As a youngster in the 1940s, I idolized the popular cowboy star Tom Mix. I attended many of his movies and faithfully listened to his fantastic radio adventures.

One memorable evening, the radio announcer offered an official pair of Tom Mix glow-in-the-dark spurs for 25 cents and two Ralston Cereal box tops.

I quickly developed an insatiable appetite for Ralston Cereal—and astonished Mom by volunteering work in exchange for the required 25 cents. Before long, my order was mailed.

Each day after school, I raced to the mailbox in search of the package containing the spurs. Weeks passed before it finally arrived...and the neighbors likely wondered about my yelling, jumping and waving antics as I retrieved it.

Tearing the box open, I found two beautiful spurs. The U-shaped part of each spur was silver, emblazoned with cowboy brands and symbols. The rotating star shone with a greenish-white tint.

We neighborhood kids played cowboys and Indians for hours that afternoon. Later, still wearing my spurs in bed, I propped my feet up to watch them magically glow in the dark.

Recently while rummaging through my boyhood toy box, I found a broken spur with the star still intact. I took it to a dark room and watched as a warm glow formed not only around the spur, but also in my heart.

—*R. Troup, McConnelsville, Ohio*

This Hero's Autograph Didn't Cost a Dime

On Saturdays during the '40s and '50s, my siblings and I would walk two miles into downtown Fort Worth, Texas, for an afternoon at the movies. We were always eager to learn how our serial heroes would escape impending doom from the previous week's episode.

We were equally thrilled when our favorite cowboys filled the silver screen. Gene, Hoppy and Roy were magical names to young wannabe cowboys of that era.

One spring day in 1952, I decided to take the 15-minute walk to Everybody's Store to buy a bag

of marbles. Once inside, I noticed a crowd in the boys' clothing department.

To my amazement, I discovered Gene Autry was appearing in person, signing little leather labels sewn into a line of blue denims he was promoting. I quickly took my place at the end of a long line of youngsters whose parents had bought jeans for them. I couldn't afford jeans but figured I'd just say hello.

Pretty soon, a soft-spoken angel of a lady who appeared to be with Gene asked if I'd like him to autograph something. I told her I had no money for jeans and just wanted to see Gene up close.

Seeing that I was alone, the lady tore a piece of paper from her notebook, placed it in my hand and, with the most heartwarming smile, said, "Gene will be happy to sign this for you."

I folded the paper and put it in my shirt pocket. The line continued to inch up, and finally I got to see Gene Autry face to face! My heart was pounding so loud that I actually wondered whether he could hear it.

Seeing that I had no denims to sign, Gene held out his hand and asked if I'd like to shake. I was struck by his blue eyes, immaculate

Gene's Cowboy Commandments

1. Never take unfair advantage of anyone.
2. Be kind to animals.
3. Be trustworthy.
4. Be truthful.
5. Have no racial or religious prejudices.
6. Be helpful to elders.
7. Be industrious.
8. Be respectful to womanhood.
9. Be patriotic.
10. Always have clean thoughts and speech.

appearance and firm grip. At a complete loss for words, I simply exclaimed, "You're my most favorite cowboy!"

"Thanks," he replied. "You're my favorite pal."

Then the kind lady winked at me and told Gene I had something I'd like him to sign. That's when I remembered the piece of paper and fished it out of my shirt pocket. He signed it "Your pal Gene Autry," then shook my hand again.

Walking away, I forgot about buying marbles. Instead, I hurried home to show family and friends Gene's autograph—and to tell them he shook my hand...twice! (Later, an uncle told me he was certain the lady at the store was Gene's wife.)

Gene Autry died at the age of 91, bringing to a close the most colorful era of true cowboy heroes. A tear glistened in the eyes of many old-timers like myself when we heard the news—Gene had ridden off into his final sunset and taken his place among the singing cowboys in the sky.

—**David Cheesman**, *Rensselaer, Indiana*

PIGTAILS & PISTOLS. Jan Parrott-Holden of Vancouver, Washington, may be wearing slippers instead of boots, but she had the gun and the hat, and was a rootin', tootin' fan of Gail Davis, who played Annie Oakley on TV. Jan even named her doll Annie.

THE COMICS CRAZE

Hobby Got Him Personalized Comics

Reading the comics was the highlight of my day when I was growing up in Blakely, a small south Georgia town.

I read the comics in the *Dothan Eagle*, which was printed across the river in Dothan, Alabama. Our local paper, the *Early County News*, was a weekly and didn't have a comic section.

I became a dedicated comics reader in 1945. The quality of the paper wasn't too good in those days, but as long as the comics were readable, that was fine with me.

As the years passed, I continued to read the comics, sometimes aloud to my grandchildren, who also enjoy them.

In 1996, while recuperating from major surgery, I turned to a hobby I'd been involved in sporadically in the past—autograph collecting.

Although I'd collected autographs from politicians, sports stars and actors, I decided to try to get those of my boyhood favorites, the creators of comic strips such as *Blondie*, *Beetle Bailey*, *The Katzenjammer Kids*, *Popeye*, *Alley Oop*, *Dick Tracy*, *Mandrake the Magician*, *The Phantom*, *Barney Google* and *Snuffy Smith*.

While not all of the artists responded, those who did more than made up for it—they often included a sketch with their autographs and sometimes a little note.

What a fantastic feeling! It was like being 9 years old again and back in Blakely. It was like Christmas and my birthday all rolled into one.

For those who want to try this hobby, I have one warning—it's contagious. Once you catch it, there is no cure. You'll be hooked!

—***Norman Smith,*** *Tampa, Florida*

TO- NORM WITH ALL BEST WISHES, DEAN YOUNG

Colorful Reading Lesson

My brother and I were children of Russian-speaking parents. In school, my mother had gone only as far as the third grade, but she could read the Sunday funnies to me on Monday from the paper Dad salvaged out of the trash at the mill where he worked.

I loved hearing about *The Katzenjammer Kids* and *Little Orphan Annie*. After she read the funnies to me, Mother had me print the alphabet and sound out the letters.

One Monday evening, while waiting for my mother to finish the supper dishes, I started to sound out the letters in *The Katzenjammer Kids*. Suddenly, much to my surprise, I was reading the funnies aloud!

—**Pete Taranoff,** *Walnut Creek, California*

Caught up in Comics

At the age of 10, I was on a 1957 trip with my mother, who was driving north on U.S. Highway 395 in California's Mono County. Mom's 1951 Jeep station wagon was struggling up a steep climb at a snail's pace.

Unappreciative of the beautiful Mono Basin outside my window, I was engrossed in *The Adventures of Superman* when I absentmindedly pulled the door handle. With little wind resistance, the door opened easy as you please.

Of course, this was long before there were seat belts in every car. So, succumbing to the law of gravity, I fell out, dropping to the pavement like a bag of pipes.

Mom was on me faster than a chicken on a june bug. Before I'd shaken off the twittering birds and twinkling stars, she had stopped the car, set the

HEY, BOO BOO! "This free comic book is the one I got in 1961 after cutting out a coupon from the back of a Kellogg's Corn Flakes box at the age of 5," notes Greg Owen of Harrisonburg, Virginia. "I remember painstakingly printing my name and address onto the coupon. I was too young to appreciate the journey my comic book took from New York City to my home in Bridgewater, Virginia—even though I had not written my last name on the coupon. How fortunate I was to grow up in small-town America—where the local post office could locate a kid by his first name (and address) alone."

brake, leaped out and raced around to face the uncertainty of her little boy's future.

Fortunately, the only thing mangled was my comic book. I suffered only minor scrapes.

Upon our return, Mom told Pop about the incident. He went down to the Army-Navy store, bought some surplus World War II Army Air Force seat belts and installed them in the Jeep.

Pop figured if those belts could keep flying cadets in their planes at 100 mph, they would surely keep me in the car.

—**Christopher Marsh,** *Poway, California*

JOIN THE CLUB!

Unofficial Member

As a huge fan of *The Mickey Mouse Club*, I loved it when the members would move their hands to open the big wooden doors while saying, "Meeska, mooska, Mouseketeer...Mousekartoon Time now is here." This ritual would introduce one of the many short cartoons featured on the show.

My favorite Mouseketeer was Karen, and I had a huge crush on Cubby. What a dreamboat Spin was, and I'm sure Marty was cute, too, but he played the bad boy and I didn't like him.

I received an unofficial Mouseketeer costume for my ninth birthday, in 1956. It was not like the ones worn on TV, and the soft ears flopped over, but I didn't care. I was thrilled to be an unofficial club member and wore my outfit whenever I watched the show.

—*Mary Kelly Boley,* East Peoria, Illinois

Duck-Billed Club

What I recall about *The Mickey Mouse Club* was the theme, where Donald Duck yelled out his name after the kids sang, "Mickey Mouse!"

Poor old Donald. He was like an older sibling who is ignored when a baby comes into the family. He just wanted to get some of the attention.

My best friend back in Townsend, Massachusetts, Evie Lumppio, and I felt sorry for the cute little cartoon bird, so we formed our own Donald Duck Club. The other club members were Evie's pooch, Vufti, and my cat, Whitey.

We even had Donald Duck hats that quacked (really more like squeaked) when you squeezed the bills.

Every weekday, we sat in front of the television set, eagerly awaiting the theme song so we could shout along with Donald, at the tops of our lungs, "Donald Duck!"

When we held our club meetings, or even when we were just playing together, we called each other Evette and Nanette after the show's most popular Mouseketeer, Annette Funicello.

We even asked our parents if we could change our names.

—*Nancy Lovell Benoit,* Auburn, Massachusetts

THEY'RE HERE! We were happy to discover, on our 1957 trip to Disneyland from our home in Monrovia, California, that the Mouseketeers were to perform and sign autographs. Roy knew I was shy and hammed it up for me (wearing the striped shirt in the bottom photo). My sister Miriam (seated in the top photo) and I also posed with Sharon and Darlene. It was so exciting to meet and chat with the real Mouseketeers!
—Linda Cerrito Peltier, Huntington Beach, California

he called himself 'sparky'

Shortly after World War II, I worked as an art director for a publisher in St. Paul, Minnesota.

While there, I met a young man and gave him his first job lettering comics. I also bought his first cartoon for publication back when he was calling himself "Sparky." Sparky was Charles Schulz, who went on to create the popular *Peanuts* comic strip.

Though he was a private person, Charles and I remained good friends over many years.

—**Roman Bates**, St. Paul, Minnesota